AIF-C01
AWS Certified AI Practitioner

AWS(아마존 웹 서비스) 국제공인 AI 전문가 자격시험

AWS(아마존 웹 서비스)
국제공인 AI 전문가
자격시험

초판 인쇄 2024년 12월 12일
초판 발행 2024년 12월 12일

출판등록 번호 제 2015-000001 호
ISBN 979-11-94000-04-4 (03800)

주소 강원도 횡성군 횡성읍 송전로 209 (고즈넉한 길)
도서문의(신한서적) 031) 942 9851 팩스 : 031) 942 9852
도서내용문의 010 8287 9388
펴낸 곳 책바세
펴낸이 이용태

지은이 책바세 IT팀
기획 책바세
진행 책임 책바세
편집 디자인 책바세
표지 디자인 책바세

인쇄 및 제본 (주)신우인쇄 / 031) 923 7333

본 도서의 저작권은 [책바세]에게 있으며, 내용 중 디자인 및 저자의 창작성이 인정되는 내용을 무단
으로 복제 및 복사하는 것은 저작권법에 의해 처리될 수 있다.
Published by chackbase Co. Ltd Printed in Korea

가장 쉽고 완벽하게

2025

비전공자합격자를 높이기

기출문제 + 적중문제

책바세 IT팀 저

AIF-C01
AWS Certified AI Practitioner

AWS(아마존 웹 서비스)
국제공인 AI 전문가
자격시험

이 책은

본 도서의 AWS Certified AI Practitioner Practice Exam Course는 시험 합격에 필요한 모든 필수 정보를 다루고 있다. 대부분의 독자들은 본 도서의 실제 시험 문제에 해당하는 모든 질문을 접할 수 있었다고 보고하였다. 각 실전 적중 문제 후 제공되는 해설을 철저히 읽을 것을 권장합니다. 이는 적중문제 정답에 대한 설명도 포함되며, 이를 통해 여러분의 이해를 높이고 점수를 크게 향상할 수 있다. 이러한 해설을 주의 깊게 검토하고 모든 시험에서 90% 이상의 점수를 받을 때까지 반복 연습하면, 실제 시험에서도 자신감을 가지고 합격할 수 있을 것이라 확신한다.

이 책에 수록된 연습 문제와 답안은 시험의 유형을 익히기 위한 목적으로 설계되었으나, 실제 시험 합격을 보장하지 않으며, 성공 여부는 독자의 사전 지식, 학습 방법 및 이해도에 따라 달라질 수 있다.

이 책의 정보는 교육적 목적을 위한 것으로 의료, 법률, 재정 등의 전문적 조언을 대신하지 않으며, 이 정보를 바탕으로 결정을 내리기 전에는 전문가의 조언을 구하는 것을 권장한다. 저자와 출판사는 이 책의 사용으로 인해 발생하는 손해에 대해 책임을 지지 않으며, 자격증 시험에서 발생할 수 있는 실패에 대해서도 손실을 보장하지 않는다.

자격증 시험 내용 및 관련 요구 사항은 언제든지 변경될 수 있으며, 저자와 출판사는 시험 내용과 책의 내용 간의 차이에 대해 책임을 지지 않습니다. 독자는 시험 요구 사항을 최신 상태로 유지할 책임이 있으며, 책의 오류나 누락이 발견될 경우 피드백을 통해 저자와 출판사에 알릴 것을 권장한다.

저자와 출판사는 피드백을 바탕으로 향후 수정과 개선을 위한 노력을 계속할 것을 약속한다.

들어가기

본 도서는 AWS 공인 AI 실무자 (AIF-C01) 시험 준비를 위한 종합 자료로서, AI와 기계 학습의 기초 개념과 AWS의 AI 관련 서비스에 대한 이해를 돕기 위해 제작되었다. AI가 산업을 변모시키는 지금, 이 자격증은 클라우드 기반 AI 솔루션 분야의 새로운 기회를 열어줄 것이다. AI 분야를 탐구하는 초보자이거나 이미 AI 기술을 검증받은 전문가라면, 이 책이 필수적인 연습과 자신감을 제공하여 여러분이 필요한 실력을 갖추는 데 도움을 줄 것이다.

이 책에는 실제 자격증 시험의 구조와 난이도를 반영한 연습 문제들이 포함되어 있으며, 각 문제는 AI와 기계 학습의 핵심 개념, AWS AI 서비스, 그리고 AI 솔루션 구현을 위한 모범 사례에 대한 이해도를 테스트하도록 설계되었다. 이 시험들은 단순히 지식을 평가할 뿐만 아니라, 추가 학습이 필요한 영역을 파악하는 데에도 도움을 줄 것이다.

적중문제에 대한 해설도 함께 제공되어, 각 솔루션의 이유를 완전히 이해할 수 있도록 도와준다. 이 접근법은 AWS AI 개념의 기초를 쌓고, 학습을 강화하며, 자격증 목표를 달성하도록 이끌어 줄 것이다. AI에 대한 수요가 지속적으로 증가하는 만큼, AWS 공인 AI 실무자 자격증은 빠르게 변화하는 기술 환경에서 여러분을 돋보이게 해 줄 것이며, 경력을 향상시키거나 새로운 AI 기회를 모색하는 분들께 이 책이 든든한 동반자가 되어줄 것이다.

시험 개요

카테고리	기초
시험 시간	90분 (변동 가능)
문제 수	65개 문항 (변동 가능)
응시료	100 USD (변동 가능). 환율을 포함한 추가 비용 정보는 시험응시료 참조
예상 응시자	AWS의 AI/ML 기술 솔루션에 익숙하지만 반드시 구축할 필요는 없는 개인
응시자 직무 예시	비즈니스 분석가, IT 지원, 마케팅 전문가, 제품 또는 프로젝트 관리자, 사업부 또는 IT 관리자, 영업 전문가
시험 옵션	Pearson VUE 테스트 센터 또는 온라인 감독 시험
제공 언어	영어, 한국어, 일본어, 포르투갈어(브라질), 중국어 간체 (2024년 말에 제공 예정)

본 자격증 시험의 목적

AWS Certified AI Practitioner 시험은 수험자가 AWS의 AI 및 머신 러닝(Machine Learning, ML) 솔루션을 이해하고 실무에서 활용할 수 있도록 돕기 위한 자격 인증 시험으로, 다양한 분야에서 AI와 ML 기술을 도입하거나 사용하는 수험자가 AWS AI 서비스를 효과적으로 이해하고 활용할 수 있는 기초 능력을 검증하고자 한다. 본 시험의 구체적인 목적은 다음과 같다.

AI 및 ML 기본 개념에 대한 이해 검증

- AI와 ML의 기초 개념을 이해하고, 이를 실무에 활용할 수 있는 역량을 평가

- 모델 학습, 딥러닝의 기본 원리, AI의 윤리적 사용 등에 대한 기본 이해를 확인하며, 머신 러닝 모델의 구조와 원리를 AWS 클라우드에서 어떻게 적용할 수 있는지를 평가

AWS AI 및 ML 서비스에 대한 숙련도 평가

- AWS가 제공하는 핵심 AI 및 ML 서비스들(Amazon SageMaker, Amazon Rekognition, Amazon Comprehend, Amazon Lex 등)에 대한 수험자의 이해를 검증

- 각 서비스의 주요 기능과 사용 사례를 알고 있으며, 실제 비즈니스 상황에서 어떤 서비스를 사용해야 하는지 판단할 수 있는 능력을 평가

실제 비즈니스 문제 해결 능력 검증

- AI/ML 솔루션을 이용해 다양한 비즈니스 문제를 해결할 수 있는지 평가

- 고객의 의견 분석, 이미지 인식, 챗봇 구축, 사기 탐지와 같은 상황에서 AWS AI/ML 서비스를 어떻게 활용할 수 있는지를 묻는 문제들을 통해 실무 적용 능력을 확인

AWS 클라우드 인프라에서 AI/ML 모델 사용 능력 평가

- AWS 클라우드 인프라에서 AI 및 ML 모델을 배포하고 관리하는 기본적인 방법을 이해하고 있는지 확인

- AWS의 클라우드 개념 (리전, 가용영역, 엣지 로케이션 등)을 이해하고, AI/ML 모델을 AWS 클라우드 환경에 맞게 최적화하고 확장할 수 있는지 평가

본 자격증 시험의 응시 대상에 대하여

AWS Certified AI Practitioner 시험은 AWS의 AI 및 ML 솔루션을 이해하고, 이를 사용하는 데 필요한 기본 지식을 갖춘 초급 수준의 수험자를 대상으로 하며, 본 시험은 주로 AWS에서 제공하는 인공지능(AI) 및 머신 러닝(ML) 기술을 사용하는 기본적인 이해를 테스트하며, 다음과 같은 조건을 만족하는 수험자를 대상으로 한다.

추천(보유)되는 AWS 지식

- AWS의 핵심 서비스(예: Amazon EC2, Amazon S3, AWS Lambda, Amazon SageMaker) 및 주요 사용 사례에 대한 친숙함

- AWS 클라우드의 보안 및 컴플라이언스를 위한 AWS 공유 책임 모델에 대한 이해

- AWS 리소스에 대한 접근 제어 및 보안을 위한 AWS Identity and Access Management(IAM)에 대한 이해

- AWS 글로벌 인프라에 대한 이해 (AWS 리전, 가용 영역, 엣지 로케이션 개념 포함)

- AWS 서비스 가격 모델에 대한 이해

대상 수험자가 수행하지 않아도 되는 업무

- AI 및 ML 모델 또는 알고리즘 개발 및 코딩

- 데이터 엔지니어링 또는 기능 엔지니어링 기술 구현

- 하이퍼파라미터 튜닝 또는 모델 최적화 수행

- AI 및 ML 파이프라인 또는 인프라 구축 및 배포

- AI 및 ML 모델의 수학적 또는 통계적 분석 수행

- AI 및 ML 시스템에 대한 보안 또는 컴플라이언스 프로토콜 구현

- AI 및 ML 솔루션을 위한 거버넌스 프레임워크 및 정책 개발 및 구현

본 자격증 취득의 장점

AWS 공인 AI 실무자(전문가) 자격증을 취득하면, 인공지능 분야에 처음 입문하는 사람부터 실력을 검증하고자 하는 전문가에 이르기까지 다양한 혜택을 누릴 수 있다. AWS 공인 AI 실무자 자격증을 취득하는 것은 미래에 대한 전략적인 투자로, 단순히 시험을 넘어서 더 많은 혜택을 제공한다. 새로운 커리어를 시작하거나 현재 직무에서 발전하고자 할 때, 이 자격증은 필요한 기술, 인정, 기회를 제공해 인공지능과 클라우드 컴퓨팅의 세계에서 성공할 수 있도록 돕는다. 다음은 본 자격증 취득의 주요 장점들이다.

산업내 인지도

AWS 공인 AI 실무자 자격증은 AWS 클라우드 내에서 AI 기초 지식의 기준으로 세계적으로 인정받고 있다. 이 자격증은 머신러닝 및 인공지능 개념을 확실히 이해하고 AWS 서비스를 활용해 이를 구현할 수 있는 능력을 고용주와 클라이언트에게 증명해 준다. 이를 통해 AI, 데이터 과학, 클라우드 컴퓨팅 분야에서 차별화된 경쟁력을 갖출 수 있다.

경력 향상

AI가 다양한 산업에 깊이 통합되면서, 클라우드 플랫폼에서 AI 솔루션을 관리하고 배포할 수 있는 전문가에 대한 수요가 증가하고 있다. 이 자격증은 AI 엔지니어, 머신러닝 개발자, 데이터 과학자와 같은 고급 직무로의 발판이 된다. 자격증을 취득함으로써 AI와 클라우드 컴퓨팅 분야에서 커리어 성장을 위한 의지를 보여주고, 더 나은 일자리와 높은 연봉을 얻을 가능성을 높일 수 있다.

향상된 기술 역량

AWS 공인 AI 실무자 시험은 머신러닝 모델, AWS AI 서비스 (예: Amazon SageMaker), AI의 윤리적 함의와 같은 필수 주제를 다룬다. 시험을 준비하며 이러한 개념을 깊이 이해하고, AI 프로젝트 수행 능력을 높일 수 있다. 최신 AI 도구와 기술에 대한 실력을 갖추게 되어, 실무에서 바로 적용 가능한 실용적인 지식을 얻을 수 있다.

AWS 리소스 및 커뮤니티 접근성

AWS는 자격증 소지자에게 전 세계 AI 전문가 네트워크, 이벤트, 리소스에 대한 독점적인 접근 기회를 제공한다. 이를 통해 동료들과 지식을 공유하고, 최신 AI 동향을 지속적으로 파악할 수 있다. 또한, AI와 클라우드 컴퓨팅 분야에서 학습을 이어나가고 전문성을 확장할 수 있는 교육 경로도 제공받을 수 있다.

전문성 검증

이미 AI 또는 클라우드 컴퓨팅 산업에 종사하고 있는 사람들에게 이 자격증은 전문성을 검증할 수 있는 방법을 제공한다. 이 자격증은 AI 관련 주제에 대한 능력을 고용주와 고객에게 증명하며, 신뢰를 높이고 더 많은 책임과 리더십 역할로 이어질 수 있다.

자신감 향상

AWS 공인 AI 실무자 시험 준비와 통과 과정은 현실적인 AI 과제를 해결할 수 있는 자신감을 제공한다. 시험 내용을 철저히 검토하고 문제를 풀며, 인공지능과 머신러닝의 기초 지식을 탄탄히 쌓게 된다. 이러한 자신감은 면접에서뿐만 아니라 AWS를 사용해 AI 솔루션을 구현하는 일상 업무에서도 도움이 된다.

지속적인 자기 개발 촉진

AWS 공인 AI 실무자 자격증을 취득한 후에도 AWS는 자격증 갱신 및 지속적인 학습을 통해 최신 기술을 유지하고 개선할 수 있는 교육 프로그램과 학습 자료를 제공한다. 이는 AI와 클라우드 컴퓨팅 분야에서 개인의 역량을 지속적으로 발전시키는 데 도움이 된다.

네트워킹 기회 확대

본 자격증 소지자는 AWS가 주최하는 각종 이벤트, 웹 세미나, AI 관련 커뮤니티에 참여할 기회가 늘어나며, 이를 통해 AI 분야에서 활동하는 전문가들과 네트워킹을 할 수 있다. 이를 통해 최신 트렌드를 공유하고, 업계에서 인정받는 전문가로 성장할 수 있는 기반을 마련할 수 있다.

미래 학습의 문을 열어줌

AWS 공인 AI 실무자 자격증은 AI 및 클라우드 컴퓨팅 여정의 시작일 뿐이다. 이 자격증을 취득한 후에는 AWS 공인 머신러닝 전문가 또는 AWS 공인 솔루션 아키텍트와 같은 고급 자격증으로 나아갈 수 있다. 각 단계마다 실력을 더욱 향상시키며, 조직에서 더욱 가치 있는 자산이 되어 줄 것이다.

본 자격증 시험 응시 방법

AWS Certified AI Practitioner 시험에 응시하기 위해서는 몇 가지 절차를 따른다. 다음은 시험 등록부터 응시 방법까지의 주요 단계이다.

1. AWS Certification 계정 생성

- 시험 응시를 위해 AWS Certification 계정을 생성하기

- AWS Certification 공식 웹사이트(https://aws.amazon.com/ko/certification)에 접속하여 로그인하거나 계정이 없는 경우 새 계정 생성하기

2. 시험 등록

- AWS Certification 웹사이트에서 '시험' 메뉴를 선택한 후, 'AWS Certified AI Practitioner' 시험 찾기

- 해당 시험을 선택하면 등록 옵션이 표시되며, 시험 등록 시 원하는 시험 장소와 일정을 선택할 수 있다. 시험 옵션으로는 Pearson VUE 시험 센터에서의 현장 시험과 온라인 원격 감독 시험이 있다.

3. 시험 유형 및 장소 선택

- **Pearson VUE 시험 센터** 오프라인 시험 센터에서 감독 하에 시험을 볼 수 있으며, 가까운 시험 센터 위치와 가능한 시간대를 선택

- **온라인 원격 감독 시험** 인터넷이 가능한 곳에서 원격으로 시험을 응시할 수 있으며, 이 경우 웹캠이 달린 컴퓨터와 안정적인 인터넷 연결 필요, 시험 중 감독자가 실시간으로 감독

4. 시험 응시 비용 결제

- AWS Certified AI Practitioner 시험의 응시 비용은 100달러 (변동 가능)

- 등록 과정 중 결제 단계에서 신용카드 등의 결제 수단을 통해 결제

- 결제가 완료되면, 확인 이메일을 통해 시험 정보와 일정 제공

5. 시험 준비

- 시험 응시 전 AWS의 AI 및 머신 러닝 기초 개념을 충분히 학습하기

- AWS에서는 학습 자료 및 연습 문제를 제공하며, AWS Skill Builder와 같은 학습 플랫폼에서 다양한 교육 과정도 이용 가능

- 시험에 대한 안내 사항과 준비물, 예를 들어 신분증 준비와 같은 사항을 숙지하고, 시험 당일 문제 없이 시험을 응시할 수 있도록 준비

6. 시험 응시

- **시험 센터 응시 시** 지정된 시험 센터에 시험 시간 15분 전까지 도착하여 신분증 등 필요한 서류를 제출하고 안내에 따라 시험

- **온라인 원격 시험 응시 시** 시험 시작 전 컴퓨터와 인터넷 연결 상태를 점검하고, AWS에서 제공하는 원격 감독 시스템을 통해 감독자와 연결한 후 시험을 시작하기 (시험 중에는 감독자의 지시에 따라야 하며, 시험 중간에 자리를 비울 수 없음)

7. 시험 결과 확인

- 시험이 끝난 후, 대부분의 경우 몇 시간 내에 결과를 확인 가능

- 결과는 AWS Certification 계정에서 확인할 수 있으며, 합격할 경우 인증서를 다운로드하고 AWS Certified 로고를 사용할 수 있는 권한 부여

AWS Certified AI Practitioner 시험에 응시하는 과정은 간단하지만, 시험 준비와 응시 방법을 미리 숙지하여 만반의 준비를 하는 것이 중요하다.

01 AI와 ML의 기본 원리

개요

이 도메인은 AI(인공지능)와 ML(머신러닝)의 기본 개념과 관련된 지식을 다룬다. 여기에는 AI 및 ML의 주요 용어와 개념, 데이터 유형, 학습 방식, 그리고 다양한 AI/ML 기술의 실제 적용 사례에 대한 이해가 포함된다.

핵심 주제

1.1 기본 AI 개념 및 용어 설명

- AI, ML, 딥러닝, 신경망, 컴퓨터 비전, 자연어 처리(NLP), 모델, 알고리즘, 학습과 추론, 편향성(Bias), 공정성(Fairness), 적합성(Fit), 대규모 언어 모델(LLM) 등 기본 AI 용어 정의

- AI, ML, 딥러닝의 유사점과 차이점 설명

- 배치 추론, 실시간 추론 등 다양한 유형의 추론 방식 설명

- AI 모델에서 사용되는 다양한 데이터 유형 설명 (예: 라벨링된 데이터, 라벨링되지 않은 데이터, 구조화된 데이터, 비구조화된 데이터 등)

- 지도학습, 비지도학습, 강화학습의 개념 설명

1.2 AI의 실용적인 사용 사례 식별

- AI 및 ML이 가치를 제공할 수 있는 응용 프로그램을 인식 (예: 인간의 의사결정 지원, 솔루션 확장성, 자동화)

- AI 및 ML 솔루션이 적합하지 않은 경우 결정 (예: 특정 결과가 필요할 때, 비용-이익 분석)

- 특정 사용 사례에 적합한 ML 기법 선택 (예: 회귀, 분류, 클러스터링)

- 실제 AI 응용 사례 예시 (예: 컴퓨터 비전, NLP, 음성 인식, 추천 시스템, 사기 탐지, 예측 분석)

- AWS 관리형 AI/ML 서비스의 기능 설명 (예: SageMaker, Amazon Transcribe, Amazon Translate, Amazon Comprehend, Amazon Lex, Amazon Polly)

1.3 ML 개발 생애 주기 설명

- ML 파이프라인의 구성 요소 설명 (예: 데이터 수집, 탐색적 데이터 분석(EDA), 데이터 전처리, 특징 엔지니어링, 모델 학습, 하이퍼파라미터 튜닝, 평가, 배포, 모니터링)

- ML 모델의 소스 설명 (예: 오픈소스 사전 학습 모델, 맞춤형 모델 학습)

- 프로덕션 환경에서 모델을 사용하는 방법 설명 (예: 관리형 API 서비스, 셀프 호스팅 API)

- ML 파이프라인 각 단계에 관련된 AWS 서비스 및 기능 식별 (예: SageMaker, SageMaker Data Wrangler, SageMaker Feature Store, SageMaker Model Monitor)

- ML 운영(MLOps)의 기본 개념 이해 (예: 실험, 반복 가능한 프로세스, 확장 가능한 시스템, 기술 부채 관리, 프로덕션 준비 상태 달성, 모델 모니터링, 모델 재학습)

- ML 모델 성능 메트릭과 비즈니스 메트릭 이해 (예: 정확도, ROC 곡선 하의 면적(AUC), F1 점수, 사용자당 비용, 개발 비용, 고객 피드백, 투자 대비 수익률(ROI))

문제 출제 방식

객관식 문제 (Multiple Choice)

객관식 문제는 한 가지의 정답과 세 가지의 오답(혼동을 유발하는 답변)이 제공된다. 주로 AI 및 ML의 기본 개념을 설명하거나, 특정 상황에서 어떤 AI/ML 기술을 사용할지 묻는 질문으로 출제된다.

복수 응답 문제 (Multiple Response)

이 문제 유형은 다섯 가지 이상의 응답 옵션 중 두 개 이상의 정답을 선택해야 한다. 예를 들어, AI의 실제 응용 사례에 대한 질문이 있을 수 있으며, 여러 선택지 중에서 두 개 이상의 맞는 답을 모두 선택해야 한다.

순서 배열 문제 (Ordering)

AI/ML 파이프라인에서 작업을 순서대로 배열하는 문제가 출제될 수 있다. 예를 들어, 데이터를 수집하고 전처리한 후 모델을 학습하는 과정을 순서대로 배열하는 문제가 포함될 수 있다.

매칭 문제 (Matching)

AI 및 ML의 기본 개념이나 용어와 그 정의를 짝짓는 문제가 나올 수 있다. 예를 들어, '지도학습'이라는 용어를 '라벨이 있는 데이터를 사용하여 모델을 학습하는 방식'과 매칭하는 형식이다.

살펴본 것처럼 이 도메인에서 출제되는 문제들은 주로 AI/ML의 기본 개념과 그 실제 활용에 대한 이해도를 평가하는 데 중점을 두고 있다.

02 생성형 AI의 기본 원리

개요

이 도메인은 생성형 AI의 기본 개념과 그 원리를 다룬다. 여기에는 생성형 AI의 작동 방식, 관련 기술, 그리고 생성형 AI가 비즈니스 문제를 해결하는 데 어떻게 사용될 수 있는지에 대한 이해가 포함되며, 생성형 AI 모델의 한계와 장점을 파악하는 능력도 이 도메인에서 평가된다.

핵심 주제

1.1 생성형 AI의 기본 개념 설명

- 생성형 AI의 기초 개념 이해 (예: 토큰, 청크, 임베딩, 벡터, 프롬프트 엔지니어링, 트랜스포머 기반 대규모 언어 모델(LLM), 기반 모델, 다중 모달 모델, 확산 모델 등)

- 생성형 AI 모델의 잠재적 사용 사례 식별 (예: 이미지 생성, 비디오 생성, 오디오 생성, 요약, 챗봇, 번역, 코드 생성, 고객 서비스 에이전트, 검색, 추천 엔진)

- 생성형 AI 모델의 생애 주기 설명 (예: 데이터 선택, 모델 선택, 사전 학습, 조정, 평가, 배포, 피드백)

1.2 생성형 AI의 비즈니스 문제 해결 능력 및 한계 이해

- 생성형 AI의 장점 설명 (예: 적응성, 반응성, 사용 편의성)

- 생성형 AI 솔루션의 단점 설명 (예: 환각(Hallucination), 해석 불가능성, 부정확성, 비결정론)

- 생성형 AI 모델 선택 시 고려해야 할 다양한 요인 이해 (예: 모델 유형, 성능 요구사항, 기능, 제약, 규정 준수 등)

- 생성형 AI 응용 프로그램의 비즈니스 가치와 성과 지표 결정 (예: 교차 도메인 성능, 효율성, 전환율, 사용자당 평균 수익, 정확성, 고객 생애 가치)

1.3 생성형 AI 애플리케이션 구축을 위한 AWS 인프라 및 기술 설명

- 생성형 AI 애플리케이션 개발을 위한 AWS 서비스 및 기능 식별 (예: Amazon SageMaker JumpStart, Amazon Bedrock, PartyRock, Amazon Bedrock Playground, Amazon Q 등)

- 생성형 AI 애플리케이션 구축 시 AWS 서비스를 사용하는 이점 설명 (예: 접근성, 낮은 진입 장벽, 효율성, 비용 효과, 시장 진출 속도, 비즈니스 목표 달성 능력)

- 생성형 AI 애플리케이션에 적합한 AWS 인프라의 이점 이해 (예: 보안, 규정 준수, 책임성, 안전성)

- AWS 생성형 AI 서비스의 비용 절감 효과와 그에 따른 트레이드오프 이해 (예: 응답성, 가용성, 중복성, 성능, 지역적 커버리지, 토큰 기반 가격 책정, 맞춤형 모델)

문제 출제 방식

객관식 문제 (Multiple Choice)

객관식 문제는 한 가지의 정답과 세 가지의 오답(혼동을 유발하는 답변)이 제공된다. 예를 들어, 생성형 AI 모델의 기본 개념이나 AWS에서 어떤 서비스가 생성형 AI 애플리케이션 구축에 적합한지 묻는 질문이 출제될 수 있다.

복수 응답 문제 (Multiple Response)

이 문제 유형은 다섯 개 이상의 응답 옵션 중 두 개 이상의 정답을 선택해야 한다. 예를 들어, 생성형 AI의 장점이나 단점에 대해 여러 선택지 중 올바른 답을 모두 고르는 문제가 출제될 수 있다.

순서 배열 문제 (Ordering)

생성형 AI 모델의 생애 주기를 설명하는 문제로, 데이터 선택부터 배포, 피드백까지의 단계를 올바른 순서로 배열하는 문제가 포함될 수 있다.

매칭 문제 (Matching)

생성형 AI 관련 용어와 그 정의를 매칭하는 문제 유형이다. 예를 들어, '트랜스포머 모델'이라는 용어를 '대규모 언어 모델(LLM)의 핵심 구성 요소'와 매칭하는 문제가 나올 수 있다.

살펴본 것처럼 이 도메인에서는 생성형 AI의 개념을 이해하고, 실제 사용 사례에 적합한 기술을 선택하는 능력과 AWS 인프라를 활용하는 방법을 묻는 데 중점을 두고 있다.

기반 모델 응용

개요

이 도메인은 기반 모델(Foundation models)의 응용과 관련된 내용을 다룬다. 기반 모델은 사전 학습된 대규모 모델로, 다양한 AI 및 ML 응용 프로그램에서 광범위하게 사용할 수 있는 모델을 의미한다. 이 도메인에서는 기반 모델의 설계, 프롬프트 엔지니어링 기술, 모델 성능 평가 방법 등을 다루며, 이 모델을 비즈니스 문제 해결에 어떻게 적용할 수 있는지 평가한다.

핵심 주제

1.1 기반 모델을 사용하는 애플리케이션의 설계 고려 사항 설명

- 사전 학습된 모델을 선택하는 기준 식별 (예: 비용, 모달리티, 지연 시간, 다국어 지원, 모델 크기, 모델 복잡성, 맞춤화 가능성, 입출력 길이 등)

- 추론 매개변수가 모델 응답에 미치는 영향 이해 (예: 온도, 입출력 길이)

- Retrieval Augmented Generation(RAG) 정의 및 비즈니스 응용 사례 설명 (예: Amazon Bedrock, 지식 기반)

- 벡터 데이터베이스에 임베딩을 저장하는 데 도움이 되는 AWS 서비스 식별 (예: Amazon OpenSearch Service, Amazon Aurora, Amazon Neptune, Amazon DocumentDB, Amazon RDS for PostgreSQL)

- 기반 모델 맞춤화 방법에 따른 비용 트레이드오프 설명 (예: 사전 학습, 미세 조정, 문맥 학습, RAG)

- 다단계 작업에서 에이전트의 역할 이해 (예: Amazon Bedrock 에이전트)

1.2 효과적인 프롬프트 엔지니어링 기술 선택

- 프롬프트 엔지니어링의 개념 및 구성요소 설명 (예: 맥락, 지시문, 부정적 프롬프트, 모델 잠재 공간)

- 프롬프트 엔지니어링 기술 이해 (예: 생각의 사슬(Chain-of-thought), 제로샷 학습, 원샷 학습, 소수샷 학습, 프롬프트 템플릿)

- 프롬프트 엔지니어링의 이점 및 모범 사례 이해 (예: 응답 품질 향상, 실험, 가드레일, 발견 과정, 구체성과 간결성, 여러 명령어 사용)

- 프롬프트 엔지니어링의 잠재적 위험과 한계 정의 (예: 데이터 노출, 프롬프트 중독, 프롬프트 탈취, 프롬프트 탈옥)

1.3 기반 모델의 학습 및 미세 조정 프로세스 설명

- 기반 모델 학습의 주요 요소 설명 (예: 사전 학습, 미세 조정, 연속 사전 학습)

- 기반 모델 미세 조정 방법 정의 (예: 지시문 튜닝, 특정 도메인에 맞춘 모델 적응, 전이 학습, 연속 사전 학습)

- 기반 모델 미세 조정을 위한 데이터 준비 방법 설명 (예: 데이터 큐레이션, 데이터 거버넌스, 데이터 크기, 라벨링, 대표성, 인간 피드백을 통한 강화 학습(RLHF))

1.4 기반 모델 성능 평가 방법 설명

- 기반 모델 성능 평가 접근법 이해 (예: 인간 평가, 벤치마크 데이터셋)

- 기반 모델 성능을 평가할 수 있는 관련 지표 식별 (예: ROUGE, BLEU, BERTScore)

- 기반 모델이 비즈니스 목표를 효과적으로 충족하는지 여부 결정 (예: 생산성, 사용자 참여도, 작업 효율성)

문제 출제 방식

객관식 문제 (Multiple Choice)

객관식 문제는 한 가지의 정답과 세 가지의 오답(혼동을 유발하는 답변)이 제공된다. 예를 들어, 기반 모델을 선택하는 기준이나 특정 상황에서 어떤 기반 모델을 사용하는 것이 적절한지를 묻는 문제가 출제될 수 있다.

복수 응답 문제 (Multiple Response)

이 문제 유형은 다섯 개 이상의 응답 옵션 중 두 개 이상의 정답을 선택해야 한다. 예를 들어, 기반 모델 성능 평가 시 사용할 수 있는 지표나 프롬프트 엔지니어링의 모범 사례에 대한 질문이 출제될 수 있다.

순서 배열 문제 (Ordering)

기반 모델 학습 또는 미세 조정 과정에서 필요한 단계를 올바른 순서로 배열하는 문제가 출제될 수 있다. 예를 들어, 사전 학습부터 미세 조정, 성능 평가까지의 단계를 배열하는 문제이다.

매칭 문제 (Matching)

기반 모델 관련 용어와 그 정의를 매칭하는 문제 유형이다. 예를 들어, '미세 조정'이라는 용어를 '기존 사전 학습된 모델에 특정 도메인 데이터를 추가 학습시키는 과정'과 매칭하는 문제이다.

살펴본 것처럼 이 도메인에서는 기반 모델을 실제 애플리케이션에 적용하는 능력, 프롬프트 엔지니어링의 이해도, 그리고 모델 성능을 평가하는 방법에 대해 깊이 있는 이해를 묻는 문제가 출제된다.

04 책임 있는 AI 가이드라인

개요

이 도메인은 AI 시스템이 사회적, 윤리적으로 올바르게 개발되고 사용되도록 보장하는 방법에 중점을 둔다. 책임 있는 AI는 편향을 줄이고, 공정하고 안전한 AI 시스템을 개발하며, 데이터 및 모델의 투명성과 설명 가능성을 강화하는 것을 목표로 한다. 또한, 법적 위험을 관리하고 AI가 사회에 미치는 부정적인 영향을 최소화하는 것이 포함된다.

핵심 주제

1.1 책임 있는 AI 시스템 개발 설명

- 책임 있는 AI의 주요 요소 식별 (예: 편향성, 공정성, 포괄성, 견고성, 안전성, 진실성)

- 책임 있는 AI의 요소를 식별하는 도구 사용 방법 이해 (예: Amazon Bedrock의 가드레일)

- 모델 선택 시 환경적 고려 사항과 지속 가능성을 포함한 책임 있는 관행 이해

- 생성형 AI 작업 시 발생할 수 있는 법적 위험 식별 (예: 지적 재산권 침해 주장, 편향된 모델 출력, 고객 신뢰 손실, 사용자 리스크, 환각 현상)

- 데이터셋의 특성 식별 (예: 포괄성, 다양성, 큐레이팅된 데이터 소스, 균형 잡힌 데이터셋)

- 편향성과 분산의 영향을 이해 (예: 인구 통계 그룹에 미치는 영향, 부정확성, 과적합, 미적합)

- 편향, 신뢰성 및 진실성을 감지하고 모니터링할 수 있는 도구 설명 (예: 라벨 품질 분석, 인간 감사, 하위 그룹 분석, Amazon SageMaker Clarify, SageMaker Model Monitor, Amazon Augmented AI)

1.2 투명하고 설명 가능한 모델의 중요성 인식

- 투명하고 설명 가능한 모델과 그렇지 않은 모델의 차이 이해

- 투명하고 설명 가능한 모델을 식별하는 도구 이해 (예: SageMaker Model Cards, 오픈 소스 모델, 데이터, 라이선스)

- 모델 안전성과 투명성 간의 트레이드오프 식별 (예: 해석 가능성과 성능의 균형)

- 설명 가능한 AI를 위한 인간 중심 디자인 원칙 이해

문제 출제 방식

객관식 문제 (Multiple Choice)

객관식 문제는 한 가지의 정답과 세 가지의 오답(혼동을 유발하는 답변)이 제공된다. 예를 들어, AI 시스템 개발 시 편향을 줄이는 방법이나, 투명한 AI 모델을 선택하는 기준을 묻는 문제가 출제될 수 있다.

복수 응답 문제 (Multiple Response)

이 문제 유형은 다섯 개 이상의 응답 옵션 중 두 개 이상의 정답을 선택해야 한다. 예를 들어, 책임 있는 AI 시스템에서 중요한 요소를 식별하거나, 편향성을 줄이기 위한 모범 사례를 묻는 문제가 출제될 수 있다.

순서 배열 문제 (Ordering)

책임 있는 AI 시스템 개발 과정에서 중요한 단계들을 올바른 순서로 배열하는 문제가 출제될 수 있다. 예를 들어, 데이터셋의 공정성 보장을 위한 단계나, 모델 안전성을 보장하기 위한 절차를 배열하는 문제가 나올 수 있다.

매칭 문제 (Matching)

책임 있는 AI 관련 용어와 그 정의를 매칭하는 문제 유형이다. 예를 들어, '편향성'이라는 용어를 '특정 그룹에 불공평한 영향을 미치는 AI 모델의 특성'과 매칭하는 문제가 출제될 수 있다.

이 도메인에서는 AI 시스템의 윤리적, 사회적 책임을 묻는 문제가 주로 출제되며, 특히 AI 모델의 공정

성, 투명성, 그리고 AI 사용에서 발생할 수 있는 법적 및 사회적 문제들을 다룬다.

05 AI 솔루션을 위한 보안, 규정 준수 및 거버넌스

개요

이 도메인은 AI 시스템을 보호하고 규정 준수 요구사항을 충족하며, 효과적인 거버넌스를 유지하는 방법에 중점을 둔다. 여기에는 AI 솔루션이 적절하게 보호되고, 데이터 보안과 개인 정보 보호가 보장되며, 규제 및 법적 요구사항을 준수하는지 확인하는 것이 포함된다. 또한, AI 솔루션을 위한 관리와 감사 체계를 효과적으로 구현하는 방법도 다룬다.

핵심 주제

1.1 AI 시스템을 보호하는 방법 설명

- AI 시스템을 보호하기 위한 AWS 서비스 및 기능 식별 (예: IAM 역할, 정책 및 권한, 암호화, Amazon Macie, AWS PrivateLink, AWS 공유 책임 모델)

- 데이터 출처를 기록하고 문서화하는 개념 이해 (예: 데이터 계보, 데이터 카탈로그화, SageMaker Model Cards)

- 보안 데이터 엔지니어링을 위한 모범 사례 설명 (예: 데이터 품질 평가, 개인정보 보호 기술 구현, 데이터 접근 제어, 데이터 무결성 보장)

- AI 시스템의 보안 및 개인정보 보호에 대한 고려사항 이해 (예: 애플리케이션 보안, 위협 탐지, 취약점 관리, 인프라 보호, 프롬프트 주입, 전송 중 및 저장 시 암호화)

1.2 투명하고 설명 가능한 모델의 중요성 인식

- AI 시스템에 적용되는 규제 준수 표준 식별 (예: 국제 표준화 기구 [ISO], 시스템 및 조직 통제 [SOC], 알고리즘 책임성 법률)

- 거버넌스 및 규정 준수를 지원하는 AWS 서비스 및 기능 식별 (예: AWS Config, Amazon Inspector, AWS Audit Manager, AWS Artifact, AWS CloudTrail, AWS Trusted Advisor)

- 데이터 거버넌스 전략 설명 (예: 데이터 생애 주기, 로깅, 데이터 레지던시, 모니터링, 관찰, 데이터 보존)

- 거버넌스 프로토콜을 따르기 위한 프로세스 설명 (예: 정책 수립, 검토 일정, 검토 전략, 거버넌스 프레임워크 [예: Generative AI Security Scoping Matrix], 투명성 기준, 팀 교육 요구 사항)

문제 출제 방식

객관식 문제 (Multiple Choice)

객관식 문제는 한 가지의 정답과 세 가지의 오답(혼동을 유발하는 답변)이 제공된다. 예를 들어, AI 시스템을 위한 보안 강화 방법이나, 특정 상황에서 AWS 서비스로 데이터를 보호하는 방법을 묻는 문제가 출제될 수 있다.

복수 응답 문제 (Multiple Response)

복수 응답 문제는 다섯 개 이상의 응답 옵션 중 두 개 이상의 정답을 선택해야 한다. 예를 들어, 데이터 보안을 보장하는 AWS 서비스를 선택하거나, 규정 준수를 지원하는 도구를 식별하는 문제가 출제될 수 있다.

순서 배열 문제 (Ordering)

AI 시스템에 대한 보안 강화 절차 또는 데이터 거버넌스 전략을 올바른 순서로 배열하는 문제가 나올 수 있다. 예를 들어, 데이터 무결성을 보장하는 단계나, 거버넌스 프로토콜을 따르기 위한 절차를 순서대로 배열하는 문제이다.

매칭 문제 (Matching)

보안, 규정 준수 및 거버넌스와 관련된 용어와 그 정의를 매칭하는 문제 유형이다. 예를 들어, 'AWS Config'라는 용어를 'AWS 리소스의 규정 준수를 평가하는 서비스'와 매칭하는 문제가 나올 수 있다.

이 도메인에서는 AI 시스템을 안전하게 보호하고 규정 준수 요구사항을 충족하는 능력을 평가하며, AWS 도구를 사용하여 AI 솔루션에 대한 보안 및 거버넌스를 효과적으로 관리하는 방법에 중점을 둔다.

AWS 웹사이트 입장하기: 아래 QR 코드를 통해 시험 응시

기출문제

—500

도메인 1: AI와 ML의 기본 원리

AI와 ML의 핵심 개념(지도, 비지도, 강화학습), ML 워크플로우의 각 단계, 데이터 처리 방법론을 이해하고 있는지를 평가하는데, 각 개념들의 정확한 정의와 차이점을 명확히 구분할 수 있어야 한다. 특히 AWS의 주요 AI 서비스들(SageMaker, Rekognition, Comprehend 등)이 이러한 개념들을 어떻게 실제로 구현하는지 이해하고 있어야 하고, 문제에서 제시된 비즈니스 시나리오에 따라 적절한 ML 접근 방식(분류, 회귀, 군집화)을 선택할 수 있어야 한다. ML 프로젝트의 5단계(문제 정의, 데이터 준비, 모델 학습 평가, 배포, 모니터링)를 순차적으로 이해하고 각 단계에서 발생할 수 있는 문제들을 해결할 수 있는 능력을 평가하므로, 단순 암기보다는 실제 사례를 통한 개념 이해와 서비스 활용 방안에 중점을 둔 학습을 권장한다.

1. Which machine learning algorithm is typically used for classification problems?
1. 어떤 유형의 학습에서 알고리즘은 예제를 통해 학습하고 학습용으로 라벨이 달린 데이터를 받는가?

a) Logistic Regression (로지스틱 회귀)
b) Linear Regression (선형 회귀)
c) Principal Component Analysis (주성분 분석)
d) K-means (K-평균)

2. What is the purpose of backpropagation in neural networks?
2. 신경망에서 역전파(backpropagation)의 목적은 무엇인가?

a) To initialize weights (가중치 초기화)
b) To calculate output values (출력값 계산)
c) To update the weights by minimizing error (오류 최소화를 통해 가중치 업데이트)
d) To normalize input data (입력 데이터를 정규화)

1번 정답: a   2번 정답: c

3. What does the term "epoch" refer to in machine learning?
3. 기계 학습에서 "epoch"이라는 용어는 무엇을 의미하는가?

a) One pass over the entire training dataset (전체 학습 데이터셋을 한 번 통과하기)
b) A hyperparameter tuning technique (하이퍼파라미터 조정 기법)
c) The number of hidden layers in a neural network (신경망의 은닉층 수)
d) A gradient descent algorithm (경사 하강 알고리즘)

4. Which type of data does unsupervised learning typically work with?
4. 비지도 학습은 일반적으로 어떤 유형의 데이터를 사용하는가?

a) Labeled data (라벨이 달린 데이터)
b) Unlabeled data (라벨이 없는 데이터)
c) Reinforcement signals (강화 신호)
d) Augmented data (증강 데이터)

5. What is the primary purpose of a clustering algorithm?
5. 군집화 알고리즘의 주요 목적은 무엇인가?

a) Predict future outcomes (미래 결과 예측)
b) Group similar items together (유사한 항목을 함께 그룹화)
c) Classify data into categories (데이터를 범주로 분류)
d) Generate new features (새로운 특징 생성)

6. Which AWS service is commonly used for building, training, and deploying machine learning models?
6. 기계 학습 모델을 구축, 학습 및 배포하는 데 일반적으로 사용되는 AWS 서비스는 무엇인가?

a) Amazon Lex (아마존 렉스)
b) AWS SageMaker (AWS 세이지메이커)
c) Amazon Polly (아마존 폴리)
d) AWS Lambda (AWS 람다)

3번 정답: a   4번 정답: b   5번 정답: b   6번 정답: b

7. Which subfield of AI is dedicated to developing systems capable of performing tasks that require human intelligence?

7. 다음 중 인간의 지능이 필요한 작업을 수행할 수 있는 시스템을 구축하는 것에 중점을 둔 AI의 하위 분야는 무엇인가?

a) Deep Learning (딥러닝)
b) Artificial Intelligence (인공지능)
c) Machine Learning (머신러닝)
d) Dropout Layer (드롭아웃 레이어)

8. What is the method for increasing a model's accuracy by expanding the training dataset?

8. 더 큰 훈련 데이터셋을 사용하여 모델의 정확도를 향상시키는 과정은 무엇인가?

a) Data augmentation (데이터 증강)
b) Hyperparameter tuning (하이퍼파라미터 튜닝)
c) Transfer learning (전이 학습)
d) Feature engineering (특성 공학)

9. In reinforcement learning, which of the following does the agent receive for performing actions in an environment?

9. 강화 학습에서 에이전트가 환경에서 행동을 수행한 후 받는 것은 무엇인가?

a) Feedback (피드백)
b) Rewards (보상)
c) Labels (레이블)
d) Predictions (예측)

10. Which AWS service provides pre-trained machine learning models that you can use for image and video analysis?

10. 이미지 및 비디오 분석에 사용할 수 있는 사전 학습된 기계 학습 모델을 제공하는 AWS 서비스는 무엇인가?

a) AWS SageMaker (AWS 세이지메이커)
b) Amazon Comprehend (아마존 컴프리헨드)
c) Amazon Rekognition (아마존 레코그니션)
d) AWS Glue (AWS 글루)

7번 정답: b   8번 정답: a   9번 정답: b   10번 정답: c

11. In which type of learning does the algorithm learn by example and receives labeled data for training?

11. 어떤 유형의 학습에서 알고리즘은 예제를 통해 학습하고 학습용으로 라벨이 달린 데이터를 받는가?

a) Unsupervised learning (비지도 학습)

b) Supervised learning (지도 학습)

c) Reinforcement learning (강화 학습)

d) Semi-supervised learning (준지도 학습)

12. What term describes a situation where an algorithm becomes overly tailored to the training data, resulting in poor performance on unseen data?

12. 알고리즘이 학습 데이터에 지나치게 특화되어 새로운 데이터에서 성능이 저하되는 문제를 나타내는 용어는 무엇인가?

a) Recurrent Neural Network (순환 신경망)

b) Overfitting (과적합)

c) Regularization (정규화)

d) Generalization (일반화)

13. What is a neural network technique where each node in one layer is connected to every node in the next layer?

13. 한 층의 각 노드가 다음 층의 모든 노드와 연결되는 신경망 기술은 무엇인가?

a) Underfitting (과소적합)

b) Convolutional Neural Network (합성곱 신경망)

c) Fully Connected Layer (완전 연결층)

d) Data Science (데이터 과학)

14. Which of the following is NOT a common algorithm for supervised learning?

14. 다음 중 지도 학습에서 일반적으로 사용되지 않는 알고리즘은 무엇인가?

a) Underfitting (과소적합)

b) Convolutional Neural Network (합성곱 신경망)

c) Fully Connected Layer (완전 연결층)

d) Data Science (데이터 과학)

11번 정답: b   12번 정답: b   13번 정답: c   14번 정답: b

15. Which machine learning model is commonly used for dimensionality reduction?
15. 차원 축소에 일반적으로 사용되는 기계 학습 모델은 무엇인가?

a) Support Vector Machine (서포트 벡터 머신)
b) K-means Clustering (K-평균 군집화)
c) Principal Component Analysis (주성분 분석)
d) Naive Bayes (나이브 베이즈)

16. What type of neural network is best suited for image processing tasks?
16. 이미지 처리 작업에 가장 적합한 신경망 유형은 무엇인가?

a) Recurrent Neural Network (순환 신경망)
b) Convolutional Neural Network (합성곱 신경망)
c) Generative Adversarial Network (생성적 적대 신경망)
d) Fully Connected Neural Network (완전 연결 신경망)

17. Which AWS service is designed to help build conversational agents?
17. 대화형 에이전트를 구축하는 데 도움을 주기 위해 설계된 AWS 서비스는 무엇인가?

a) Amazon Comprehend (아마존 컴프리헨드)
b) AWS SageMaker (AWS 세이지메이커)
c) Amazon Lex (아마존 렉스)
d) Amazon Transcribe (아마존 트랜스크라이브)

18. In natural language processing (NLP), what does tokenization refer to?
18. 자연어 처리(NLP)에서 토크나이제이션이 의미하는 것은 무엇인가?

a) Assigning numerical values to words (단어에 숫자 값을 할당하는 것)
b) Splitting text into meaningful units (텍스트를 의미 있는 단위로 나누는 것)
c) Reducing words to their base forms (단어를 기본 형태로 줄이는 것)
d) Removing stop words from text (텍스트에서 불용어를 제거하는 것)

15번 정답: c   16번 정답: b   17번 정답: c   18번 정답: b

19. What is the role of a hyperparameter in machine learning?
19. 기계 학습에서 하이퍼파라미터의 역할은 무엇인가?

a) A parameter whose value is set before training begins (훈련이 시작되기 전에 값이 설정되는 매개변수)
b) A parameter learned from the training data (훈련 데이터로부터 학습되는 매개변수)
c) A technique to reduce overfitting (과적합을 줄이는 기술)
d) A method to initialize the weights (가중치를 초기화하는 방법)

20. Which of the following is a common activation function used in deep learning?
20. 다음 중 딥러닝에서 일반적으로 사용되는 활성화 함수는 무엇인가?

a) Softmax (소프트맥스)
b) ReLU (렐루)
c) Sigmoid (시그모이드)
d) All of the above (위의 모든 것)

21. What is the difference between supervised and unsupervised learning?
21. 지도 학습과 비지도 학습의 차이는 무엇인가?

a) Supervised learning requires labeled data, while unsupervised learning does not (지도 학습은 라벨이 달린 데이터를 요구하지만, 비지도 학습은 그렇지 않음)
b) Unsupervised learning is more accurate than supervised learning (비지도 학습이 지도 학습보다 더 정확함)
c) Supervised learning does not require training data (지도 학습은 훈련 데이터를 필요로 하지 않음)
d) Unsupervised learning uses reinforcement signals (비지도 학습은 강화 신호를 사용함)

22. Which of the following is an unsupervised learning algorithm?
22. 다음 중 비지도 학습 알고리즘은 무엇인가?

a) Decision Trees (의사결정 트리)
b) K-means Clustering (K-평균 군집화)
c) Logistic Regression (로지스틱 회귀)
d) Random Forests (랜덤 포레스트)

19번 정답: a   20번 정답: d   21번 정답: a   22번 정답: b

23. What is one benefit of using AWS SageMaker for machine learning?
23. AWS SageMaker를 기계 학습에 사용할 때의 장점 중 하나는 무엇인가?

a) It provides pre-built AI solutions for specific business use cases (특정 비즈니스 사용 사례에 맞춘 사전 구축된 AI 솔루션을 제공)

b) It allows users to build and train machine learning models quickly (사용자가 기계 학습 모델을 빠르게 구축하고 학습)

c) It automatically generates feature importance scores (특성 중요도 점수를 자동으로 생성)

d) It manages all data preprocessing tasks automatically (모든 데이터 전처리 작업을 자동으로 관리)

24. Which machine learning model is best suited for binary classification tasks?
24. 이진 분류 작업에 가장 적합한 기계 학습 모델은 무엇인가?

a) Linear Regression (선형 회귀)

b) Logistic Regression (로지스틱 회귀)

c) K-means (K-평균 군집화)

d) Decision Tree (의사결정 트리)

25. Which type of machine learning uses a system of rewards and punishments to teach the model?
25. 보상과 처벌 시스템을 사용하여 모델을 학습시키는 기계 학습 유형은 무엇인가?

a) Supervised learning (지도 학습)

b) Unsupervised learning (비지도 학습)

c) Reinforcement learning (강화 학습)

d) Semi-supervised learning (반지도 학습)

26. What is the term for reducing the dimensions of the feature space while maintaining the essence of the data?
26. 데이터의 본질을 유지하면서 특성 공간의 차원을 줄이는 용어는 무엇인가?

a) Normalization (정규화)

b) Dimensionality reduction (차원 축소)

c) Feature engineering (특성 공학)

d) Regularization (정규화)

23번 정답: b   24번 정답: b   25번 정답: c   26번 정답: b

27. Which of the following is a commonly used distance metric in clustering algorithms?
27. 다음 중 군집화 알고리즘에서 일반적으로 사용되는 거리 측정 지표는 무엇인가?

a) Euclidean distance (유클리드 거리)
b) Pearson correlation (피어슨 상관 계수)
c) Cosine similarity (코사인 유사도)
d) Hamming distance (해밍 거리)

28. What is the main purpose of the softmax function in a neural network?
28. 신경망에서 소프트맥스 함수의 주요 목적은 무엇인가?

a) To perform regression tasks (회귀 작업을 수행하기 위해)
b) To reduce overfitting (과적합을 줄이기 위해)
c) To convert logits into probabilities (로짓을 확률로 변환하기 위해)
d) To initialize weights (가중치를 초기화하기 위해)

29. What type of learning algorithm is K-nearest neighbors (KNN)?
29. K-최근접 이웃(KNN)은 어떤 유형의 학습 알고리즘인가?

a) Supervised learning (지도 학습)
b) Unsupervised learning (비지도 학습)
c) Semi-supervised learning (반지도 학습)
d) Reinforcement learning (강화 학습)

30. What is overfitting in machine learning?
30. 기계 학습에서 과적합이란 무엇인가?

a) When the model performs well on training data but poorly on unseen data (모델이 훈련 데이터에서는 잘 작동하지만, 보지 못한 데이터에서는 성능이 저하되는 경우)
b) When the model cannot learn from the training data (모델이 훈련 데이터에서 학습할 수 없는 경우)
c) When the model underestimates the complexity of the task (모델이 작업의 복잡성을 과소평가하는 경우)
d) When the model performs well on unseen data but poorly on training data (모델이 보지 못한 데이터에서는 잘 작동하지만, 훈련 데이터에서는 성능이 저하되는 경우)

27번 정답: a   28번 정답: c   29번 정답: a   30번 정답: a

31. Which of the following is an example of a loss function used in regression problems?
31. 다음 중 회귀 문제에서 사용되는 손실 함수의 예는 무엇인가?

a) Cross-entropy loss (교차 엔트로피 손실)
b) Mean Squared Error (MSE) (평균 제곱 오차)
c) Hinge loss (힌지 손실)
d) F1 score (F1 점수)

32. Which of the following is a key difference between deep learning and traditional machine learning algorithms?
32. 다음 중 딥러닝과 전통적인 기계 학습 알고리즘의 주요 차이점은 무엇인가?

a) Deep learning relies on structured data, while traditional algorithms do not (딥러닝은 구조화된 데이터에 의존하지만, 전통적인 알고리즘은 그렇지 않음)
b) Deep learning requires more manual feature extraction (딥러닝은 더 많은 수작업 특성 추출을 필요함)
c) Deep learning can automatically learn features from data (딥러닝은 데이터로부터 특성을 자동으로 학습할 수 있음)
d) Traditional algorithms are more scalable than deep learning (전통적인 알고리즘은 딥러닝보다 확장성이 더 높음)

33. What is the function of a learning rate in an optimization algorithm?
33. 최적화 알고리즘에서 학습률의 기능은 무엇인가?

a) It controls how much the weights are updated with each step (각 단계마다 가중치가 얼마나 업데이트되는지 제어)
b) It determines the size of the training data (훈련 데이터의 크기를 결정)
c) It defines the number of hidden layers in the model (모델의 은닉층 수를 정의)
d) It reduces the overfitting of the model (모델의 과적합을 줄임)

34. Which AWS service is designed to extract text and data from documents?
34. 문서에서 텍스트와 데이터를 추출하도록 설계된 AWS 서비스는 무엇인가?

a) Amazon Polly (아마존 폴리)
b) Amazon Comprehend (아마존 컴프리헨드)
c) Amazon Textract (아마존 텍스트랙트)
d) Amazon Rekognition (아마존 레코그니션)

31번 정답: b   32번 정답: c   33번 정답: a   34번 정답: c

35. What is the purpose of the dropout technique in deep learning?

35. 딥러닝에서 드롭아웃 기법의 목적은 무엇인가?

a) To reduce the size of the dataset (데이터셋의 크기를 줄이기 위해)

b) To prevent overfitting by randomly dropping neurons during training (훈련 중 무작위로 뉴런을 드롭하여 과적합을 방지하기 위해)

c) To accelerate the convergence of the model (모델의 수렴을 가속화하기 위해)

d) To reduce the number of layers in the model (모델의 층 수를 줄이기 위해)

36. Which of the following best describes gradient descent?

36. 다음 중 경사 하강법을 가장 잘 설명하는 것은 무엇인가?

a) A method for normalizing input data (입력 데이터를 정규화하는 방법)

b) An algorithm for optimizing the weights of a model (모델의 가중치를 최적화하는 알고리즘)

c) A technique for data augmentation (데이터 증강 기법)

d) A method for reducing the complexity of a neural network (신경망의 복잡성을 줄이는 방법)

37. What is a common use case for generative adversarial networks (GANs)?

37. 생성적 적대 신경망(GANs)의 일반적인 사용 사례는 무엇인가?

a) Classification of text data (텍스트 데이터 분류)

b) Identification of clusters (군집 식별)

c) Prediction of numerical values (수치 예측)

d) Generation of synthetic images (합성 이미지 생성)

38. Which of the following is a major challenge in working with time-series data?

38. 다음 중 시계열 데이터를 다루는 데 있어 주요 도전 과제는 무엇인가?

a) High dimensionality (고차원성)

b) Lack of labeled data (라벨이 없는 데이터 부족)

c) Temporal dependencies between observations (관측 간의 시간 의존성)

d) Overfitting the model (모델의 과적합)

35번 정답: b   36번 정답: b   37번 정답: d   38번 정답: c

39. What is a common evaluation metric used for classification problems?
39. 분류 문제에서 일반적으로 사용되는 평가 지표는 무엇인가?

a) Mean Squared Error (MSE: 평균 제곱 오차)
b) Root Mean Squared Error (RMSE: 제곱근 평균 제곱 오차)
c) F1 Score (F1 점수)
d) Mean Absolute Error (MAE: 평균 절대 오차)

40. Which AWS service can transcribe audio into text using machine learning?
40. 어떤 AWS 서비스가 기계 학습을 사용하여 오디오를 텍스트로 변환할 수 있는가?

a) Amazon Translate (아마존 트랜스레이트)
b) Amazon Polly (아마존 폴리)
c) Amazon Transcribe (아마존 트랜스크라이브)
d) Amazon Rekognition (아마존 레코그니션)

41. What is the main difference between reinforcement learning and supervised learning?
41. 강화 학습과 지도 학습의 주요 차이점은 무엇인가?

a) Reinforcement learning works with labeled data, while supervised learning does not (강화 학습은 라벨이 있는 데이터로 작동하고, 지도 학습은 그렇지 않음)
b) Supervised learning uses reward signals to improve models (지도 학습은 모델을 개선하기 위해 보상 신호 사용)
c) Reinforcement learning focuses on sequential decision-making (강화 학습은 순차적 의사 결정에 중점을 둠)
d) Reinforcement learning requires a large amount of training data (강화 학습은 대량의 훈련 데이터를 필요로 함)

42. Which of the following algorithms is best suited for text classification?
42. 다음 중 텍스트 분류에 가장 적합한 알고리즘은 무엇인가?

a) Naive Bayes (나이브 베이즈)
b) K-means (K-평균)
c) Principal Component Analysis (주성분 분석)
d) Linear Regression (선형 회귀)

39번 정답: c   40번 정답: c   41번 정답: c   42번 정답: a

43. What is the goal of normalization in machine learning?
43. 기계 학습에서 정규화의 목적은 무엇인가?

a) To reduce the dimensionality of data (데이터의 차원을 줄이기 위해)
b) To scale input features to a specific range (입력 특성을 특정 범위로 스케일링하기 위해)
c) To remove irrelevant features (관련 없는 특성을 제거하기 위해)
d) To optimize the learning rate (학습 속도를 최적화하기 위해)

44. What is the role of a kernel function in support vector machines (SVM)?
44. 서포트 벡터 머신(SVM)에서 커널 함수의 역할은 무엇인가?

a) To map the input data into a higher-dimensional space (입력 데이터를 고차원 공간에 매핑하는 것)
b) To reduce overfitting (과적합을 줄이는 것)
c) To normalize the data (데이터를 정규화하는 것)
d) To initialize weights in the model (모델의 가중치를 초기화하는 것)

45. In unsupervised learning, which algorithm is commonly used to group similar data points?
45. 비지도 학습에서 유사한 데이터 포인트를 그룹화하는 데 일반적으로 사용되는 알고리즘은 무엇인가?

a) Logistic Regression (로지스틱 회귀)
b) Decision Tree (의사결정 트리)
c) K-means Clustering (K-평균 군집화)
d) Random Forest (랜덤 포레스트)

46. What is the purpose of a confusion matrix in classification problems?
46. 분류 문제에서 혼동 행렬의 목적은 무엇인가?

a) To identify clusters in the data (데이터에서 군집을 식별하는 것)
b) To summarize the performance of a classification algorithm (분류 알고리즘의 성능을 요약하는 것)
c) To reduce overfitting in a model (모델의 과적합을 줄이는 것)
d) To calculate the loss function (손실 함수를 계산하는 것)

43번 정답: b   44번 정답: a   45번 정답: c   46번 정답: b

47. Which type of problem is best suited for regression analysis?
47. 회귀 분석에 가장 적합한 문제 유형은 무엇인가?

a) Predicting a continuous value (연속 값을 예측하는 것)

b) Classifying data into categories (데이터를 범주로 분류하는 것)

c) Grouping similar items together (유사한 항목을 그룹화하는 것)

d) Identifying relationships between variables (변수 간의 관계를 식별하는 것)

48. What is the main purpose of regularization in machine learning?
48. 기계 학습에서 정규화의 주요 목적은 무엇인가?

a) To prevent overfitting by penalizing large weights (큰 가중치에 대한 패널티로 과적합을 방지하는 것)

b) To reduce the number of layers in a neural network (신경망의 층 수를 줄이는 것)

c) To decrease the size of the dataset (데이터셋의 크기를 줄이는 것)

d) To improve the speed of training (훈련 속도를 개선하는 것)

49. Which AWS service can be used to detect patterns and anomalies in time series data?
49. 시계열 데이터에서 패턴과 이상치를 탐지하는 데 사용할 수 있는 AWS 서비스는 무엇인가?

a) Amazon Lookout for Metrics (아마존 룩아웃 포 메트릭스)

b) Amazon Transcribe (아마존 트랜스크라이브)

c) Amazon Polly (아마존 폴리)

d) Amazon Rekognition (아마존 레코그니션)

50. In which type of machine learning task would you typically use classification algorithms?
50. 어떤 유형의 기계 학습 작업에서 주로 분류 알고리즘을 사용하는가?

a) Predicting numerical values (수치 예측)

b) Grouping data into categories (데이터를 범주로 그룹화)

c) Identifying trends over time (시간에 따른 추세 식별)

d) Generating new features (새로운 특성 생성)

47번 정답: a   48번 정답: a   49번 정답: a   50번 정답: b

51. What is the main goal of unsupervised learning algorithms?

51. 비지도 학습 알고리즘의 주요 목적은 무엇인가?

a) To learn from labeled data (라벨이 있는 데이터에서 학습)
b) To find hidden patterns in data (데이터에서 숨겨진 패턴을 찾기)
c) To predict future values (미래 값을 예측)
d) To optimize model performance (모델 성능 최적화)

52. What is the advantage of using ensemble learning techniques?

52. 앙상블 학습 기법을 사용하는 장점은 무엇인가?

a) They are faster to train than individual models (개별 모델보다 훈련이 빠름)
b) They improve prediction accuracy by combining multiple models (여러 모델을 결합하여 예측 정확도 향상)
c) They require less training data (훈련 데이터가 적게 필요)
d) They are less prone to overfitting (과적합의 가능성이 낮음)

53. Which of the following is an example of a deep learning architecture?

53. 다음 중 딥러닝 아키텍처의 예는 무엇인가?

a) Support Vector Machine (서포트 벡터 머신)
b) Decision Tree (의사결정 트리)
c) Convolutional Neural Network (CNN) (합성곱 신경망)
d) K-means Clustering (K-평균 군집화)

54. What is the main challenge with using high-dimensional data in machine learning?

54. 기계 학습에서 고차원 데이터를 사용할 때의 주요 문제는 무엇인가?

a) It can cause underfitting (과소적합을 일으킬 수 있음)
b) It can lead to the curse of dimensionality (차원의 저주를 일으킬 수 있음)
c) It simplifies model training (모델 훈련 단순화)
d) It improves model generalization (모델 일반화 향상)

51번 정답: b   52번 정답: b   53번 정답: c   54번 정답: b

55. What type of learning involves an agent taking actions to maximize a reward signal?
55. 보상 신호를 극대화하기 위해 에이전트가 행동을 취하는 학습 유형은 무엇인가?

a) Unsupervised learning (비지도 학습)

b) Supervised learning (지도 학습)

c) Reinforcement learning (강화 학습)

d) Transfer learning (전이 학습)

56. What is the main difference between a classification and regression task?
56. 분류 작업과 회귀 작업의 주요 차이점은 무엇인가?

a) Regression requires more data than classification (회귀는 분류보다 더 많은 데이터를 요구)

b) Classification deals with discrete labels, while regression deals with continuous values (분류는 이산적인 라벨을 다루고, 회귀는 연속적인 값을 다룸)

c) Classification predicts numerical outcomes, while regression predicts categories (분류는 수치적 결과를 예측하고, 회귀는 범주를 예측)

d) Classification always requires unsupervised learning (분류는 항상 비지도 학습을 필요)

57. What is a hyperparameter in machine learning?
57. 기계 학습에서 하이퍼파라미터란 무엇인가?

a) A parameter learned during the training process (훈련 과정에서 학습된 매개변수)

b) A parameter set before the training process begins (훈련 과정 시작 전에 설정된 매개변수)

c) A variable that affects the output of the model (모델의 출력을 영향을 미치는 변수)

d) A feature of the input data (입력 데이터의 특성)

58. What type of neural network is commonly used for processing sequential data like text or time-series?
58. 텍스트나 시계열 데이터와 같은 순차 데이터를 처리하는 데 일반적으로 사용되는 신경망 유형은 무엇인가?

a) Convolutional Neural Network (CNN) (합성곱 신경망)

b) Recurrent Neural Network (RNN) (순환 신경망)

c) K-Nearest Neighbors (KNN) (K-최근접 이웃)

d) Support Vector Machine (SVM) (서포트 벡터 머신)

55번 정답: c   56번 정답: b   57번 정답: b   58번 정답: b

59. What is the purpose of feature scaling in machine learning?
59. 기계 학습에서 특성 스케일링의 목적은 무엇인가?

a) To increase the size of the dataset (데이터셋의 크기를 늘리기 위해)
b) To make sure features have similar magnitudes (특성들이 유사한 크기를 가지도록 하기 위해)
c) To enhance the model's interpretability (모델의 해석 가능성을 향상시키기 위해)
d) To reduce overfitting (과적합을 줄이기 위해)

60. Which AWS service uses machine learning to automatically translate text between different languages?
60. 기계 학습을 사용하여 언어 간 자동 번역을 가능하게 하는 AWS 서비스는 무엇인가?

a) Amazon Polly (아마존 폴리)
b) Amazon Translate (아마존 트랜슬레이트)
c) Amazon Comprehend (아마존 컴프리헨드)
d) AWS SageMaker (아마존 세이지메이커)

61. What is a key characteristic of reinforcement learning?
61. 강화 학습의 주요 특성은 무엇인가?

a) It uses labeled data for training (라벨이 있는 데이터를 사용하여 학습)
b) It learns from interactions with an environment to maximize rewards (환경과의 상호작용을 통해 보상을 극대화하는 학습)
c) It focuses on clustering similar data points (유사한 데이터 포인트를 군집화하는 데 중점)
d) It applies transfer learning techniques (전이 학습 기법 적용)

62. In a neural network, what is the purpose of backpropagation?
62. 신경망에서 역전파의 목적은 무엇인가?

a) To initialize the weights of the network (네트워크의 가중치를 초기화하기 위해)
b) To update the weights based on the loss function (손실 함수에 따라 가중치를 업데이트하기 위해)
c) To evaluate the performance of the model (모델의 성능을 평가하기 위해)
d) To reduce the dimensionality of input data (입력 데이터의 차원을 줄이기 위해)

59번 정답: b   60번 정답: b   61번 정답: b   62번 정답: b

63. What is the primary goal of natural language processing (NLP)?
63. 자연어 처리(NLP)의 주요 목표는 무엇인가?

a) To extract insights from structured numerical data (구조화된 수치 데이터에서 인사이트 추출하기 위해)
b) To understand and process human language (인간 언어를 이해하고 처리하기 위해)
c) To improve the performance of neural networks (신경망의 성능을 개선하기 위해)
d) To create realistic visual representations (사실적인 시각적 표현을 생성하기 위해)

64. Which of the following is a popular deep learning library for Python?
64. 다음 중 Python에서 인기 있는 딥러닝 라이브러리는 무엇인가?

a) TensorFlow (텐서플로우)
b) NumPy (넘파이)
c) SciPy (사이파이)
d) Matplotlib (맷플롯립)

65. What is a major challenge when using deep learning models for real-time applications?
65. 실시간 애플리케이션에 딥러닝 모델을 사용할 때의 주요 과제는 무엇인가?

a) Lack of sufficient data (충분한 데이터 부족)
b) High computational requirements (높은 계산 요구 사항)
c) Poor model accuracy (모델 정확도 저하)
d) Overfitting issues (과적합 문제)

66. Which AWS service allows you to build and deploy machine learning models without having to manage infrastructure?
66. 인프라를 관리하지 않고도 기계 학습 모델을 구축하고 배포할 수 있는 AWS 서비스는 무엇인가?

a) Amazon Comprehend (아마존 컴프리헨드)
b) AWS SageMaker (아마존 세이지메이커)
c) Amazon Translate (아마존 트랜슬레이트)
d) Amazon Rekognition (아마존 레코그니션)

63번 정답: b   56번 정답: a   65번 정답: b   66번 정답: b

67. What is the role of a dropout layer in a neural network?

67. 신경망에서 드롭아웃 층의 역할은 무엇인가?

a) To reduce overfitting by randomly dropping units during training (훈련 중 무작위로 유닛을 드롭하여 과적합을 줄이기 위해)
b) To increase the learning rate during backpropagation (역전파 중 학습 속도를 높이기 위해)
c) To add more layers to the network (네트워크에 더 많은 층을 추가하기 위해)
d) To decrease the dimensionality of input data (입력 데이터의 차원을 줄이기 위해)

68. Which AWS service is primarily used for sentiment analysis of text data?

68. 텍스트 데이터의 감정 분석에 주로 사용되는 AWS 서비스는 무엇인가?

a) Amazon Polly (아마존 폴리)
b) Amazon Comprehend (아마존 컴프리헨드)
c) AWS Lambda (아마존 람다)
d) Amazon Lex (아마존 렉스)

69. What is an epoch in the context of machine learning?

69. 기계 학습에서 에폭(epoch)이란 무엇인가?

a) The process of initializing the model's weights (모델의 가중치를 초기화하는 과정)
b) The time it takes to process one batch of data (하나의 배치를 처리하는 데 걸리는 시간)
c) One complete pass through the training data (훈련 데이터를 한 번 완전히 통과하는 것)
d) The number of hidden layers in a neural network (신경망의 은닉층 수)

70. What is the main challenge of using reinforcement learning in real-world environments?

70. 실제 환경에서 강화 학습을 사용하는 데 주요 과제는 무엇인가?

a) Limited availability of labeled data (라벨이 달린 데이터의 제한된 가용성)
b) High computational cost and time for training (훈련에 높은 계산 비용과 시간이 소요됨)
c) Difficulty in hyperparameter tuning (하이퍼파라미터 조정의 어려움)
d) Lack of appropriate optimization algorithms (적절한 최적화 알고리즘 부족)

67번 정답: a   68번 정답: b   69번 정답: c   70번 정답: b

71. What is a major advantage of transfer learning in deep learning?
71. 딥러닝에서 전이 학습의 주요 장점은 무엇인가?

a) It eliminates the need for large training datasets (대규모 훈련 데이터셋의 필요성 제거)
b) It allows models to be trained faster by using pre-trained weights (사전 학습된 가중치를 사용하여 모델을 더 빠른 훈련)
c) It automatically tunes hyperparameters (하이퍼파라미터 자동 조정)
d) It reduces the risk of overfitting in regression tasks (회귀 작업에서 과적합의 위험 감소)

72. In machine learning, what is the purpose of cross-validation?
72. 기계 학습에서 교차 검증의 목적은 무엇인가?

a) To improve model interpretability (모델의 해석 가능성을 개선하기 위해)
b) To evaluate the model's performance on unseen data (보지 못한 데이터에서 모델 성능 평가를 위해)
c) To enhance model training speed (모델 훈련 속도를 높이기 위해)
d) To reduce the dimensionality of features (특성의 차원을 줄이기 위해)

73. Which AWS service allows you to build conversational interfaces for applications?
73. 애플리케이션을 위한 대화형 인터페이스를 구축할 수 있는 AWS 서비스는 무엇인가?

a) Amazon Polly (아마존 폴리)
b) Amazon Rekognition (아마존 레코그니션)
c) Amazon Lex (아마존 렉스)
d) AWS Lambda (아마존 람다)

74. What is the purpose of using word embeddings in natural language processing?
74. 자연어 처리에서 워드 임베딩을 사용하는 목적은 무엇인가?

a) To represent words in a lower-dimensional space (단어를 저차원 공간에서 표현하기 위해)
b) To normalize text data (텍스트 데이터를 정규화하기 위해)
c) To cluster similar text documents (유사한 텍스트 문서를 클러스터링하기 위해)
d) To convert text data into image features (텍스트 데이터를 이미지 특징으로 변환하기 위해)

71번 정답: b   72번 정답: b   73번 정답: c   74번 정답: a

75. What is the key advantage of using AWS Lambda for AI applications?
75. AI 애플리케이션에 AWS Lambda를 사용하는 주요 장점은 무엇인가?

a) It enables serverless architecture, reducing infrastructure management (서버리스 아키텍처를 가능하게 하여 인프라 관리 줄이기)

b) It allows for real-time model training (실시간 모델 훈련 가능)

c) It is optimized for large-scale batch processing (대규모 배치 처리를 위한 최적화)

d) It automatically generates machine learning models (기계 학습 모델 자동 생성)

76. What is the main challenge of using reinforcement learning in real-world environments?
76. 실제 환경에서 강화 학습을 사용하는 데 주요 과제는 무엇인가?

a) Limited availability of labeled data (라벨이 달린 데이터의 제한된 가용성)

b) High computational cost and time for training (훈련에 높은 계산 비용과 시간이 소요됨)

c) Difficulty in hyperparameter tuning (하이퍼파라미터 조정의 어려움)

d) Lack of appropriate optimization algorithms (적절한 최적화 알고리즘 부족)

77. What is the primary function of Amazon Polly?
77. 아마존 폴리(Amazon Polly)의 주요 기능은 무엇인가?

a) Text-to-speech conversion (텍스트 음성 변환)

b) Image recognition (이미지 인식)

c) Text summarization (텍스트 요약)

d) Sentiment analysis (감정 분석)

78. Which machine learning technique is used to group similar items together without labeled data?
78. 라벨이 없는 데이터로 유사한 항목을 함께 그룹화하는 데 사용되는 기계 학습 기법은 무엇인가?

a) Supervised learning (지도 학습)

b) Reinforcement learning (강화 학습)

c) Clustering (군집화)

d) Classification (분류)

75번 정답: a   76번 정답: b   77번 정답: a   78번 정답: c

79. What is the purpose of a confusion matrix in evaluating a machine learning model?
79. 기계 학습 모델을 평가할 때 혼동 행렬의 목적은 무엇인가?

a) To track the number of epochs during training (훈련 중 에폭 수 추적)
b) To measure the difference between predicted and actual values (예측 값과 실제 값 간의 차이 측정)
c) To summarize the performance of a classification model (분류 모델의 성능 요약)
d) To tune hyperparameters during model training (모델 훈련 중 하이퍼파라미터 조정)

80. In which AWS service can you use pre-built algorithms to train your machine learning models?
80. 기계 학습 모델을 훈련하기 위해 사전 구축된 알고리즘을 사용할 수 있는 AWS 서비스는 무엇인가?

a) AWS Lambda (아마존 람다)
b) Amazon SageMaker (아마존 세이지메이커)
c) Amazon Translate (아마존 트랜슬레이트)
d) Amazon Kinesis (아마존 키네시스)

81. What is overfitting in machine learning?
81. 기계 학습에서 과적합이란 무엇인가?

a) When a model performs well on training data but poorly on new data (모델이 훈련 데이터에서는 잘 작동하지만 새로운 데이터에서는 성능이 저하될 때)
b) When a model has too few features (모델이 너무 적은 특성을 가졌을 때)
c) When a model is not complex enough (모델이 충분히 복잡하지 않을 때)
d) When a model uses too much memory (모델이 너무 많은 메모리를 사용할 때)

82. Which technique can help prevent overfitting in machine learning models?
82. 기계 학습 모델에서 과적합을 방지하는 데 도움이 되는 기법은 무엇인가?

a) Increasing the number of training epochs (훈련 에폭 수를 늘리는 것)
b) Decreasing the number of hidden layers in a neural network (신경망의 은닉층 수를 줄이는 것)
c) Using regularization techniques like L2 (L2와 같은 정규화 기법을 사용하는 것)
d) Reducing the size of the training dataset (훈련 데이터셋의 크기를 줄이는 것)

79번 정답: c   80번 정답: b   81번 정답: a   82번 정답: c

83. What is a key advantage of using managed services like Amazon Comprehend for NLP tasks?
83. NLP 작업에 아마존 컴프리헨드와 같은 관리형 서비스를 사용할 때의 주요 장점은 무엇인가?

a) It eliminates the need for custom model training (맞춤형 모델 훈련의 필요성 제거)
b) It automatically generates new training data (새로운 훈련 데이터를 자동으로 생성)
c) It is optimized for large-scale image processing (대규모 이미지 처리에 최적화)
d) It simplifies real-time video analysis (실시간 비디오 분석을 간소화)

84. What is the role of hyperparameters in machine learning models?
84. 기계 학습 모델에서 하이퍼파라미터의 역할은 무엇인가?

a) They control the training process and model complexity (훈련 과정과 모델의 복잡성을 제어)
b) They serve as the input features for a model (모델의 입력 특성으로 사용)
c) They evaluate the performance of a model (모델의 성능을 평가)
d) They store intermediate data during training (훈련 중 중간 데이터 저장)

85. In AWS SageMaker, what is a benefit of using automatic model tuning?
85. AWS SageMaker에서 자동 모델 튜닝을 사용하는 이점은 무엇인가?

a) It tunes the hyperparameters to optimize model performance (모델 성능을 최적화하기 위해 하이퍼파라미터를 조정)
b) It generates new training data from existing data (기존 데이터에서 새로운 훈련 데이터를 생성)
c) It automatically selects the best model architecture (최적의 모델 아키텍처를 자동으로 선택)
d) It reduces the need for feature engineering (특성 엔지니어링의 필요성을 감소)

86. Which AWS service would you use to detect objects and faces in images?
86. 이미지에서 객체와 얼굴을 감지하는 데 사용할 AWS 서비스는 무엇인가?

a) Amazon Comprehend (아마존 컴프리헨드)
b) Amazon SageMaker (아마존 세이지메이커)
c) Amazon Rekognition (아마존 레코그니션)
d) AWS Lambda (아마존 람다)

83번 정답: a   84번 정답: a   85번 정답: a   86번 정답: c

87. In a neural network, what is the function of an activation function?
87. 신경망에서 활성화 함수의 역할은 무엇인가?

a) It initializes the weights of the network (네트워크의 가중치를 초기화)
b) It determines the output of each neuron (각 뉴런의 출력을 결정)
c) It adjusts the learning rate during training (훈련 중 학습 속도를 조정)
d) It reduces the number of hidden layers (은닉층 수 감소)

88. What is a key characteristic of unsupervised learning?
88. 비지도 학습의 주요 특성은 무엇인가?

a) It uses labeled data for training (라벨이 있는 데이터를 사용하여 학습)
b) It focuses on clustering and association tasks (군집화 및 연관 작업에 중점)
c) It requires large amounts of training data (많은 양의 훈련 데이터를 요구)
d) It is primarily used for regression tasks (주로 회귀 작업에 사용)

89. Which AWS service provides real-time video and image analysis?
82. 기계 학습 모델에서 과적합을 방지하는 데 도움이 되는 기법은 무엇인가?

a) Amazon Polly (아마존 폴리)
b) Amazon Kinesis Video Streams (아마존 키네시스 비디오 스트림)
c) Amazon Rekognition (아마존 레코그니션)
d) Amazon Lex (아마존 렉스)

90. What is the purpose of using cross-entropy loss in machine learning?
90. 기계 학습에서 교차 엔트로피 손실을 사용하는 목적은 무엇인가?

a) To calculate the error in classification tasks (분류 작업에서 오류를 계산하기 위해)
b) To measure the distance between predicted and actual values in regression (회귀에서 예측 값과 실제 값 간의 거리를 측정하기 위해)
c) To initialize the model weights (모델 가중치를 초기화하기 위해)
d) To perform feature scaling (특성 스케일링을 수행하기 위해)

87번 정답: b   88번 정답: b   89번 정답: c   90번 정답: a

91. Which AWS service helps create interactive chatbots for customer support?
91. 고객 지원을 위한 대화형 챗봇을 만드는 데 도움이 되는 AWS 서비스는 무엇인가?

a) Amazon Polly (아마존 폴리)
b) Amazon Rekognition (아마존 레코그니션)
c) AWS Lambda (아마존 람다)
d) Amazon Lex (아마존 렉스)

92. In the context of machine learning, what is dimensionality reduction?
92. 기계 학습에서 차원 축소란 무엇인가?

a) Reducing the number of features in the dataset (데이터셋의 특성 수를 줄이는 것)
b) Decreasing the size of the training dataset (훈련 데이터셋의 크기를 줄이는 것)
c) Adding more hidden layers to a neural network (신경망에 더 많은 은닉층을 추가하는 것)
d) Increasing the number of epochs during training (훈련 중 에폭 수를 늘리는 것)

93. What is a common approach to improving the performance of an underfitting machine learning model?
93. 과소적합된 기계 학습 모델의 성능을 향상시키기 위한 일반적인 접근 방식은 무엇인가?

a) Decreasing the complexity of the model (모델의 복잡성을 줄이기)
b) Increasing the amount of training data (훈련 데이터의 양을 늘리기)
c) Reducing the number of features in the dataset (데이터셋의 특성 수를 줄이기)
d) Decreasing the number of training epochs (훈련 에폭 수를 줄이기)

94. What is the key role of the optimizer in training a machine learning model?
94. 기계 학습 모델 훈련에서 옵티마이저의 주요 역할은 무엇인가?

a) To minimize the loss function by updating the weights (가중치를 업데이트하여 손실 함수 최소화하기)
b) To generate new training data from the existing data (기존 데이터에서 새로운 훈련 데이터 생성하기)
c) To select the most important features from the dataset (데이터셋에서 가장 중요한 특성을 선택하기)
d) To reduce overfitting during training (훈련 중 과적합을 줄이기)

91번 정답: d   92번 정답: a   93번 정답: b   94번 정답: a

95. Which of the following is an unsupervised learning algorithm?
95. 다음 중 비지도 학습 알고리즘은 무엇인가?

a) Linear regression (선형 회귀)
b) Decision tree (의사결정 트리)
c) K-means clustering (K-평균 군집화)
d) Logistic regression (로지스틱 회귀)

96. What is the purpose of one-hot encoding in machine learning?
96. 기계 학습에서 원-핫 인코딩의 목적은 무엇인가?

a) To convert categorical data into a numerical format (범주형 데이터를 수치 형식으로 변환하기 위해)
b) To normalize numerical data (수치 데이터를 정규화하기 위해)
c) To reduce the dimensionality of input data (입력 데이터의 차원을 줄이기 위해)
d) To enhance the interpretability of model predictions (모델 예측의 해석 가능성을 향상시키기 위해)

97. Which AWS service can be used to process large-scale streaming data in real-time?
97. 대규모 스트리밍 데이터를 실시간으로 처리하는 데 사용할 수 있는 AWS 서비스는 무엇인가?

a) AWS Lambda (아마존 람다)
b) Amazon Kinesis (아마존 키네시스)
c) Amazon Polly (아마존 폴리)
d) Amazon SageMaker (아마존 세이지메이커)

98. Which AWS service offers pre-trained models specifically for translating languages?
98. 언어 번역을 위한 사전 훈련된 모델을 제공하는 AWS 서비스는 무엇인가?

a) Amazon Polly (아마존 폴리)
b) AWS Lambda (아마존 람다)
c) Amazon Translate (아마존 트랜슬레이트)
d) Amazon Lex (아마존 렉스)

95번 정답: c   96번 정답: a   97번 정답: b   98번 정답: c

99. What is a benefit of using AWS SageMaker for machine learning?
99. 기계 학습에서 AWS SageMaker를 사용하는 이점은 무엇인가?

a) It allows easy integration with deep learning frameworks like TensorFlow and PyTorch (텐서플로우 및 파이토치와 같은 딥러닝 프레임워크와의 쉬운 통합을 가능)

b) It automatically generates labeled data for training (훈련을 위한 라벨이 달린 데이터를 자동으로 생성)

c) It eliminates the need for hyperparameter tuning (하이퍼파라미터 튜닝의 필요성을 제거)

d) It performs feature selection during training (훈련 중에 특성 선택을 수행)

100. What is a key difference between classification and regression tasks?
100. 분류 작업과 회귀 작업의 주요 차이점은 무엇인가?

a) Classification predicts continuous values, while regression predicts categories (분류는 연속 값을 예측하고 회귀는 범주를 예측)

b) Classification predicts categories, while regression predicts continuous values (분류는 범주를 예측하고 회귀는 연속 값을 예측)

c) Classification requires labeled data, while regression uses unlabeled data (분류는 라벨이 있는 데이터를 요구하고 회귀는 라벨이 없는 데이터를 사용)

d) Classification is used for clustering, while regression is used for ranking (분류는 군집화에 사용되고 회귀는 순위 매김에 사용)

99번 정답: a   100번 정답: b

도메인 2: 생성형 AI의 기본 원리

기초적인 생성형 AI 개념(transformer 아키텍처, 프롬프트 엔지니어링, LLM의 작동 방식 등)과 Amazon Bedrock, Amazon CodeWhisperer, Amazon Lex와 같은 AWS의 생성형 AI 서비스들의 특징 및 활용 사례를 이해하고 있는지 평가하며, 특히 프롬프트 작성 기법(Few-shot learning, Chain-of-thought 등)과 생성형 AI 모델의 한계점(환각, 편향성, 보안 문제 등)을 정확히 파악하고 이를 실제 비즈니스 상황에 적용할 수 있는지를 중점적으로 테스트하므로, 시험 준비 시에는 생성형 AI의 기술적 원리뿐만 아니라 실제 서비스 구현 시 발생할 수 있는 다양한 문제점들과 이에 대한 해결 방안, 그리고 책임있는 AI 구현을 위한 모범 사례들을 함께 학습하는 것을 권장한다.

1. What does the discriminator do in a GAN?
1. GAN에서 판별자의 역할은 무엇인가?

a) Generates new data samples (새로운 데이터 샘플을 생성)
b) Predicts future data points (미래 데이터 포인트를 예측)
c) Discriminates between real and fake data (진짜 데이터와 가짜 데이터를 구별)
d) Classifies images (이미지 분류)

2. What is a common challenge in training GANs?
2. GAN을 훈련할 때 흔히 발생하는 문제는 무엇인가?

a) Overfitting the model (모델 과적합)
b) Mode collapse (모드 붕괴)
c) Data imbalance (데이터 불균형)
d) Lack of labeled data (라벨이 없는 데이터 부족)

1번 정답: c   2번 정답: b

3. What does a Generative Adversarial Network (GAN) consist of?
3. 생성적 적대 신경망(GAN)은 무엇으로 구성되어 있는가?

a) A generator and discriminator (생성자와 판별자)
b) A classifier and detector (분류기와 탐지기)
c) A predictor and optimizer (예측기와 최적화기)
d) An encoder and decoder (인코더와 디코더)

4. Which of the following is an example of a generative AI task?
4. 다음 중 생성 AI 작업의 예는 무엇인가?

a) Sentiment analysis (감정 분석)
b) Image classification (이미지 분류)
c) Text translation (텍스트 번역)
d) Image synthesis (이미지 합성)

5. In a GAN, what is the role of the generator?
5. GAN에서 생성자의 역할은 무엇인가?

a) To evaluate the generated data (생성된 데이터를 평가하기 위해)
b) To generate fake data samples (가짜 데이터 샘플을 생성하기 위해)
c) To train a predictive model (예측 모델을 훈련하기 위해)
d) To classify real data from fake data (진짜 데이터를 가짜 데이터와 구분하기 위해)

6. Which of the following is an application of generative AI in the entertainment industry?
6. 다음 중 엔터테인먼트 산업에서 생성 AI의 응용 사례는 무엇인가?

a) Fraud detection (사기 탐지)
b) Image captioning (이미지 캡셔닝)
c) Movie script generation (영화 대본 생성)
d) Spam filtering (스팸 필터링)

3번 정답: a   4번 정답: d   5번 정답: b   6번 정답: c

7. What is the primary purpose of generative AI models?

7. 생성 AI 모델의 주요 목적은 무엇인가?

a) To classify data into predefined categories (데이터를 미리 정의된 범주로 분류하기 위해)
b) To generate new data based on existing patterns (기존 패턴을 기반으로 새로운 데이터를 생성하기 위해)
c) To segment and analyze datasets (데이터셋을 세분화하고 분석하기 위해)
d) To perform supervised learning tasks (지도 학습 작업을 수행하기 위해)

8. Which type of neural network is commonly used for generative AI applications?

8. 생성 AI 애플리케이션에 일반적으로 사용되는 신경망 유형은 무엇인가?

a) Convolutional Neural Networks (CNNs) (합성곱 신경망)
b) Recurrent Neural Networks (RNNs) (순환 신경망)
c) Generative Adversarial Networks (GANs) (생성적 적대 신경망)
d) Deep Q-Networks (DQNs) (딥 Q-네트워크)

9. What type of data does a generative AI model typically use during training?

9. 생성 AI 모델이 훈련 중에 일반적으로 사용하는 데이터 유형은 무엇인가?

a) Supervised data with labeled outcomes (라벨이 있는 지도 데이터)
b) Unlabeled data for self-supervised learning (자기 지도 학습을 위한 라벨이 없는 데이터)
c) Real-world data to learn patterns (패턴을 학습하기 위한 실제 데이터)
d) Only synthetic data generated by the model (모델이 생성한 합성 데이터만)

10. Which of the following techniques is NOT commonly used in generative AI?

10. 다음 중 생성 AI에서 일반적으로 사용되지 않는 기술은 무엇인가?

a) Autoencoders (오토인코더)
b) GANs (생성적 적대 신경망)
c) LSTMs (장기-단기 메모리)
d) K-Means Clustering (K-평균 군집화)

7번 정답: b   8번 정답: c   9번 정답: c   10번 정답: d

11. What is a popular generative AI architecture used for text generation?

11. 텍스트 생성을 위해 널리 사용되는 생성 AI 아키텍처는 무엇인가?

a) Transformer model (트랜스포머 모델)
b) Convolutional Neural Networks (CNNs) (합성곱 신경망)
c) Long Short-Term Memory (LSTM) (장기-단기 메모리)
d) Decision Trees (의사 결정 나무)

12. Which of the following generative models can be used for generating high-quality text?

12. 다음 중 고품질 텍스트 생성을 위해 사용할 수 있는 생성 모델은 무엇인가?

a) LSTM (장기-단기 메모리)
b) BERT (버트)
c) GPT (Generative Pre-trained Transformer) (생성적 사전 학습 트랜스포머)
d) Naive Bayes (나이브 베이즈)

13. Variational Autoencoders (VAEs) are primarily used for which type of generative AI task?

13. 변이형 오토인코더(VAE)는 주로 어떤 유형의 생성 AI 작업에 사용되는가?

a) Image classification (이미지 분류)
b) Dimensionality reduction (차원 축소)
c) Data generation (데이터 생성)
d) Speech recognition (음성 인식)

14. In the context of generative AI, what does "latent space" refer to?

14. 생성 AI에서 "잠재 공간"은 무엇을 의미하는가?

a) A high-dimensional space where data points are represented in a compressed form (데이터 포인트가 압축된 형태로 표현되는 고차원 공간)
b) The space where the discriminator operates in a GAN (GAN에서 판별자가 작동하는 공간)
c) The output space of a neural network (신경망의 출력 공간)
d) The real-world environment used to generate data (데이터 생성을 위해 사용되는 실제 환경)

11번 정답: a   12번 정답: c   13번 정답: c   14번 정답: a

15. What is the purpose of the "reconstruction loss" in autoencoders?
15. 오토인코더에서 "재구성 손실"의 목적은 무엇인가?

a) To measure the difference between generated and real data (생성된 데이터와 실제 데이터의 차이를 측정)
b) To reconstruct real-world labels (실제 라벨 재구성)
c) To penalize wrong classifications (잘못된 분류에 대해 페널티를 부과)
d) To calculate the accuracy of predictions (예측의 정확도를 계산)

16. Which of the following is a benefit of using pre-trained generative models?
16. 다음 중 사전 학습된 생성 모델을 사용할 때의 이점은 무엇인가?

a) Reduced training time (훈련 시간 단축)
b) Improved labeled data availability (라벨링된 데이터의 가용성 향상)
c) Guaranteed accuracy (정확도 보장)
d) Complete avoidance of overfitting (과적합 완전 회피

17. In generative AI, what does "overfitting" typically lead to?
17. 생성 AI에서 "과적합"은 일반적으로 무엇으로 이어지는가?

a) The model becoming too generalized (모델이 지나치게 일반화됨)
b) The model capturing noise in training data (모델이 훈련 데이터의 노이즈를 포착함)
c) Increased accuracy in unseen data (보지 못한 데이터에서 정확도 증가)
d) The ability to generate completely novel data (완전히 새로운 데이터를 생성할 수 있는 능력)

18. Which generative AI model is most associated with creating deepfake videos?
18. 딥페이크 비디오 생성과 가장 관련이 있는 생성 AI 모델은 무엇인가?

a) CNNs (합성곱 신경망들)
b) GANs (생성적 적대 신경망들)
c) LSTMs (장기 단기 메모리 신경망들)
d) Decision Trees (결정 트리)

15번 정답: a   16번 정답: a   17번 정답: b   18번 정답: b

19. Which of the following is a potential ethical concern associated with generative AI?
19. 다음 중 생성 AI와 관련된 잠재적인 윤리적 문제는 무엇인가?

a) Improving classification accuracy (분류 정확도 향상)
b) Reducing training costs (훈련 비용 절감)
c) The creation of synthetic data for malicious use (악의적인 사용을 위한 합성 데이터 생성)
d) Using too much computing power (과도한 컴퓨팅 파워 사용)

20. What is the main advantage of using generative AI models in design and creativity industries?
20. 디자인 및 창의성 산업에서 생성 AI 모델을 사용할 때의 주요 이점은 무엇인가?

a) Reduced need for manual classification (수동 분류의 필요성 감소)
b) Increased data processing speed (데이터 처리 속도 향상)
c) Creation of novel and unique content (새롭고 독창적인 콘텐츠 생성)
d) Elimination of data labeling (데이터 라벨링 제거)

21. Which of the following is a core challenge when training a GAN?
21. GAN을 훈련할 때의 핵심 과제는 무엇인가?

a) Slow processing speed (느린 처리 속도)
b) Generator overpowering the discriminator (생성자가 판별자를 압도함)
c) Mode collapse (모드 붕괴)
d) Lack of sufficient labeled data (충분한 라벨링된 데이터 부족)

22. What is the role of the latent vector in a GAN model?
22. GAN 모델에서 잠재 벡터의 역할은 무엇인가?

a) It represents the training labels (훈련 레이블을 나타내기)
b) It is the input to the generator for creating new samples (새로운 샘플을 생성하기 위한 생성기의 입력)
c) It measures the accuracy of the discriminator (판별기의 정확도를 측정)
d) It adjusts the learning rate of the model (모델의 학습률을 조정)

19번 정답: c   20번 정답: c   21번 정답: c   22번 정답: b

23. Generative AI models are typically designed to do which of the following?
23. 생성 AI 모델은 일반적으로 다음을 위해 설계된다. 이중 맞는 것은?

a) Classify data into predefined categories (데이터를 미리 정의된 범주로 분류하기 위해)

b) Predict the next item in a sequence (시퀀스에서 다음 항목을 예측하기 위해)

c) Generate new and unseen data (새롭고 보이지 않는 데이터를 생성하기 위해)

d) Detect anomalies in datasets (데이터셋에서 이상치를 감지하기 위해)

24. Which neural network architecture is most commonly used for generative image tasks?
24. 생성 이미지 작업에 가장 많이 사용되는 신경망 아키텍처는 무엇인가?

a) CNN (합성곱 신경망)

b) RNN (순환 신경망)

c) GAN (생성적 적대 신경망)

d) Q-Learning (Q-러닝)

25. What distinguishes a Variational Autoencoder (VAE) from a regular Autoencoder?
25. 변분 오토인코더(VAE)와 일반 오토인코더의 차이점은 무엇인가?

a) The use of a probabilistic latent space (확률적 잠재 공간의 사용)

b) The ability to classify data (데이터를 분류하는 능력)

c) The capacity to perform reinforcement learning tasks (강화 학습 작업을 수행하는 능력)

d) The architecture that includes convolution layers (컨볼루션 레이어를 포함한 아키텍처)

26. In the context of natural language processing, which generative model has demonstrated high success in text generation tasks?
26. 자연어 처리의 맥락에서 텍스트 생성 작업에서 높은 성공을 보여준 생성 모델은 무엇인가?

a) Naive Bayes (나이브 베이즈)

b) GPT (Generative Pre-trained Transformer)

c) Logistic Regression (로지스틱 회귀)

d) RNN

23번 정답: c   24번 정답: c   25번 정답: a   26번 정답: b

27. Which of the following is a common loss function used in GANs?
27. 다음 중 GAN에서 흔히 사용되는 손실 함수는 무엇인가?

a) Cross-entropy loss (교차 엔트로피 손실)
b) Mean squared error (평균 제곱 오차)
c) Binary classification loss (이진 분류 손실)
d) Hinge loss (힌지 손실)

28. What is the "latent space" in generative AI?
28. 생성 AI에서 "잠재 공간"이란 무엇인가?

a) A compressed representation of input data (입력 데이터의 압축 표현)
b) The output layer in neural networks (신경망의 출력 레이어)
c) A separate space used to label data (데이터에 레이블을 지정하기 위해 사용되는 별도의 공간)
d) A place where AI data is stored (AI 데이터가 저장되는 장소)

29. Which model is best suited for generating synthetic images of faces?
29. 얼굴의 합성 이미지를 생성하는 데 가장 적합한 모델은 무엇인가?

a) RNN (순환 신경망)
b) CNN (합성곱 신경망)
c) GAN (생성적 적대 신경망)
d) BERT (버트)

30. In a Variational Autoencoder, what is the purpose of the encoder?
30. 변이형 오토인코더에서 인코더의 목적은 무엇인가?

a) To reconstruct data from the latent space (잠재 공간에서 데이터를 재구성하기 위해)
b) To map input data into a latent space (입력 데이터를 잠재 공간으로 매핑하기 위해)
c) To predict the class of the input data (입력 데이터의 클래스를 예측하기 위해)
d) To generate new data samples (새로운 데이터 샘플을 생성하기 위해)

27번 정답: a   28번 정답: a   29번 정답: c   30번 정답: b

31. What is the main purpose of the generator in a GAN?
31. GAN에서 생성자의 주요 목적은 무엇인가?

a) To evaluate the loss function (손실 함수를 평가하기 위해)
b) To generate new data samples (새로운 데이터 샘플을 생성하기 위해)
c) To classify images (이미지를 분류하기 위해)
d) To adjust the learning rate (학습률을 조정하기 위해)

32. Generative models like VAEs and GANs fall under which category of machine learning?
32. VAE 및 GAN과 같은 생성 모델은 기계 학습의 어떤 범주에 속하는가?

a) Supervised learning (지도 학습)
b) Reinforcement learning (강화 학습)
c) Unsupervised learning (비지도 학습)
d) Semi-supervised learning (반지도 학습)

33. Which type of neural network architecture is commonly used for sequence-to-sequence modeling in generative tasks?
33. 생성 작업에서 시퀀스-투-시퀀스 모델링에 일반적으로 사용되는 신경망 아키텍처 유형은 무엇인가?

a) Transformer (트랜스포머)
b) CNN
c) GAN
d) Naive Bayes (나이브 베이즈)

34. In GANs, what is the primary goal of the discriminator?
34. GAN에서 판별자의 주요 목표는 무엇인가?

a) To minimize the loss (손실을 최소화하기 위해)
b) To classify generated data as fake or real (생성된 데이터를 가짜 또는 실제로 분류하기 위해)
c) To generate high-quality data (고품질 데이터를 생성하기 위해)
d) To optimize the latent vector (잠재 벡터를 최적화하기 위해)

31번 정답: b   32번 정답: c   33번 정답: a   34번 정답: b

35. Which of the following is an application of generative AI in the healthcare industry?
35. 다음 중 의료 산업에서 생성 AI의 응용 분야는 무엇인가?

a) Generating synthetic patient data (합성 환자 데이터를 생성하기 위해)
b) Classifying patient health records (환자 건강 기록을 분류하기 위해)
c) Optimizing treatment plans (치료 계획을 최적화하기 위해)
d) Segmenting MRI scans (MRI 스캔을 세분화하기 위해)

36. What does "mode collapse" refer to in the context of training a GAN?
36. "모드 붕괴"는 GAN을 훈련하는 맥락에서 무엇을 무엇인가?

a) A situation where the generator produces limited types of outputs (생성자가 제한된 유형의 출력을 생성하는 상황)
b) The failure of the discriminator to distinguish real from fake data (판별자가 진짜와 가짜 데이터를 구별하지 못하는 상황)
c) The inability to optimize the learning rate (학습률을 최적화할 수 없는 상황)
d) The collapse of all network weights to zero (모든 네트워크 가중치가 0으로 붕괴하는 상황)

37. Which generative AI technique allows the interpolation of data in a latent space to generate new, meaningful samples?
37. 어떤 생성 AI 기법이 잠재 공간에서 데이터를 보간하여 새로운 의미 있는 샘플을 생성하는가?

a) LSTM (장단기 메모리)
b) VAE (변분 오토인코더)
c) CNN (합성곱 신경망)
d) DQN (심층 Q-네트워크)

38. The Transformer model is widely known for which of the following applications?
39. Transformer 모델은 다음 응용 프로그램 중 어떤 것으로 널리 알려져 있는가?

a) Time series forecasting (시계열 예측)
b) Image classification (이미지 분류)
c) Natural language processing (자연어 처리)
d) Fraud detection (사기 탐지)

35번 정답: a   36번 정답: a   37번 정답: b   38번 정답: c

39. Which generative AI model is designed to encode input into a compressed format and then decode it back?
39. 어떤 생성 AI 모델이 입력을 압축 형식으로 인코딩한 다음 다시 디코딩하도록 설계되어있는가?

a) VAE (변분 오토인코더)
b) GAN (생성적 적대 신경망)
c) RNN (순환 신경망)
d) DQN (심층 Q-네트워크)

40. What is a common application of generative AI in the gaming industry?
40. 게임 산업에서 생성 AI의 일반적인 응용은 무엇인가?

a) Classification of player behaviors (플레이어 행동 분류)
b) Creation of in-game assets like characters or landscapes (캐릭터나 배경과 같은 게임 내 자산 생성)
c) Optimizing in-game purchases (게임 내 구매 최적화)
d) Recommending strategies (전략 추천)

41. Which of the following is NOT an application of generative AI?
41. 다음 중 생성 AI의 응용이 아닌 것은 무엇인가?

a) Creating synthetic images (합성 이미지 생성)
b) Detecting anomalies in data (데이터 이상 감지)
c) Generating audio for music (음악용 오디오 생성)
d) Producing human-like text (사람과 유사한 텍스트 생성)

42. What is the advantage of using GANs in image generation?
42. 이미지 생성에서 GAN을 사용하는 장점은 무엇인가?

a) GANs can classify images more accurately (GAN은 이미지를 더 정확하게 분류할 수 있습니다)
b) GANs generate high-quality and realistic images (GAN은 고품질의 현실적인 이미지를 생성합니다)
c) GANs reduce the amount of training data needed (GAN은 필요한 훈련 데이터의 양을 줄입니다)
d) GANs are easier to train than other models (GAN은 다른 모델보다 훈련이 쉽습니다)

39번 정답: a   40번 정답: b   41번 정답: b   42번 정답: b

43. Which of the following is an example of a generative AI system creating content from scratch?
43. 다음 중 생성 AI 시스템이 처음부터 콘텐츠를 생성하는 예는 무엇인가?

a) A recommender system suggesting movies (영화를 추천하는 추천 시스템)
b) A language model generating a poem (시를 생성하는 언어 모델)
c) A chatbot responding to a customer query (고객 문의에 응답하는 챗봇)
d) A spam filter classifying emails (이메일을 분류하는 스팸 필터)

44. In the context of generative AI, what does "latent variable" represent?
44. 생성 AI의 맥락에서 "잠재 변수"는 무엇을 나타내는가?

a) A hidden feature that can explain variations in the data (데이터의 변화를 설명할 수 있는 숨겨진 특징)
b) The output of a fully connected neural network (완전 연결 신경망의 출력)
c) The difference between real and synthetic data (실제 데이터와 합성 데이터 간의 차이)
d) A parameter that controls the training rate of a model (모델의 학습 속도를 제어하는 매개변수)

45. What is the purpose of using regularization techniques in generative AI models?
45. 생성 AI 모델에서 정규화 기법을 사용하는 목적은 무엇인가?

a) To enhance the model's ability to overfit (모델의 과적합 능력을 향상시키기 위해)
b) To prevent mode collapse during training (훈련 중 모드 붕괴를 방지하기 위해)
c) To ensure model convergence (모델 수렴을 보장하기 위해)
d) To reduce the complexity of the model and prevent overfitting (모델의 복잡성을 줄이고 과적합을 방지)

46. What is the key difference between a standard Autoencoder and a Variational Autoencoder (VAE)?
46. 기본 오토인코더와 변이형 오토인코더(VAE)의 주요 차이점은 무엇인가?

a) VAEs use a stochastic approach to sample data (VAE는 확률적 접근 방식을 사용하여 데이터를 샘플링)
b) Autoencoders use GANs to create output (오토인코더는 출력을 생성하기 위해 GAN을 사용한다)
c) VAEs do not compress data (VAE는 데이터를 압축하지 않는다)
d) VAEs do not reconstruct data (VAE는 데이터를 재구성하지 않는다)

43번 정답: b   44번 정답: a   45번 정답: d   46번 정답: a

47. Which generative AI architecture has been most successful in generating high-quality text in natural language processing?
47. 자연어 처리에서 고품질 텍스트 생성에 가장 성공적인 생성 AI 아키텍처는 무엇인가?

a) CNN (합성곱 신경망)

b) GAN (생성적 적대 신경망)

c) GPT (생성형 사전 학습 모델)

d) Naive Bayes (나이브 베이즈)

48. Which of the following tasks is NOT typically performed using generative AI?
48. 다음 중 생성 AI를 사용하여 일반적으로 수행되지 않는 작업은 무엇인가?

a) Image generation (이미지 생성)

b) Data augmentation (데이터 증강)

c) Fraud detection (사기 탐지)

d) Text-to-image conversion (텍스트-이미지 변환)

49. The "discriminator" in a GAN serves what role?
49. GAN에서 "판별기"는 어떤 역할을 하는가?

a) It predicts the class of the data (데이터의 클래스를 예측한다)

b) It generates synthetic data (합성 데이터를 생성한다)

c) It distinguishes real data from synthetic data (실제 데이터와 합성 데이터를 구분한다)

d) It evaluates the loss function (손실 함수를 평가한다)

50. How does a GAN improve over time?
50. GAN은 시간이 지남에 따라 어떻게 개선되는가?

a) The discriminator gets stronger while the generator weakens (판별자가 강해지고 생성자는 약해진다)

b) The generator and discriminator compete, improving each other's performance (생성자와 판별자가 경쟁하여 서로의 성능을 향상시킨다)

c) The generator starts producing random data (생성자가 무작위 데이터를 생성하기 시작한다)

d) The discriminator's accuracy decreases with more training (판별자의 정확도가 훈련이 진행될수록 감소)

47번 정답: c   48번 정답: c   49번 정답: c   50번 정답: b

51. Which loss function is commonly used in GAN training?
51. GAN 훈련에서 일반적으로 사용되는 손실 함수는 무엇인가?

a) Mean Squared Error (평균 제곱 오차)
b) Cross-Entropy Loss (크로스 엔트로피 손실)
c) Hinge Loss (힌지 손실)
d) L1 Regularization (L1 정규화)

52. What is an advantage of Variational Autoencoders (VAEs) in generating data?
52. 데이터 생성에서 변이형 오토인코더(VAE)의 장점은 무엇인가?

a) VAEs are more computationally efficient than GANs (VAE는 GAN보다 계산 효율이 높다)
b) VAEs can generate data based on probabilistic sampling (VAE는 확률적 샘플링을 기반으로 데이터를 생성)
c) VAEs perform better than CNNs in image classification (VAE는 이미지 분류에서 CNN보다 우수한 성능)
d) VAEs are designed to generate labeled data (VAE는 레이블이 있는 데이터를 생성하도록 설계)

53. What is one benefit of using transfer learning with pre-trained generative models?
53. 사전 학습된 생성 모델과 함께 전이 학습을 사용할 때의 한 가지 이점은 무엇인가?

a) The model automatically generates data without training (모델이 학습 없이 자동으로 데이터를 생성한다)
b) It reduces the amount of data needed to train the model (모델을 학습하는 데 필요한 데이터 양을 줄인다)
c) It guarantees accurate predictions (정확한 예측을 보장한다)
d) It increases model overfitting (모델 과적합을 증가)

54. What is a common application of generative AI in e-commerce?
54. 전자상거래에서 생성 AI의 일반적인 응용 사례는 무엇인가?

a) Customer segmentation (고객 세분화)
b) Generating personalized product recommendations (개인화된 제품 추천 생성)
c) Predicting stock prices (주가 예측)
d) Monitoring website performance (웹사이트 성능 모니터링)

51번 정답: b   52번 정답: b   53번 정답: b   54번 정답: b

55. Which generative AI technique can create interpolated images between two different styles?
55. 두 가지 다른 스타일 사이에 보간된 이미지를 생성할 수 있는 생성 AI 기법은 무엇인가?

a) GAN (생성적 적대 신경망)
b) Transformer (트랜스포머)
c) Autoencoder (오토인코더)
d) Reinforcement Learning (강화 학습)

56. Which of the following is an ethical concern related to generative AI?
56. 다음 중 생성 AI와 관련된 윤리적 문제는 무엇인가?

a) Reducing bias in predictive models (예측 모델의 편향 줄이기)
b) Generating realistic but fake content (사실적이지만 가짜 콘텐츠 생성)
c) Improving data storage efficiency (데이터 저장 효율성 향상)
d) Lowering computational costs (계산 비용 절감)

57. How does a Variational Autoencoder (VAE) ensure that the generated samples are diverse?
57. 변이형 오토인코더(VAE)가 생성된 샘플이 다양하도록 보장하는 방법은 무엇인가?

a) By using a deterministic latent space (결정론적 잠재 공간을 사용)
b) By sampling from a probability distribution in the latent space (잠재 공간에서 확률 분포에서 샘플링)
c) By including noise in the decoder (디코더에 노이즈를 포함)
d) By adjusting the learning rate constantly (학습률을 지속적으로 조정)

58. Which of the following is a major drawback of training a GAN?
58. GAN을 훈련할 때의 주요 단점은 무엇인가?

a) It requires less computational power (계산 능력이 적게 필요)
b) GANs can easily generate overfitted models (GAN은 쉽게 과적합된 모델 생성)
c) Training can be unstable and lead to mode collapse (훈련이 불안정하고, 모드 붕괴 가능성)
d) GANs cannot produce realistic results (GAN은 사실적인 결과를 생성할 수 없음)

55번 정답: a 56번 정답: b 57번 정답: b 58번 정답: c

59. Which generative AI model has been most associated with text generation applications like chatbots?

59. 채팅 봇과 같은 텍스트 생성 응용 프로그램과 가장 관련이 있는 생성 AI 모델은 무엇인가?

a) GPT (생성 사전 훈련 변환기)

b) CNN (합성곱 신경망)

c) RNN (순환 신경망)

d) Decision Trees (결정 트리)

60. In generative AI, which technique is commonly used for data augmentation?

60. 생성 AI에서 데이터 증강에 일반적으로 사용되는 기술은 무엇인가?

a) GANs (생성적 적대 신경망들)

b) CNNs (합성곱 신경망들)

c) SVM (서포트 벡터 머신)

d) RNNs (순환 신경망들)

61. What is a major application of GANs in the medical field?

61. 의료 분야에서 GAN의 주요 응용 사례는 무엇인가?

a) Detecting fraudulent activity in healthcare claims (의료 청구서에서 사기 행위 탐지)

b) Synthesizing medical images for training purposes (훈련을 위한 의료 이미지 합성)

c) Diagnosing diseases from images (이미지를 통한 질병 진단)

d) Performing sentiment analysis on patient reviews (환자 리뷰에 대한 감정 분석 수행)

62. Which of the following describes the process of backpropagation in training generative models?

62. 다음 중 생성 모델 훈련에서 역전파 과정을 설명하는 것은 무엇인가?

a) It involves computing the gradient of the loss function with respect to each weight. (각 가중치에 대한 손실 함수의 기울기를 계산하는 것을 포함)

b) It generates new data samples (새로운 데이터 샘플 생성)

c) It adjusts the learning rate dynamically during training. (훈련 중 학습률을 동적으로 조정)

d) It evaluates the performance of the discriminator in a GAN. (GAN에서 판별기의 성능 평가)

59번 정답: a   60번 정답: a   61번 정답: b   62번 정답: a

63. Why is unsupervised learning commonly associated with generative AI?
63. 왜 비지도 학습이 생성 AI와 일반적으로 연관되는가?

a) Generative AI models require a large number of labels to function. (생성 AI 모델은 기능을 위해 많은 레이블 필요)

b) The models are trained to learn from unlabeled data and create new data. (모델이 레이블 없는 데이터에서 학습하고 새로운 데이터를 생성하도록 훈련)

c) Unsupervised learning speeds up the training process. (비지도 학습이 훈련 과정 가속화)

d) Unsupervised learning ensures better performance in real-time applications. (비지도 학습이 실시간 응용 프로그램에서 더 나은 성능 보장)

64. What type of neural network is primarily used in image-based generative tasks?
64. 이미지 기반 생성 작업에 주로 사용되는 신경망 유형은 무엇인가?

a) RNN

b) CNN

c) Transformer (트랜스포머)

d) LSTM

65. Which of the following is a common challenge when training generative models?
65. 생성 모델을 훈련할 때 흔히 겪는 문제는 무엇인가?

a) Overfitting on training data (훈련 데이터에 과적합하는 것)

b) Mode collapse (모드 붕괴)

c) Increasing model variance (모델 분산 증가)

d) Reducing model complexity (모델 복잡성 감소)

66. What is the latent space used for in a generative model like a VAE?
66. VAE와 같은 생성 모델에서 잠재 공간은 무엇을 위해 사용되는가?

a) It stores the model weights. (모델 가중치 저장)

b) It is a representation that encodes meaningful features from the input data. (입력 데이터에서 의미 있는 특징을 인코딩하는 표현)

c) It improves the accuracy of the classification tasks. (분류 작업의 정확도 향상)

d) It speeds up the training process. (훈련 과정 가속화)

63번 정답: b   64번 정답: b   65번 정답: b   66번 정답: b

67. Which of the following best describes a VAE's ability to reconstruct data?
67. 다음 중 VAE가 데이터를 재구성하는 능력을 가장 잘 설명하는 것은 무엇인가?

a) It generates entirely new data points from scratch. (처음부터 완전히 새로운 데이터 포인트를 생성)

b) It samples from a probability distribution to reconstruct data. (데이터를 재구성하기 위해 확률 분포에서 샘플링)

c) It creates exact replicas of input data. (입력 데이터의 정확한 복제본을 생성)

d) It uses deterministic values to ensure precise reconstruction. (정확한 재구성을 보장하기 위해 결정적 값을 사용)

68. Which of the following is a common challenge when training generative models?
68. 생성 모델을 훈련할 때 흔히 겪는 문제는 무엇인가?

a) Overfitting on training data (훈련 데이터에 과적합하는 것)

b) Mode collapse (모드 붕괴)

c) Increasing model variance (모델 분산 증가)

d) Reducing model complexity (모델 복잡성 감소)

69. Which model is most commonly used in generative natural language processing tasks like text generation?
69. 텍스트 생성과 같은 생성적 자연어 처리 작업에 가장 많이 사용되는 모델은 무엇인가?

a) CNN

b) GPT

c) Naive Bayes

d) SVM

70. What is the primary advantage of Variational Autoencoders (VAEs) over traditional Autoencoders?
70. 전통적인 오토인코더에 비해 변형 오토인코더(VAE)의 주요 장점은 무엇인가?

a) VAEs can classify data more effectively. (VAE는 데이터를 더 효과적으로 분류)

b) VAEs use probabilistic techniques to generate new data points. (VAE는 확률적 기법을 사용하여 새로운 데이터 포인트를 생성)

c) VAEs require labeled data for training. (VAE는 훈련을 위해 레이블이 지정된 데이터 필요)

d) VAEs are easier to train than traditional Autoencoders. (VAE는 전통적인 오토인코더보다 훈련이 더 쉬움)

67번 정답: b   68번 정답: b   69번 정답: b   70번 정답: b

71. How does generative AI contribute to the creation of synthetic data?
71. 생성 AI는 합성 데이터 생성에 어떻게 기여하는가?

a) By classifying data from real datasets (실제 데이터셋에서 데이터를 분류하여)
b) By generating new, artificial data that resembles real data (실제 데이터와 유사한 새로운 인공 데이터를 생성)
c) By improving data labeling processes (데이터 레이블링 프로세스를 개선)
d) By filtering real data for errors (실제 데이터를 오류 검출을 위해 필터링)

72. What is a practical application of generative AI in the finance industry?
72. 금융 산업에서 생성 AI의 실질적인 응용은 무엇인가?

a) Creating personalized banking experiences (개인 맞춤형 은행 경험 제공)
b) Generating synthetic financial data for modeling (모델링을 위한 합성 금융 데이터 생성)
c) Detecting fraudulent transactions (사기 거래 탐지)
d) Predicting stock market trends (주식 시장 동향 예측)

73. Which of the following describes the purpose of the discriminator in a GAN?
73. 다음 중 GAN에서 판별기의 목적을 설명하는 것은 무엇인가?

a) It generates new data samples. (새로운 데이터 샘플 생성)
b) It distinguishes between real and synthetic data. (실제 데이터와 합성 데이터 구분)
c) It evaluates the loss of the generator. (생성기의 손실 평가)
d) It encodes the input data into a latent space. (입력 데이터를 잠재 공간에 인코딩)

74. Which of the following techniques can be used to mitigate mode collapse in GANs?
74. 다음 중 GAN에서 모드 붕괴를 완화하는 데 사용할 수 있는 기법은 무엇인가?

a) Increasing the learning rate (학습률 증가)
b) Using a diverse training dataset (다양한 훈련 데이터셋 사용)
c) Using convolutional layers (컨볼루션 레이어 사용)
d) Applying dropout regularization (드롭아웃 정규화 적용)

71번 정답: b   72번 정답: b   73번 정답: b   74번 정답: b

75. In a GAN, what is the generator's primary objective?
75. GAN에서 생성기는 다음을 목표로 한다. 맞는 것은?

a) Maximize the loss of the discriminator (판별기의 손실을 최대화)

b) Minimize the difference between real and generated data (실제 데이터와 생성된 데이터 간의 차이를 최소화)

c) Predict the class of an image (이미지의 클래스를 예측)

d) Maximize classification accuracy (분류 정확도 최대화)

76. What distinguishes GPT models from traditional RNNs in language generation?
76. 언어 생성에서 GPT 모델과 기존 RNN의 차이점은 무엇인가?

a) GPT models use transformers, allowing them to process text in parallel. (GPT 모델은 트랜스포머를 사용하여 텍스트를 병렬로 처리)

b) GPT models are not suitable for generating human-like text. (GPT 모델은 인간과 유사한 텍스트 생성에 부적합)

c) GPT models require less training data than RNNs. (GPT 모델은 RNN보다 더 적은 훈련 데이터 필요)

d) GPT models focus only on image generation tasks. (GPT 모델은 이미지 생성 작업에만 집중)

77. Which type of model is commonly used for image generation in generative AI?
77. 생성 AI에서 이미지 생성을 위해 일반적으로 사용되는 모델 유형은 무엇인가?

a) CNN (합성곱 신경망)

b) RNN (순환 신경망)

c) GPT (생성형 사전 학습 모델)

d) Transformer (트랜스포머)

78. In generative AI, what is "zero-shot learning"?
78. 생성 AI에서 "제로샷 학습"이란 무엇인가?

a) A method where a model learns without any labeled data (레이블이 없는 상태에서 모델이 학습하는 방법)

b) The ability of a model to generate outputs without being specifically trained on those categories (특정 범주에 대해 별도로 훈련되지 않고도 출력을 생성할 수 있는 능력)

c) A training process where no training data is used (훈련 데이터가 전혀 사용되지 않는 훈련 과정)

d) The process of fine-tuning a pre-trained model (사전 훈련된 모델을 미세 조정하는 과정)

75번 정답: b   76번 정답: a   77번 정답: a   78번 정답: b

79. How can generative AI be used in product design?
79. 생성 AI는 제품 디자인에 어떻게 활용될 수 있는가?

a) By predicting customer preferences (고객의 선호도를 예측하여)

b) By generating new design concepts based on existing patterns (기존 패턴을 기반으로 새로운 디자인 개념 생성하여)

c) By classifying design prototypes (디자인 시안을 분류하여)

d) By optimizing production workflows (생산 워크플로우 최적화하여)

80. What is the main challenge when training a Transformer-based generative model?
80. Transformer 기반 생성 모델을 훈련할 때 주요 어려움은 무엇인가?

a) Ensuring mode collapse does not occur (모드 붕괴가 발생하지 않도록 보장)

b) Handling large datasets and computational power requirements (대규모 데이터셋과 컴퓨팅 파워 요구 사항 처리)

c) Generating images in real-time (실시간으로 이미지 생성)

d) Optimizing hyperparameters (하이퍼파라미터 최적화)

81. What is the role of the decoder in a VAE?
81. VAE에서 디코더의 역할은 무엇인가?

a) To encode the input data into latent variables (입력 데이터를 잠재 변수로 인코딩)

b) To classify input data (입력 데이터를 분류)

c) To reconstruct the data from the latent variables (잠재 변수로부터 데이터를 재구성)

d) To distinguish between real and fake data (실제 데이터와 가짜 데이터를 구분)

82. Which of the following is a limitation of GANs in generative AI?
82. 생성 AI에서 GAN의 한계 중 하나는 무엇인가?

a) GANs require labeled data (GAN은 레이블된 데이터 필요)

b) GANs can suffer from mode collapse (GAN은 모드 붕괴의 영향을 받음)

c) GANs cannot generate high-resolution images (GAN은 고해상도 이미지를 생성할 수 없음)

d) GANs are unsupervised learning models (GAN은 비지도 학습 모델임)

79번 정답: b   80번 정답: b   81번 정답: c   82번 정답: b

83. What is a typical application of generative AI in the fashion industry?
83. 패션 산업에서 생성 AI의 일반적인 응용 사례는 무엇인가?

a) Predicting seasonal sales trends (계절별 판매 트렌드 예측)
b) Generating new clothing designs based on trends (트렌드를 기반으로 새로운 의류 디자인 생성)
c) Classifying customer preferences (고객 선호도를 분류)
d) Reducing production waste (생산 폐기물 감소)

84. In the context of generative AI, what is interpolation?
84. 생성 AI의 맥락에서 보간은 무엇을 의미하는가?

a) Training a model on multiple datasets (여러 데이터셋에서 모델을 훈련)
b) Generating new samples by blending features from two data points (두 데이터 포인트의 특징을 혼합하여 새로운 샘플 생성)
c) Predicting future data trends (미래 데이터 트렌드 예측)
d) Reducing overfitting in a model (모델의 과적합 감소)

85. How can a trained generative model like a GAN contribute to data privacy?
85. GAN과 같은 훈련된 생성 모델이 데이터 프라이버시에 어떻게 기여할 수 있는가?

a) By classifying data more efficiently (데이터를 더 효율적으로 분류)
b) By generating synthetic data to avoid using real, sensitive data (실제 민감 데이터를 사용하지 않고 가상 데이터를 생성)
c) By encrypting sensitive user data (사용자 민감 데이터를 암호화)
d) By predicting data breaches in advance (데이터 유출을 사전에 예측)

86. Which of the following statements about GPT models is correct?
86. 다음 중 GPT 모델에 대한 설명으로 올바른 것은 무엇인가?

a) GPT models can process text and generate human-like language. (GPT 모델은 텍스트를 처리하고 인간과 유사한 언어를 생성)
b) GPT models are primarily used for image recognition tasks. (GPT 모델은 주로 이미지 인식 작업에 사용)
c) GPT models require supervised learning for text generation. (GPT 모델은 텍스트 생성을 위해 지도 학습이 필요)
d) GPT models rely on convolutional neural networks for text processing. (GPT 모델은 텍스트 처리를 위해 컨볼루션 신경망을 사용)

83번 정답: b   84번 정답: b   85번 정답: b   86번 정답: a

87. What does the latent space in a VAE represent?
87. VAE의 잠재 공간은 무엇을 나타내는가?

a) A fixed value used for classification (분류에 사용되는 고정 값)

b) A probabilistic distribution encoding input data features (입력 데이터 특성을 인코딩하는 확률 분포)

c) The number of layers in a model (모델의 레이어 수)

d) A method of reducing dimensionality (차원 축소 방법)

88. How does a GAN improve the realism of generated data?
88. GAN은 생성된 데이터의 현실성을 어떻게 향상하는가?

a) By using a reinforcement learning algorithm (강화 학습 알고리즘을 사용)

b) By optimizing both the generator and discriminator during training (훈련 중 생성기와 판별기를 최적화)

c) By using a larger latent space (더 큰 잠재 공간을 사용하여)

d) By increasing the learning rate over time (시간이 지남에 따라 학습률을 증가)

89. Which generative AI model is known for its ability to handle sequential data, such as text?
89. 텍스트와 같은 순차 데이터를 처리하는 능력으로 잘 알려진 생성 AI 모델은 무엇인가?

a) Convolutional Neural Network (CNN) (합성곱 신경망)

b) Recurrent Neural Network (RNN) (순환 신경망)

c) Generative Adversarial Network (GAN) (생성적 적대 신경망)

d) Autoencoder (오토인코더)

90. What is a key advantage of using generative AI models in creative industries like art and music?
90. 예술과 음악 같은 창의적 산업에서 생성 AI 모델을 사용하는 주요 이점은 무엇인가?

a) Increased speed in classifying existing data (기존 데이터 분류 속도 증가)

b) The ability to generate entirely new and unique creative content (완전히 새롭고 독창적인 창작 콘텐츠 생성 능력)

c) Reducing the computational power needed for creativity (창의성에 필요한 계산 능력 감소)

d) Improving the accuracy of traditional predictive models (전통적인 예측 모델의 정확도 향상)

87번 정답: b   88번 정답: b   89번 정답: b   90번 정답: b

91. What is the main objective of a generative adversarial network (GAN) during training?
91. GAN의 훈련 중 주요 목표는 무엇인가?

a) To improve classification accuracy (분류 정확도 향상)

b) To generate realistic data samples that the discriminator cannot distinguish from real data (판별자가 실제 데이터와 구별할 수 없는 현실적인 데이터 샘플 생성)

c) To reduce the dimensionality of the input data (입력 데이터의 차원 축소)

d) To categorize data into predefined classes (데이터를 미리 정의된 클래스에 분류)

92. In a Variational Autoencoder (VAE), what does the "variational" part refer to?
92. VAE에서 "변분" 부분은 무엇을 의미하는가?

a) The use of variational calculus in the model (모델에서 변분 계산의 사용)

b) The introduction of random noise in training (훈련 중 임의의 노이즈 도입)

c) The probabilistic approach to encoding and decoding data (데이터 인코딩과 디코딩에 대한 확률적 접근법)

d) The ability to vary the learning rate dynamically (학습률을 동적으로 조절하는 능력)

93. Which type of generative model is most commonly used for image synthesis tasks?
93. 이미지 합성 작업에 가장 일반적으로 사용되는 생성 모델 유형은 무엇인가?

a) Variational Autoencoder (VAE) (변분 오토인코더)

b) Generative Adversarial Network (GAN) (생성적 적대 신경망)

c) Recurrent Neural Network (RNN) (순환 신경망)

d) Long Short-Term Memory (LSTM) (장단기 메모리)

94. Which approach helps in improving the stability of GAN training?
94. GAN 훈련의 안정성을 향상하는 데 도움이 되는 접근 방식은 무엇인가?

a) Using a single neural network for both generator and discriminator (생성기와 판별기에 하나의 신경망 사용)

b) Employing different architectures for the generator and discriminator (생성기와 판별기에 다른 아키텍처 사용)

c) Training both models independently without feedback (피드백 없이 두 모델을 독립적으로 훈련)

d) Reducing the complexity of the discriminator (판별기의 복잡성 감소)

91번 정답: b   92번 정답: c   93번 정답: b   94번 정답: b

95. What does "mode collapse" refer to in the context of GANs?
95. GAN에서 "모드 붕괴"는 무엇을 의미하는가?

a) The generator produces a wide variety of samples (생성기가 다양한 샘플을 생성함)

b) The discriminator fails to learn and provides inaccurate feedback (판별기가 학습하지 못하고 부정확한 피드백을 제공함)

c) The generator creates limited types of samples, lacking diversity (생성기가 다양성이 부족한 제한된 유형의 샘플을 생성함)

d) The model overfits to the training data (모델이 훈련 데이터에 과적합됨)

96. How does the use of transfer learning benefit generative AI models?
96. 전이 학습의 사용이 생성 AI 모델에 어떤 이점을 주는가?

a) By allowing models to generate data without prior training (모델이 사전 훈련 없이 데이터를 생성할 수 있도록 함)

b) By leveraging pre-trained models to improve performance with less data (사전 학습된 모델을 활용하여 적은 데이터로 성능 향상)

c) By avoiding the need for any data during training (훈련 중 데이터가 전혀 필요하지 않도록 함)

d) By simplifying the architecture of generative models (생성 모델의 구조를 단순화함)

97. What does "style transfer" in generative AI refer to?
97. 생성 AI에서 "스타일 전이"는 무엇을 의미하는가?

a) Transferring a model's parameters to another model (모델의 파라미터를 다른 모델로 전이)

b) Applying the style of one image to the content of another image (한 이미지의 스타일을 다른 이미지의 콘텐츠에 적용)

c) Shifting the focus from image generation to text generation (이미지 생성에서 텍스트 생성으로 초점을 이동)

c) Shifting the focus from image generation to text generation (이미지 생성에서 텍스트 생성으로 초점을 이동)

d) Transferring learned features between different datasets (다른 데이터 세트 간에 학습된 특징을 전이)

95번 정답: c   96번 정답: b   97번 정답: b

98. What is the role of the "encoder" in a Variational Autoencoder (VAE)?

98. VAE에서 "인코더"의 역할은 무엇인가?

a) To generate new samples from the latent space (잠재 공간에서 새로운 샘플 생성)

b) To encode input data into a probabilistic latent space representation (입력 데이터를 확률적 잠재 공간 표현으로 인코딩)

c) To evaluate the performance of the decoder (디코더의 성능 평가)

d) To classify data into predefined categories (데이터를 미리 정의된 범주로 분류)

99. What does "fine-tuning" involve in the context of generative AI models?

99. 생성 AI 모델의 문맥에서 "파인 튜닝"이란 무엇을 포함하는가?

a) Training a model from scratch (모델을 처음부터 훈련)

b) Adjusting a pre-trained model on a new dataset to improve performance (새 데이터 세트에서 사전 훈련된 모델을 조정하여 성능 향상)

c) Simplifying the model architecture for faster training (더 빠른 훈련을 위해 모델 구조를 단순화)

d) Increasing the complexity of the model (모델의 복잡성 증가)

100. In generative AI, what is "data augmentation" and how is it related to generative models?

100. 생성 AI에서 "데이터 증강"이란 무엇이며 생성 모델과는 어떤 관련이 있는가?

a) The process of creating synthetic data to enhance the training dataset (훈련 데이터셋을 확장하기 위해 합성 데이터를 생성하는 과정)

b) The technique of reducing the size of the dataset (데이터셋의 크기를 줄이는 기법)

c) The method of normalizing data to improve model performance (모델 성능을 향상시키기 위해 데이터를 정규화하는 방법)

d) The use of additional features to improve classification accuracy (분류 정확도를 높이기 위해 추가 특성을 사용하는 것)

98번 정답: b   99번 정답: b   100번 정답: a

도메인 3: 기반 모델 응용

기반 모델(Foundation Models)의 핵심 개념과 특징을 이해하고 Amazon Bedrock, Titan, Claude 등의 AWS 기반 모델 서비스들을 실제 비즈니스 요구사항에 맞게 선택하고 적용할 수 있는 능력을 평가하며, 특히 기반 모델의 선택 기준(모델 크기, 처리 속도, 비용, 특화 분야 등), 커스터마이징 방법(프롬프트 튜닝, RAG 등), 모델 평가 방법, 그리고 실제 구현 시 고려해야 할 보안, 거버넌스, 비용 최적화 전략에 대한 이해도를 테스트하므로, 시험 준비 시에는 각 기반 모델의 기술적 특징뿐만 아니라 실제 비즈니스 시나리오에서 어떤 모델이 가장 적합한지 판단할 수 있는 분석력과 함께 AWS의 기반 모델 서비스들의 구체적인 활용 사례와 모범 사례들을 중점적으로 학습하는 것을 권장한다.

1. What's a standard implementation of foundation models in natural language processing?
1. 자연어 처리에서 기초 모델의 일반적인 사용 사례는 무엇인가?

a) Language translation (언어 번역)
b) Sentiment analysis (감정 분석)
c) Time-series forecasting (시계열 예측)
d) Audio signal processing (오디오 신호 처리)

2. Which AWS service provides pre-trained models for text analysis tasks?
2. 어떤 AWS 서비스가 텍스트 분석 작업을 위한 사전 학습된 모델을 제공하는가?

a) Amazon Lex (아마존 렉스)
b) Amazon Rekognition (아마존 레코그니션)
c) Amazon Polly (아마존 폴리)
d) Amazon Comprehend (아마존 컴프리헨드)

1번 정답: b   2번 정답: d

3. For which type of task is a foundation model typically not well-suited?
3. 기초 모델이 일반적으로 적합하지 않은 작업 유형은 무엇인가?

a) Image recognition (이미지 인식)
b) Anomaly detection in time series (시계열의 이상 탐지)
c) Image captioning (이미지 캡션 생성)
d) Text summarization (텍스트 요약)

4. What is the primary advantage of using pre-trained foundation models?
4. 사전 학습된 기초 모델을 사용하는 주요 이점은 무엇인가?

a) Reduced training time (훈련 시간 단축)
b) Customizability (사용자 맞춤화)
c) Increased hardware requirements (하드웨어 요구 사항 증가)
d) Higher accuracy on niche tasks (특정 작업에서의 높은 정확도)

5. How can foundation models be used in customer service applications?
5. 기초 모델이 고객 서비스 애플리케이션에 어떻게 사용될 수 있는가?

a) Automating responses with chatbots (챗봇을 사용한 응답 자동화)
b) Generating audio content (오디오 콘텐츠 생성)
c) Creating video content (비디오 콘텐츠 생성)
d) Analyzing financial data (재무 데이터 분석)

6. What type of foundation model would you use for speech-to-text applications?
6. 음성 인식 애플리케이션에 사용할 수 있는 기초 모델 유형은 무엇인가?

a) Image segmentation models (이미지 분할 모델)
b) Speech recognition models (음성 인식 모델)
c) Text summarization models (텍스트 요약 모델)
d) Object detection models (객체 탐지 모델)

3번 정답: b   4번 정답: a   5번 정답: a   6번 정답: b

7. What type of foundation model is used for generating human-like text?
7. 인간과 유사한 텍스트를 생성하는 데 사용되는 기초 모델 유형은 무엇인가?

a) Convolutional Neural Networks (CNNs) (합성곱 신경망)
b) Generative Pre-trained Transformers (GPT) (생성 사전 학습 변환기)
c) Recurrent Neural Networks (RNNs) (순환 신경망)
d) Generative Adversarial Networks (GANs) (생성적 적대 신경망)

8. What is a common application of image classification models?
8. 이미지 분류 모델의 일반적인 응용 사례는 무엇인가?

a) Text translation (텍스트 번역)
b) Speech recognition (음성 인식)
c) Identifying objects in images (이미지 내 객체 식별)
d) Predicting stock prices (주가 예측)

9. Which AWS service provides managed training and deployment for machine learning models?
9. AWS에서 기계 학습 모델을 위한 관리형 교육 및 배포를 제공하는 서비스는 무엇인가?

a) Amazon S3 (아마존 S3)
b) AWS Glue (AWS 글루)
c) Amazon SageMaker (아마존 세이지메이커)
d) AWS CloudFormation (AWS 클라우드포메이션)

10. For which of the following tasks is Amazon Rekognition best suited?
10. Amazon Rekognition이 가장 적합한 작업은 무엇인가?

a) Text summarization (텍스트 요약)
b) Image and video analysis (이미지 및 비디오 분석)
c) Voice synthesis (음성 합성)
d) Data warehousing (데이터 웨어하우징)

7번 정답: b   8번 정답: c   9번 정답: c   10번 정답: b

11. What is the main benefit of transfer learning in the context of foundation models?
11. 기초 모델에서 전이 학습의 주요 이점은 무엇인가?

a) Training models from scratch (모델을 처음부터 학습하기)
b) Reducing the need for large datasets (대규모 데이터셋 필요성 줄이기)
c) Increasing model complexity (모델 복잡성 증가)
d) Enhancing real-time processing capabilities (실시간 처리 능력 강화)

12. Which AWS service offers a high-level API for conversational AI models?
12. 대화형 AI 모델을 위한 고급 API를 제공하는 AWS 서비스는 무엇인가?

a) Amazon Lex (아마존 렉스)
b) Amazon Polly (아마존 폴리)
c) Amazon Rekognition (아마존 레코그니션)
d) AWS Glue (AWS 글루)

13. Which AWS service can be used to fine-tune a pre-trained language model for a specific use case?
13. 특정 사용 사례에 맞춰 사전 학습된 언어 모델을 미세 조정하는 데 사용할 수 있는 AWS 서비스는 무엇인가?

a) Amazon SageMaker (아마존 세이지메이커)
b) Amazon Polly (아마존 폴리)
c) Amazon Lex (아마존 렉스)
d) AWS Lambda (AWS 람다)

14. How does Amazon Polly differ from other foundation models?
14. 아마존 폴리는 다른 기초 모델과 어떻게 다른가?

a) It provides text-to-speech capabilities (텍스트 음성 변환 기능 제공)
b) It offers image recognition (이미지 인식 제공)
c) It performs sentiment analysis (감정 분석 수행)
d) It generates text summaries (텍스트 요약 생성)

11번 정답: b   12번 정답: a   13번 정답: a   14번 정답: a

15. What AWS service provides tools for visualizing and interacting with machine learning models?

15. AWS에서 기계 학습 모델을 시각화하고 상호작용하는 도구를 제공하는 서비스는 무엇인가?

a) Amazon SageMaker Studio (아마존 세이지메이커 스튜디오)

b) Amazon Rekognition (아마존 레코그니션)

c) Amazon Lex (아마존 렉스)

d) AWS Step Functions (AWS 스텝 함수)

16. Which foundation model is best for generating human-like speech from text?

16. 텍스트로부터 인간과 유사한 음성을 생성하는 데 가장 적합한 기초 모델은 무엇인가?

a) Amazon Comprehend (아마존 컴프리헨드)

b) Amazon Lex (아마존 렉스)

c) Amazon Polly (아마존 폴리)

d) Amazon SageMaker (아마존 세이지메이커)

17. What is a common use case for a language generation model?

17. 언어 생성 모델의 일반적인 사용 사례는 무엇인가?

a) Predicting weather patterns (날씨 패턴 예측)

b) Generating product descriptions (제품 설명 생성)

c) Identifying spam emails (스팸 이메일 식별)

d) Analyzing sales data (판매 데이터 분석)

18. Which AWS service provides capabilities for creating and managing machine learning workflows?

18. 기계 학습 워크플로를 생성하고 관리하는 기능을 제공하는 AWS 서비스는 무엇인가?

a) AWS Step Functions (AWS 스텝 함수)

b) Amazon Redshift (아마존 레드시프트)

c) AWS CloudFormation (AWS 클라우드포메이션)

d) Amazon SageMaker (아마존 세이지메이커)

15번 정답: a   16번 정답: c   17번 정답: b   18번 정답: d

19. How can foundation models improve content recommendation systems?
19. 기초 모델이 콘텐츠 추천 시스템을 어떻게 개선할 수 있는가?

a) By analyzing user behavior and preferences (사용자 행동 및 선호도 분석)
b) By generating financial reports (재무 보고서 생성)
c) By optimizing network performance (네트워크 성능 최적화)
d) By detecting fraudulent activities (사기 행위 감지)

20. What kind of models would you use for visual object detection tasks?
20. 시각적 객체 탐지 작업에 사용할 수 있는 모델 유형은 무엇인가?

a) Text generation models (텍스트 생성 모델)
b) Speech synthesis models (음성 합성 모델)
c) Convolutional Neural Networks (CNNs) (합성곱 신경망)
d) Recurrent Neural Networks (RNNs) (순환 신경망)

21. In which scenario would you use a generative adversarial network (GAN)?
21. 생성적 적대 신경망(GAN)을 사용할 수 있는 시나리오는 무엇인가?

a) Text translation (텍스트 번역)
b) Image generation (이미지 생성)
c) Speech recognition (음성 인식)
d) Time-series forecasting (시계열 예측)

22. Which AWS service can be used for sentiment analysis of customer feedback?
22. 고객 피드백의 감정 분석에 사용할 수 있는 AWS 서비스는 무엇인가?

a) Amazon Lex (아마존 렉스)
b) Amazon Comprehend (아마존 컴프리헨드)
c) Amazon Rekognition (아마존 레코그니션)
d) Amazon Polly (아마존 폴리)

19번 정답: a   20번 정답: c   21번 정답: b   22번 정답: b

23. What is a common application of foundation models in the financial sector?
23. 금융 부문에서 기초 모델의 일반적인 적용 사례는 무엇인가?

a) Fraud detection (사기 탐지)
b) Video editing (비디오 편집)
c) Audio generation (오디오 생성)
d) Image enhancement (이미지 향상)

24. What is the main purpose of Amazon Comprehend?
24. 아마존 컴프리헨드의 주요 목적은 무엇인가?

a) Speech synthesis (음성 합성)
b) Text analysis (텍스트 분석)
c) Image recognition (이미지 인식)
d) Video analysis (비디오 분석)

25. Which type of model would you use for generating artistic images?
25. 예술적 이미지를 생성하는 데 사용할 모델 유형은 무엇인가?

a) Generative Adversarial Networks (GANs) (생성적 적대 신경망)
b) Convolutional Neural Networks (CNNs) (합성곱 신경망)
c) Recurrent Neural Networks (RNNs) (순환 신경망)
d) Long Short-Term Memory (LSTM) networks (장단기 메모리 신경망)

26. What is the main function of Amazon Lex?
26. 아마존 렉스의 주요 기능은 무엇인가?

a) Text summarization (텍스트 요약)
b) Conversational interfaces (대화형 인터페이스)
c) Image processing (이미지 처리)
d) Audio analysis (오디오 분석)

23번 정답: a   24번 정답: b   25번 정답: a   26번 정답: b

27. Which AWS service helps with creating automated workflows for data processing and model training?
27. 데이터 처리 및 모델 학습을 위한 자동화된 워크플로를 생성하는 데 도움이 되는 AWS 서비스는 무엇인가?

a) AWS Glue (AWS 글루)

b) Amazon S3 (아마존 S3)

c) AWS CodePipeline (AWS 코드파이프라인)

d) Amazon SageMaker (아마존 세이지메이커)

28. What type of foundation model is suitable for creating chatbots?
28. 챗봇을 생성하는 데 적합한 기초 모델 유형은 무엇인가?

a) Text-to-speech models (텍스트 음성 변환 모델)

b) Language understanding models (언어 이해 모델)

c) Image classification models (이미지 분류 모델)

d) Time-series prediction models (시계열 예측 모델)

29. How can foundation models be used in healthcare applications?
29. 기초 모델이 의료 애플리케이션에서 어떻게 사용될 수 있는가?

a) Analyzing medical images (의료 이미지 분석)

b) Generating financial reports (재무 보고서 생성)

c) Creating marketing content (마케팅 콘텐츠 생성)

d) Enhancing video streaming quality (비디오 스트리밍 품질 향상)

30. What is the main use case of Amazon Rekognition in security applications?
30. 보안 애플리케이션에서 Amazon Rekognition의 주요 사용 사례는 무엇인가?

a) Fraud detection (사기 감지)

b) Object and facial recognition (객체 및 얼굴 인식)

c) Sentiment analysis (감정 분석)

d) Speech synthesis (음성 합성)

27번 정답: a   28번 정답: b   29번 정답: a   30번 정답: b

31. Which AWS service provides tools for deploying machine learning models at scale?
31. AWS에서 머신 러닝 모델을 대규모로 배포하기 위한 도구를 제공하는 서비스는 무엇인가?

a) Amazon Elastic Container Service (ECS) (아마존 엘라스틱 컨테이너 서비스)
b) Amazon Elastic Kubernetes Service (EKS) (아마존 엘라스틱 쿠버네티스 서비스)
c) Amazon SageMaker (아마존 세이지메이커)
d) AWS CloudTrail (AWS 클라우드트레일)

32. What kind of model would you use for real-time speech translation?
32. 실시간 음성 번역을 위해 어떤 종류의 모델을 사용하는가?

a) Speech-to-text models (음성을 텍스트로 변환하는 모델)
b) Text-to-speech models (텍스트를 음성으로 변환하는 모델)
c) Machine translation models (기계 번역 모델)
d) Image recognition models (이미지 인식 모델)

33. Which AWS service is best for building scalable machine learning workflows?
33. 대규모 확장 가능한 머신러닝 워크플로를 구축하는 데 가장 적합한 AWS 서비스는 무엇인가?

a) AWS Step Functions (AWS 스텝 펑션)
b) Amazon RDS (아마존 RDS)
c) AWS CloudFormation (AWS 클라우드포메이션)
d) Amazon SageMaker (아마존 세이지메이커)

34. How can foundation models assist in e-commerce applications?
34. 기초 모델은 전자상거래 애플리케이션에서 어떻게 활용될 수 있는가?

a) By generating personalized product recommendations (개인 맞춤형 제품 추천 생성)
b) By optimizing video streaming (비디오 스트리밍 최적화)
c) By analyzing network traffic (네트워크 트래픽 분석)
d) By improving database performance (데이터베이스 성능 향상)

31번 정답: c   32번 정답: c   33번 정답: d   34번 정답: a

35. What type of model is used for generating voice responses in virtual assistants?
35. 가상 비서에서 음성 응답을 생성하는 데 사용되는 모델 유형은 무엇인가?

a) Text-to-speech models (텍스트를 음성으로 변환하는 모델)
b) Image recognition models (이미지 인식 모델)
c) Object detection models (객체 감지 모델)
d) Time-series prediction models (시계열 예측 모델)

36. What is the main advantage of using Amazon Polly for text-to-speech tasks?
36. 텍스트를 음성으로 변환하는 작업에서 Amazon Polly를 사용하는 주요 장점은 무엇인가?

a) High accuracy in sentiment analysis (감성 분석의 높은 정확도)
b) Realistic and natural-sounding voices (사실적이고 자연스러운 음성)
c) Advanced image processing capabilities (고급 이미지 처리 기능)
d) Real-time text translation (실시간 텍스트 번역)

37. Which foundation model is used for creating conversational agents?
37. 대화형 에이전트를 만드는 데 사용되는 기초 모델은 무엇인가?

a) Generative Pre-trained Transformers (GPT) (사전 학습된 생성 변환기)
b) Convolutional Neural Networks (CNNs) (합성곱 신경망)
c) Recurrent Neural Networks (RNNs) (순환 신경망)
d) Generative Adversarial Networks (GANs) (생성적 적대 신경망)

38. How does Amazon SageMaker support model deployment?
38. Amazon SageMaker는 모델 배포를 어떻게 지원하는가?

a) By providing managed endpoints for real-time inference (실시간 추론을 위한 관리형 엔드포인트 제공)
b) By offering data visualization tools (데이터 시각화 도구 제공)
c) By performing data integration (데이터 통합 수행)
d) By managing data warehousing (데이터 웨어하우징 관리)

35번 정답: a   36번 정답: b   37번 정답: a   38번 정답: a

39. What is the purpose of using Amazon Comprehend in text analysis?
39. 텍스트 분석에서 Amazon Comprehend를 사용하는 목적은 무엇인가?

a) Identifying key phrases and entities (주요 구문 및 개체 식별)
b) Generating human-like speech (사람과 유사한 음성 생성)
c) Detecting objects in images (이미지에서 객체 감지)
d) Translating text in real-time (실시간 텍스트 번역)

40. Which AWS service is designed for building and training machine learning models with minimal code?
40. 코드 작성을 최소화하여 머신 러닝 모델을 구축하고 훈련하기 위한 AWS 서비스는 무엇인가?

a) Amazon SageMaker Autopilot (아마존 세이지메이커 오토파일럿)
b) AWS Glue (AWS 글루)
c) Amazon Lex (아마존 렉스)
d) Amazon Rekognition (아마존 레코그니션)

41. How can foundation models enhance automated customer support systems?
41. 기초 모델은 자동화된 고객 지원 시스템을 어떻게 개선할 수 있는가?

a) By providing accurate responses to customer inquiries (고객 문의에 정확한 응답 제공)
b) By generating promotional content (홍보 콘텐츠 생성)
c) By improving video resolution (비디오 해상도 개선)
d) By optimizing network bandwidth (네트워크 대역폭 최적화)

42. What type of model is most effective for predicting stock market trends?
42. 주식 시장 동향 예측에 가장 효과적인 모델 유형은 무엇인가?

a) Time-series forecasting models (시계열 예측 모델)
b) Image classification models (이미지 분류 모델)
c) Text generation models (텍스트 생성 모델)
d) Speech recognition models (음성 인식 모델)

39번 정답: a   40번 정답: a   41번 정답: a   42번 정답: a

43. Which AWS service provides a suite of tools for building and training machine learning models?
43. 머신 러닝 모델을 구축하고 훈련하기 위한 도구 세트를 제공하는 AWS 서비스는 무엇인가?

a) Amazon SageMaker (아마존 세이지메이커)

b) AWS Lambda (AWS 람다)

c) Amazon Polly (아마존 폴리)

d) AWS Glue (AWS 글루)

44. What is a key feature of AWS Rekognition?
44. AWS Rekognition의 주요 기능은 무엇인가?

a) Text analysis (텍스트 분석)

b) Facial recognition and object detection (안면 인식 및 객체 감지)

c) Speech synthesis (음성 합성)

d) Time-series forecasting (시계열 예측)

45. Which AWS service is best suited for creating and managing AI-powered chatbots?
45. AI 기반 챗봇을 만들고 관리하는 데 가장 적합한 AWS 서비스는 무엇인가?

a) Amazon Lex (아마존 렉스)

b) Amazon Polly (아마존 폴리)

c) Amazon SageMaker (아마존 세이지메이커)

d) Amazon Rekognition (아마존 레코그니션)

46. What is the role of transfer learning in the application of foundation models?
46. 기초 모델 적용에서 전이 학습의 역할은 무엇인가?

a) Adapting pre-trained models to new tasks (사전 학습된 모델을 새로운 작업에 적응시키기)

b) Creating new models from scratch (새로운 모델을 처음부터 만들기)

c) Enhancing real-time processing (실시간 처리 강화)

d) Generating high-resolution images (고해상도 이미지 생성)

43번 정답: a   44번 정답: b   45번 정답: a   46번 정답: a

47. Which AWS service helps in automating workflows for machine learning tasks?
47. 어떤 AWS 서비스가 머신 러닝 작업을 위한 워크플로우 자동화를 지원하는가?

a) AWS Step Functions (AWS 스텝 함수)
b) Amazon RDS (아마존 RDS)
c) Amazon CloudWatch (아마존 클라우드와치)
d) Amazon S3 (아마존 S3)

48. What type of foundation model is commonly used for generating text-based content?
48. 텍스트 기반 콘텐츠 생성을 위해 일반적으로 사용되는 기초 모델 유형은 무엇인가?

a) Language models like GPT (GPT와 같은 언어 모델)
b) Object detection models (객체 감지 모델)
c) Speech recognition models (음성 인식 모델)
d) Image enhancement models (이미지 향상 모델)

49. How does Amazon Polly benefit applications requiring voice interactions?
49. 아마존 폴리는 음성 상호 작용이 필요한 애플리케이션에 어떤 이점을 제공하는가?

a) By providing lifelike voice responses (사실적인 음성 응답을 제공함으로써)
b) By analyzing text sentiment (텍스트 감정을 분석함으로써)
c) By detecting objects in videos (비디오에서 객체를 감지함으로써)
d) By translating spoken language (음성 언어를 번역함으로써)

50. What type of model would be used for extracting entities from text?
50. 텍스트에서 개체를 추출하는 데 사용되는 모델 유형은 무엇인가?

a) Named Entity Recognition models (명명된 개체 인식 모델)
b) Image segmentation models (이미지 분할 모델)
c) Time-series prediction models (시계열 예측 모델)
d) Speech synthesis models (음성 합성 모델)

47번 정답: a   48번 정답: a   49번 정답: a   50번 정답: a

51. What is a primary use case for Amazon Lex in conversational AI?
51. Amazon Lex의 주요 대화형 AI 사용 사례는 무엇인가?

a) Building chatbots and virtual assistants (챗봇과 가상 비서 구축)
b) Analyzing financial transactions (금융 거래 분석)
c) Recognizing objects in images (이미지에서 객체 인식)
d) Generating real-time weather forecasts (실시간 날씨 예보 생성)

52. How can foundation models be applied in content moderation?
52. 콘텐츠 관리에 기초 모델을 어떻게 적용할 수 있는가?

a) By detecting inappropriate content in text or images (텍스트나 이미지에서 부적절한 콘텐츠 감지)
b) By generating marketing campaigns (마케팅 캠페인 생성)
c) By optimizing network traffic (네트워크 트래픽 최적화)
d) By enhancing audio quality (오디오 품질 향상)

53. Which AWS service offers a suite of pre-built algorithms for machine learning?
53. 어떤 AWS 서비스가 머신 러닝을 위한 사전 구축된 알고리즘 모음을 제공하는가?

a) Amazon SageMaker (아마존 세이지메이커)
b) Amazon Comprehend (아마존 컴프리헨드)
c) AWS Lambda (AWS 람다)
d) AWS Glue (AWS 글루)

54. What type of model is commonly used for visual object detection tasks?
54. 시각적 객체 감지 작업에 일반적으로 사용되는 모델 유형은 무엇인가?

a) Convolutional Neural Networks (CNNs) (합성곱 신경망)
b) Recurrent Neural Networks (RNNs) (순환 신경망)
c) Generative Adversarial Networks (GANs) (생성적 적대 신경망)
d) Text generation models (텍스트 생성 모델)

51번 정답: a   52번 정답: a   53번 정답: a   54번 정답: a

55. Which AWS service provides APIs for analyzing text documents?
55. 어떤 AWS 서비스가 텍스트 문서 분석을 위한 API를 제공하는가?

a) Amazon Comprehend (아마존 컴프리헨드)
b) Amazon Rekognition (아마존 레코그니션)
c) Amazon Polly (아마존 폴리)
d) Amazon Lex (아마존 렉스)

56. What type of foundation model is typically used for generating human-like text responses?
56. 사람과 유사한 텍스트 응답을 생성하는 데 일반적으로 사용되는 기초 모델 유형은 무엇인가?

a) Transformer-based models (트랜스포머 기반 모델)
b) Convolutional Neural Networks (CNNs) (합성곱 신경망)
c) Recurrent Neural Networks (RNNs) (순환 신경망)
d) Generative Adversarial Networks (GANs) (생성적 적대 신경망)

57. How can foundation models assist in automating data entry tasks?
57. 데이터 입력 작업을 자동화하는 데 기초 모델이 어떻게 도움을 줄 수 있는가?

a) By extracting relevant information from documents (문서에서 관련 정보 추출)
b) By generating marketing materials (마케팅 자료 생성)
c) By optimizing network performance (네트워크 성능 최적화)
d) By enhancing video quality (비디오 품질 향상)

58. Which AWS service can be used for real-time analysis of streaming data?
58. 스트리밍 데이터의 실시간 분석에 사용할 수 있는 AWS 서비스는 무엇인가?

a) Amazon Kinesis (아마존 키네시스)
b) Amazon RDS (아마존 RDS)
c) Amazon Comprehend (아마존 컴프리헨드)
d) Amazon Polly (아마존 폴리)

55번 정답: a   56번 정답: a   57번 정답: a   58번 정답: a

59. What type of model would be used for generating realistic audio from text?
59. 텍스트에서 현실감 있는 오디오를 생성하는 데 사용할 모델 유형은 무엇인가?

a) Text-to-speech models (텍스트-음성 변환 모델)
b) Image classification models (이미지 분류 모델)
c) Object detection models (객체 탐지 모델)
d) Time-series forecasting models (시계열 예측 모델)

60. What is the main advantage of using foundation models for machine translation?
60. 기계 번역에 기초 모델을 사용하는 주요 장점은 무엇인가?

a) Leveraging pre-trained knowledge to translate text efficiently (사전 학습된 지식을 활용하여 텍스트를 효율적으로 번역)
b) Creating new models from scratch (새 모델을 처음부터 생성)
c) Enhancing image resolution (이미지 해상도 향상)
d) Analyzing audio signals (오디오 신호 분석)

61. Which AWS service provides pre-trained models for object detection in images?
61. 이미지에서 객체 탐지를 위한 사전 학습된 모델을 제공하는 AWS 서비스는 무엇인가?

a) Amazon Rekognition (아마존 레코그니션)
b) Amazon Lex (아마존 렉스)
c) Amazon Polly (아마존 폴리)
d) AWS Glue (AWS 글루)

62. What is a key benefit of using foundation models in healthcare applications?
62. 헬스케어 애플리케이션에서 기초 모델을 사용할 때의 주요 이점은 무엇인가?

a) Analyzing medical images for diagnosis (진단을 위한 의료 이미지 분석)
b) Generating financial forecasts (재무 예측 생성)
c) Creating marketing content (마케팅 콘텐츠 생성)
d) Enhancing video streaming quality (비디오 스트리밍 품질 향상)

59번 정답: a   60번 정답: a   61번 정답: a   62번 정답: a

63. Which AWS service is used for building scalable machine learning applications?
63. 확장 가능한 머신 러닝 애플리케이션을 구축하는 데 사용하는 AWS 서비스는 무엇인가?

a) Amazon SageMaker (아마존 세이지메이커)
b) Amazon RDS (아마존 RDS)
c) AWS Glue (AWS 글루)
d) Amazon Polly (아마존 폴리)

64. What type of model is best suited for creating text-based chatbots?
64. 텍스트 기반 챗봇을 만드는 데 가장 적합한 모델 유형은 무엇인가?

a) Language models like GPT (GPT와 같은 언어 모델)
b) Image recognition models (이미지 인식 모델)
c) Object detection models (객체 탐지 모델)
d) Time-series prediction models (시계열 예측 모델)

65. How can foundation models be used in fraud detection systems?
65. 기초 모델이 사기 탐지 시스템에 사용될 수 있는 방법은 무엇인가?

a) By analyzing patterns and anomalies in data (데이터의 패턴 및 이상 탐지를 통해)
b) By generating marketing content (마케팅 콘텐츠 생성)
c) By enhancing video resolution (비디오 해상도 향상)
d) By optimizing network bandwidth (네트워크 대역폭 최적화)

66. Which AWS service helps in managing machine learning workflows and deployments?
66. AWS에서 머신 러닝 워크플로와 배포를 관리하는 데 도움이 되는 서비스는 무엇인가?

a) Amazon SageMaker (아마존 세이지메이커)
b) Amazon Comprehend (아마존 컴프리헨드)
c) Amazon Rekognition (아마존 레코그니션)
d) AWS Glue (AWS 글루)

63번 정답: a   64번 정답: a   65번 정답: a   66번 정답: a

67. What type of foundation model is typically used for generating personalized content?
67. 개인화된 콘텐츠 생성을 위해 일반적으로 사용되는 기초 모델 유형은 무엇인가?

a) Generative Pre-trained Transformers (GPT) (사전 학습된 생성형 변환기)
b) Convolutional Neural Networks (CNNs) (합성곱 신경망)
c) Recurrent Neural Networks (RNNs) (순환 신경망)
d) Speech recognition models (음성 인식 모델)

68. How can foundation models enhance recommendation systems?
68. 기초 모델이 추천 시스템을 개선할 수 있는 방법은 무엇인가?

a) By analyzing user behavior and preferences (사용자 행동 및 선호 분석을 통해)
b) By optimizing database queries (데이터베이스 쿼리 최적화)
c) By detecting network intrusions (네트워크 침입 감지)
d) By enhancing audio quality (오디오 품질 향상)

69. Which AWS service provides tools for managing and deploying models at scale?
69. AWS에서 대규모 모델 관리 및 배포 도구를 제공하는 서비스는 무엇인가?

a) Amazon SageMaker (아마존 세이지메이커)
b) AWS CodeDeploy (AWS 코드디플로이)
c) AWS CloudFormation (AWS 클라우드포메이션)
d) Amazon CloudWatch (아마존 클라우드와치)

70. What type of model would you use for generating creative writing?
70. 창의적인 글 생성을 위해 사용할 수 있는 모델 유형은 무엇인가?

a) Language models like GPT (GPT와 같은 언어 모델)
b) Image recognition models (이미지 인식 모델)
c) Time-series prediction models (시계열 예측 모델)
d) Speech synthesis models (음성 합성 모델)

67번 정답: a   68번 정답: a   69번 정답: a   70번 정답: a

71. How can foundation models assist in generating automated responses for customer service?
71. 기초 모델이 고객 서비스에서 자동 응답을 생성하는 데 어떻게 도움이 될 수 있는가?

a) By leveraging pre-trained knowledge to understand and respond to queries (사전 학습된 지식을 활용하여 질문을 이해하고 응답)
b) By creating new models from scratch (새 모델을 처음부터 생성)
c) By enhancing video resolution (비디오 해상도 향상)
d) By detecting network anomalies (네트워크 이상 탐지)

72. Which AWS service provides capabilities for analyzing and understanding speech?
72. AWS에서 음성을 분석하고 이해하는 기능을 제공하는 서비스는 무엇인가?

a) Amazon Transcribe (아마존 트랜스크라이브)
b) Amazon Lex (아마존 렉스)
c) Amazon Rekognition (아마존 레코그니션)
d) Amazon Polly (아마존 폴리)

73. What is the main purpose of using Amazon Rekognition in video analysis?
73. 비디오 분석에서 Amazon Rekognition을 사용하는 주요 목적은 무엇인가?

a) Identifying and labeling objects and people (객체 및 사람 식별 및 라벨링)
b) Generating text summaries (텍스트 요약 생성)
c) Enhancing audio quality (오디오 품질 향상)
d) Translating text (텍스트 번역)

74. What type of foundation model is effective for real-time translation of spoken language?
74. 음성 언어의 실시간 번역에 효과적인 기초 모델 유형은 무엇인가?

a) Speech-to-text models (음성을 텍스트로 변환하는 모델)
b) Image classification models (이미지 분류 모델)
c) Object detection models (객체 탐지 모델)
d) Time-series prediction models (시계열 예측 모델)

71번 정답: a   72번 정답: a   73번 정답: a   74번 정답: a

75. How does Amazon Comprehend help in sentiment analysis?

75. Amazon Comprehend는 감성 분석에서 어떻게 도움이 되는가?

a) By detecting emotions and opinions in text (텍스트에서 감정과 의견 감지)
b) By recognizing objects in images (이미지에서 객체 인식)
c) By synthesizing human-like speech (인간과 같은 음성 합성)
d) By translating text (텍스트 번역)

76. What is a key advantage of using pre-trained foundation models for text generation?

76. 텍스트 생성에 사전 학습된 기초 모델을 사용할 때의 주요 장점은 무엇인가?

a) Reducing the need for extensive training data and computational resources (대규모 학습 데이터와 계산 자원의 필요성 감소)
b) Enhancing image resolution (이미지 해상도 향상)
c) Improving real-time video processing (실시간 비디오 처리 향상)
d) Optimizing network bandwidth (네트워크 대역폭 최적화)

77. Which AWS service can be used to integrate machine learning models into web applications?

77. 웹 애플리케이션에 머신러닝 모델을 통합하는 데 사용할 수 있는 AWS 서비스는 무엇인가?

a) Amazon SageMaker (아마존 세이지메이커)
b) AWS Lambda (AWS 람다)
c) Amazon RDS (아마존 RDS)
d) AWS Step Functions (AWS 스텝 함수)

78. How can foundation models be applied in content recommendation engines?

78. 콘텐츠 추천 엔진에서 기초 모델은 어떻게 적용될 수 있는가?

a) By analyzing user behavior and suggesting relevant content (사용자 행동을 분석하고 관련 콘텐츠 추천)
b) By enhancing network security (네트워크 보안 강화)
c) By optimizing video streaming quality (비디오 스트리밍 품질 최적화)
d) By improving database performance (데이터베이스 성능 향상)

75번 정답: a   76번 정답: a   77번 정답: a   78번 정답: a

79. What is the purpose of using Amazon Lex for conversational interfaces?
79. 대화형 인터페이스를 위해 Amazon Lex를 사용하는 목적은 무엇인가?

a) Creating natural language interactions with users (사용자와 자연어 상호작용 생성)
b) Analyzing financial data (금융 데이터 분석)
c) Recognizing objects in images (이미지 내 객체 인식)
d) Generating real-time weather forecasts (실시간 날씨 예측 생성)

80. Which AWS service provides tools for generating human-like speech from text?
80. 텍스트로부터 인간 같은 음성을 생성하기 위한 도구를 제공하는 AWS 서비스는 무엇인가?

a) Amazon Polly (아마존 폴리)
b) Amazon Comprehend (아마존 컴프리헨드)
c) Amazon Rekognition (아마존 레코그니션)
d) Amazon Lex (아마존 렉스)

81. What type of foundation model is used for automatic summarization of text?
81. 텍스트의 자동 요약에 사용되는 기초 모델 유형은 무엇인가?

a) Transformer-based models (트랜스포머 기반 모델)
b) Convolutional Neural Networks (CNNs) (합성곱 신경망)
c) Recurrent Neural Networks (RNNs) (순환 신경망)
d) Object detection models (객체 감지 모델)

82. How can foundation models be used in financial forecasting?
82. 기초 모델이 금융 예측에 어떻게 사용될 수 있는가?

a) By analyzing historical data and predicting future trends (과거 데이터를 분석하고 미래 트렌드를 예측함으로써)
b) By generating marketing content (마케팅 콘텐츠 생성)
c) By optimizing video streaming (비디오 스트리밍 최적화)
d) By enhancing network performance (네트워크 성능 향상)

79번 정답: a   80번 정답: a   81번 정답: a   82번 정답: a

83. Which AWS service provides APIs for image and video analysis?

83. 이미지 및 비디오 분석을 위한 API를 제공하는 AWS 서비스는 무엇인가?

a) Amazon Rekognition (아마존 레코그니션)
b) Amazon Polly (아마존 폴리)
c) Amazon Lex (아마존 렉스)
d) AWS Glue (AWS 글루)

84. What type of model is effective for detecting anomalies in network traffic?

84. 네트워크 트래픽에서 이상을 감지하는 데 효과적인 모델 유형은 무엇인가?

a) Anomaly detection models (이상 탐지 모델)
b) Image classification models (이미지 분류 모델)
c) Speech recognition models (음성 인식 모델)
d) Text generation models (텍스트 생성 모델)

85. How can foundation models enhance virtual assistants?

85. 기초 모델이 가상 비서를 어떻게 향상시킬 수 있는가?

a) By providing accurate and context-aware responses (정확하고 상황에 맞는 응답 제공)
b) By optimizing video resolution (비디오 해상도 최적화)
c) By detecting network intrusions (네트워크 침입 감지)
d) By generating financial forecasts (금융 예측 생성)

86. Which AWS service is used for real-time speech recognition?

78. 콘텐츠 추천 엔진에서 기초 모델은 어떻게 적용될 수 있는가?

a) Amazon Transcribe (아마존 트랜스크라이브)
b) Amazon Comprehend (아마존 컴프리헨드)
c) Amazon Rekognition (아마존 리코그니션)
d) Amazon Polly (아마존 폴리)

83번 정답: a   84번 정답: a   85번 정답: a   86번 정답: a

87. What is a primary application of generative models in creative industries?
87. 창작 산업에서 생성 모델의 주요 응용 분야는 무엇인가?

a) Generating text, images, and music (텍스트, 이미지, 음악 생성)
b) Analyzing network traffic (네트워크 트래픽 분석)
c) Optimizing video streaming (비디오 스트리밍 최적화)
d) Detecting fraud (사기 탐지)

88. How can foundation models be applied in automated content generation?
88. 자동화된 콘텐츠 생성에 기초 모델을 어떻게 적용할 수 있는가?

a) By creating articles, blogs, and other textual content (기사, 블로그 및 기타 텍스트 콘텐츠 생성)
b) By optimizing database performance (데이터베이스 성능 최적화)
c) By enhancing audio quality (오디오 품질 향상)
d) By detecting network intrusions (네트워크 침입 탐지)

89. Which AWS service provides tools for building and deploying conversational agents?
89. 대화형 에이전트를 구축하고 배포하는 도구를 제공하는 AWS 서비스는 무엇인가?

a) Amazon Lex (아마존 렉스)
b) AWS Glue (AWS 글루)
c) Amazon Rekognition (아마존 리코그니션)
d) Amazon Polly (아마존 폴리)

90. How can foundation models improve personalized marketing efforts?
90. 기초 모델이 개인 맞춤형 마케팅 노력을 어떻게 향상시킬 수 있는가?

a) By analyzing user preferences and generating targeted content (사용자 선호도 분석 및 타겟 콘텐츠 생성)
b) By enhancing image resolution (이미지 해상도 향상)
c) By optimizing network bandwidth (네트워크 대역폭 최적화)
d) By generating real-time weather forecasts (실시간 날씨 예보 생성)

87번 정답: a   88번 정답: a   89번 정답: a   90번 정답: a

91. What type of foundation model is used for translating text into different languages?
91. 텍스트를 다른 언어로 번역하는 데 사용되는 기초 모델 유형은 무엇인가?

a) Machine translation models (기계 번역 모델)
b) Object detection models (객체 감지 모델)
c) Speech synthesis models (음성 합성 모델)
d) Image classification models (이미지 분류 모델)

92. How does Amazon Polly contribute to creating engaging audio content?
92. Amazon Polly는 매력적인 오디오 콘텐츠를 생성하는 데 어떻게 기여하는가?

a) By converting text into lifelike speech (텍스트를 생동감 있는 음성으로 변환)
b) By analyzing sentiment in text (텍스트에서 감정 분석)
c) By detecting objects in images (이미지에서 객체 감지)
d) By translating text (텍스트 번역)

93. What is a common use case for foundation models in the entertainment industry?
93. 엔터테인먼트 산업에서 기초 모델의 일반적인 사용 사례는 무엇인가?

a) Generating music, scripts, and visuals (음악, 스크립트 및 시각 자료 생성)
b) Analyzing financial data (재무 데이터 분석)
c) Enhancing video quality (비디오 품질 향상)
d) Detecting network anomalies (네트워크 이상 탐지)

94. Which AWS service offers real-time analytics for streaming video content?
94. 스트리밍 비디오 콘텐츠에 대한 실시간 분석을 제공하는 AWS 서비스는 무엇인가?

a) Amazon Kinesis Video Streams (아마존 키네시스 비디오 스트림)
b) Amazon Comprehend (아마존 컴프리헨드)
c) Amazon Rekognition (아마존 레코그니션)
d) AWS Lambda (AWS 람다)

91번 정답: a   92번 정답: a   93번 정답: a   94번 정답: a

95. How can foundation models be used to enhance customer feedback analysis?
95. 고객 피드백 분석을 강화하기 위해 기초 모델을 어떻게 사용할 수 있는가?

a) By extracting sentiment and key insights from feedback (피드백에서 감정 및 주요 인사이트 추출)
b) By generating marketing content (마케팅 콘텐츠 생성)
c) By optimizing network performance (네트워크 성능 최적화)
d) By enhancing video quality (비디오 품질 향상)

96. What type of model is used for predicting future sales trends based on historical data?
96. 과거 데이터를 기반으로 미래 판매 경향을 예측하는 데 사용되는 모델 유형은 무엇인가?

a) Time-series forecasting models (시계열 예측 모델)
b) Image recognition models (이미지 인식 모델)
c) Speech synthesis models (음성 합성 모델)
d) Object detection models (객체 탐지 모델)

97. Which AWS service helps in integrating machine learning models with mobile and web applications?
97. 머신 러닝 모델을 모바일 및 웹 애플리케이션과 통합하는 데 도움이 되는 AWS 서비스는 무엇인가?

a) Amazon SageMaker (아마존 세이지메이커)
b) Amazon RDS (아마존 RDS)
c) AWS Step Functions (AWS 스텝 펑션)
d) Amazon CloudWatch (아마존 클라우드와치)

98. How can foundation models improve the accuracy of search engines?
98. 검색 엔진의 정확성을 기초 모델이 어떻게 향상시킬 수 있는가?

a) By understanding and ranking search queries effectively (검색 쿼리를 효과적으로 이해하고 순위 지정)
b) By optimizing video streaming (비디오 스트리밍 최적화)
c) By enhancing image resolution (이미지 해상도 향상)
d) By detecting network intrusions (네트워크 침입 감지)

95번 정답: a   96번 정답: a   97번 정답: a   98번 정답: a

99. What is a primary application of generative models in the healthcare sector?

99. 의료 분야에서 생성 모델의 주요 응용 분야는 무엇인가?

a) Generating patient reports and medical summaries (환자 보고서 및 의료 요약 생성)

b) Enhancing network security (네트워크 보안 강화)

c) Analyzing financial data (재무 데이터 분석)

d) Optimizing video quality (비디오 품질 최적화)

100. Which AWS service provides tools for managing and deploying machine learning models in production?

100. 프로덕션 환경에서 머신 러닝 모델을 관리하고 배포하는 도구를 제공하는 AWS 서비스는 무엇인가?

a) Amazon SageMaker (아마존 세이지메이커)

b) Amazon Comprehend (아마존 컴프리헨드)

c) AWS Lambda (AWS 람다)

d) Amazon Polly (아마존 폴리)

99번 정답: a   100번 정답: a

도메인 4: 책임 있는 AI 가이드라인

AI 시스템의 윤리적 설계, 개발, 배포에 관한 AWS의 핵심 원칙들(공정성, 투명성, 설명 가능성, 프라이버시, 보안 등)을 이해하고 AI 모델의 편향성 감지 및 완화 방법, 데이터 프라이버시 보호 전략, 모델 의사결정의 투명성 확보 방안, AWS의 관련 도구들(SageMaker Clarify, Amazon Macie 등)의 활용법을 평가하며, 특히 실제 비즈니스 상황에서 발생할 수 있는 윤리적 문제들을 식별하고 이를 AWS의 책임있는 AI 프레임워크에 따라 적절히 해결할 수 있는 능력을 테스트하므로, 시험 준비 시에는 AWS의 책임있는 AI 원칙들을 단순 암기하는 것을 넘어 실제 사례를 통해 이러한 원칙들이 어떻게 적용되고 구현되는지, 그리고 관련 규제 준수와 거버넌스 체계 수립 방안에 대해 종합적으로 이해하는 것이 중요하다.

1. What is a primary goal of responsible AI?

1. 책임 있는 AI의 주요 목표는 무엇인가?

a) To maximize profits (이익을 극대화하기)
b) To ensure AI operates as intended without harm (AI가 의도된 대로 작동하며 해를 끼치지 않도록 보장하기)
c) To reduce the number of AI models in production (프로덕션 AI 모델 수 줄이기)
d) To develop AI that requires minimal human oversight (최소한의 인간 감독이 필요한 AI 개발하기)

2. Which principle of responsible AI focuses on ensuring that AI systems do not perpetuate biases?

2. AI 시스템이 편향을 지속하지 않도록 보장하는 데 중점을 둔 책임 있는 AI의 원칙은 무엇인가?

a) Accountability (책임성)
b) Fairness (공정성)
c) Transparency (투명성)
d) Security (보안)

1번 정답: b   2번 정답: b

3. What is an important consideration when developing AI to ensure it is inclusive?
3. AI를 개발할 때 포괄성을 보장하기 위한 중요한 고려 사항은 무엇인가?

a) Maximizing computational efficiency (계산 효율성 극대화)

b) Engaging diverse stakeholders in the development process (개발 과정에 다양한 이해관계자 참여시키기)

c) Reducing the complexity of the AI model (AI 모델의 복잡성 줄이기)

d) Increasing the speed of data processing (데이터 처리 속도 높이기)

4. How should an organization approach the transparency of AI systems?
4. 조직은 AI 시스템의 투명성을 어떻게 접근해야 하는가?

a) By keeping the AI model and data proprietary (AI 모델과 데이터를 독점적으로 유지하기)

b) By documenting and sharing how the AI system makes decisions (AI 시스템의 의사 결정 방식을 문서화하고 공유하기)

c) By minimizing the amount of information about the AI system (AI 시스템에 대한 정보의 양 최소화하기)

d) By limiting access to AI system outputs (AI 시스템 출력에 대한 접근 제한하기)

5. What does the principle of accountability in responsible AI emphasize?
5. 책임 있는 AI의 책임 원칙이 강조하는 것은 무엇인가?

a) Automating as many processes as possible (가능한 많은 프로세스 자동화)

b) Ensuring that there are clear lines of responsibility and mechanisms for addressing issues (명확한 책임 구분 및 문제 해결 메커니즘 보장)

c) Reducing the need for human intervention in AI systems (AI 시스템에서 인간 개입 필요성 줄이기)

d) Decreasing the number of stakeholders involved in AI projects (AI 프로젝트에 참여하는 관계자 축소)

6. What should be considered when evaluating the impact of an AI system on society?
6. AI 시스템이 사회에 미치는 영향을 평가할 때 고려해야 할 사항은 무엇인가?

a) The financial benefits alone (재정적 이익만)

b) The potential social, economic, and ethical impacts (사회적, 경제적, 윤리적 잠재적 영향)

c) The technical specifications of the AI system (AI 시스템의 기술 사양)

d) The ease of deployment (배포 용이성)

3번 정답: b   4번 정답: b   5번 정답: b   6번 정답: b

7. Why is it important to regularly monitor and audit AI systems?
7. AI시스템을 정기적으로 모니터링하고 감사하는 것이 중요한 이유는 무엇인가?

a) To identify and mitigate any unintended consequences or biases (예기치 않은 결과나 편향을 식별하고 완화하기 위해)

b) To increase the model's training time (모델의 학습 시간 증가시키기 위해)

c) To reduce the model's accuracy (모델의 정확도 줄이기 위해)

d) To limit the number of users interacting with the system (시스템과 상호 작용 사용자 수 제한하기 위해)

8. Which practice is essential for ensuring AI models are fair and unbiased?
8. AI 모델이 공정하고 편향되지 않도록 보장하는 데 필수적인 실천은 무엇인가?

a) Using only historical data (오직 과거 데이터만 사용하기)

b) Implementing rigorous data validation and fairness assessments (엄격한 데이터 검증 및 공정성 평가 수행)

c) Limiting the diversity of the data (데이터 다양성 제한하기)

d) Reducing the number of features in the model (모델의 특징 수 줄이기)

9. What role does human oversight play in responsible AI?
9. 책임 있는 AI에서 인간 감독의 역할은 무엇인가?

a) It is optional if the AI system is highly accurate (AI 시스템이 매우 정확한 경우 선택 사항임)

b) It ensures that AI decisions are aligned with ethical standards and can be adjusted if needed (AI 결정이 윤리적 기준과 일치하며 필요 시 조정 가능하도록 보장함)

c) It complicates the AI development process (AI 개발 과정을 복잡하게 만듦)

d) It is only necessary for AI systems used in high-risk applications (고위험 응용 프로그램에서 사용되는 AI 시스템에만 필요함)

10. How can organizations ensure that their AI systems respect user privacy?
10. 조직이 AI시스템이 사용자 프라이버시를 존중하도록 보장하는 방법은 무엇인가?

a) By collecting as much user data as possible (가능한 많은 사용자 데이터 수집하기)

b) By implementing data protection measures and minimizing data collection (데이터 보호 조치를 구현하고 데이터 수집 최소화하기)

c) By using AI systems without any privacy considerations (프라이버시 고려 없이 AI 시스템 사용하기)

d) By anonymizing all data after processing (처리 후 모든 데이터를 익명화하기)

7번 정답: a   8번 정답: b   9번 정답: b   10번 정답: b

12. What is the purpose of establishing ethical guidelines for AI development?
11. AI 개발을 위한 윤리적 지침을 설정하는 목적은 무엇인가?

a) To streamline the development process (개발 과정을 간소화하기)

b) To provide a framework for making responsible decisions and addressing ethical issues (책임 있는 결정을 내리고 윤리적 문제를 해결하기 위한 프레임워크 제공)

c) To reduce the cost of AI projects (AI 프로젝트 비용 절감하기)

d) To limit the number of AI applications (AI 응용 프로그램 수 제한하기)

12. Which of the following is a key factor in ensuring the security of AI systems?
12. AI 시스템의 보안을 보장하는 주요 요소는 무엇인가?

a) Implementing robust access controls and encryption (강력한 접근 제어 및 암호화 구현)

b) Using outdated security practices (구식 보안 관행 사용)

c) Ignoring potential security vulnerabilities (잠재적 보안 취약점 무시)

d) Reducing the frequency of security updates (보안 업데이트 빈도 줄이기)

13. Why is it important to engage with stakeholders during the AI development process?
13. AI 개발 과정에서 이해관계자와 소통하는 것이 중요한 이유는 무엇인가?

a) To speed up the development timeline (개발 일정을 앞당기기 위해)

b) To gather diverse perspectives and ensure that the AI system meets the needs and values of all affected parties (다양한 관점을 수렴하여 AI 시스템이 모든 관련자의 요구와 가치를 충족하도록 보장하기 위해)

c) To reduce the cost of the project (프로젝트 비용을 줄이기 위해)

d) To limit the number of features in the AI system (AI 시스템의 기능 수 제한하기 위해)

14. Which of the following is an example of a responsible AI practice?
14. 다음 중 책임 있는 AI 관행의 예는 무엇인가?

a) Developing AI systems without considering ethical implications (윤리적 함의 고려 없이 AI 시스템 개발)

b) Providing clear explanations for AI decisions to users (AI 결정에 대해 사용자에게 명확한 설명 제공)

c) Using biased data to train AI models (편향된 데이터를 사용하여 AI 모델 훈련하기)

d) Limiting transparency in AI systems (AI 시스템에서 투명성 제한하기)

11번 정답: b   12번 정답: a   13번 정답: b   14번 정답: b

15. How can AI developers ensure that their models are robust and resilient?

15. AI 개발자가 모델이 견고하고 탄력적임을 보장하는 방법은 무엇인가?

a) By designing models that are highly specialized and inflexible (매우 특화되고 유연하지 않은 모델 설계하기)

b) By testing models extensively under various conditions and scenarios (다양한 조건과 시나리오에서 모델을 광범위하게 테스트하기)

c) By minimizing the use of validation data (검증 데이터 사용 최소화하기)

d) By ignoring performance metrics (성능 메트릭 무시하기)

16. What is the benefit of creating an AI ethics board?

16. AI 윤리위원회를 만드는 이점은 무엇인가?

a) To monitor financial performance of AI projects (AI 프로젝트의 재무 성과를 모니터링하기 위해)

b) To provide oversight and guidance on ethical issues and ensure responsible AI practices (윤리적 문제에 대한 감독과 지침을 제공하고 책임 있는 AI 관행을 보장하기 위해)

c) To manage the technical details of AI systems (AI 시스템의 기술 세부 사항을 관리하기 위해)

d) To reduce the number of stakeholders involved (참여하는 이해관계자의 수를 줄이기 위해)

17. Which principle focuses on the ability of AI systems to explain their decisions and actions?

17. AI 시스템이 그들의 결정과 행동을 설명할 수 있는 능력에 중점을 두는 원칙은 무엇인가?

a) Fairness (공정성)

b) Transparency (투명성)

c) Security (보안)

d) Accountability (책임성)

18. What should organizations do to address potential biases in AI systems?

18. 조직이 AI 시스템의 잠재적 편향을 해결하기 위해 해야 할 일은 무엇인가?

a) Avoid analyzing the data for biases (데이터에서 편향을 분석하는 것을 피하기)

b) Regularly review and update the data and algorithms to identify and mitigate biases (편향을 식별하고 완화하기 위해 데이터와 알고리즘을 정기적으로 검토하고 업데이트하기)

c) Use only one source of data (단일 데이터 소스만 사용하기)

d) Limit the diversity of the data (데이터의 다양성을 제한하기)

15번 정답: b   16번 정답: b   17번 정답: b   18번 정답: b

19. Which action is crucial for maintaining user trust in AI systems?
19. AI 시스템에서 사용자 신뢰를 유지하는 데 중요한 행동은 무엇인가?

a) Providing frequent updates about AI system performance and any changes (AI 시스템 성능 및 모든 변경 사항에 대해 자주 업데이트 제공하기)

b) Keeping the AI system's decision-making process hidden (AI 시스템의 의사결정 과정을 숨기기)

c) Reducing user access to system features (시스템 기능에 대한 사용자 접근 줄이기)

d) Ignoring user feedback (사용자 피드백 무시하기)

20. Why is it important to have clear documentation of AI systems?
20. AI 시스템의 명확한 문서화가 중요한 이유는 무엇인가?

a) To make the AI system less transparent (AI 시스템을 덜 투명하게 만들기 위해)

b) To ensure that the AI system's design, functionality, and decision-making process are well understood and can be reviewed (AI 시스템 설계, 기능, 의사결정 과정이 잘 이해되고 검토될 수 있도록 보장하기 위해)

c) To limit the amount of information available about the AI system (AI 시스템에 대한 정보 제한하기 위해)

d) To speed up the development process (개발 과정을 가속화하기 위해)

21. What is a potential risk of not addressing ethical considerations in AI development?
21. AI 개발에서 윤리적 고려사항을 다루지 않을 때 발생할 수 있는 잠재적 위험은 무엇인가?

a) Increased development time (개발 시간 증가)

b) Development of AI systems that may cause harm or perpetuate unfairness (해를 끼치거나 불공정을 지속할 수 있는 AI 시스템 개발)

c) Higher computational costs (더 높은 계산 비용)

d) Reduced model accuracy (모델 정확도 감소)

22. Which of the following practices helps ensure responsible use of AI in decision-making processes?
22. 의사 결정 과정에서 AI의 책임 있는 사용을 보장하는 관행은 무엇인가?

a) Allowing AI to make decisions without human oversight (사람 없이 AI가 결정을 내리도록 허용하기)

b) Incorporating human review and accountability mechanisms for critical decisions (중요한 결정에 대해 사람의 검토와 책임 메커니즘 포함하기)

c) Using AI systems only in non-critical areas (비중요 영역에서만 AI 시스템 사용하기)

d) Minimizing the involvement of domain experts (도메인 전문가의 참여 최소화하기)

19번 정답: a   20번 정답: b   21번 정답: b   22번 정답: b

23. How can organizations address the challenge of model interpretability in AI systems?
23. 조직이 AI 시스템에서 모델 해석 가능성의 과제를 해결할 수 있는 방법은 무엇인가?

a) By using complex, opaque models (복잡하고 불투명한 모델 사용)

b) By developing methods and tools that enhance the interpretability and explainability of models (모델의 해석 가능성과 설명 가능성을 높이는 방법 및 도구 개발)

c) By focusing solely on model accuracy (모델 정확성에만 집중)

d) By limiting the use of interpretability techniques (해석 가능성 기법 사용 제한)

24. What should be included in a responsible AI strategy?
24. 책임 있는 AI 전략에 포함되어야 할 것은 무엇인가?

a) Only technical specifications of the AI system (AI 시스템의 기술 사양만 포함)

b) Guidelines for ethical considerations, risk management, and stakeholder engagement (윤리적 고려사항, 위험 관리 및 이해관계자 참여에 대한 지침 포함)

c) Financial projections for AI projects (AI 프로젝트에 대한 재무 예측 포함)

d) A list of AI technologies used (사용된 AI 기술 목록 포함)

25. Which practice helps to mitigate the risks associated with AI system deployment?
25. AI 시스템 배포와 관련된 위험을 완화하는 데 도움이 되는 관행은 무엇인가?

a) Skipping the testing phase (테스트 단계 건너뛰기)

b) Conducting thorough testing and validation before deployment (배포 전 철저한 테스트와 검증 수행)

c) Using outdated algorithms (구식 알고리즘 사용)

d) Ignoring user feedback (사용자 피드백 무시)

26. What is an essential component of an AI governance framework?
26. AI 거버넌스 프레임워크의 필수 구성 요소는 무엇인가?

a) Ignoring regulatory requirements (규제 요구 사항 무시)

b) Establishing policies and procedures for the ethical and responsible use of AI (AI의 윤리적이고 책임 있는 사용을 위한 정책과 절차 수립)

c) Focusing solely on technical performance (기술 성능에만 집중)

d) Limiting stakeholder involvement (이해관계자 참여 제한)

23번 정답: b   24번 정답: b   25번 정답: b   26번 정답: b

27. How can AI systems be designed to support fairness?
27. AI 시스템이 공정성을 지원하도록 설계할 수 있는 방법은 무엇인가?

a) By using homogeneous data sets (동질적인 데이터 세트 사용)

b) By implementing fairness-aware algorithms and ensuring diverse representation in training data (공정성을 인식하는 알고리즘을 구현하고 훈련 데이터에서 다양한 표현 보장)

c) By minimizing the number of data sources (데이터 소스 수 최소화)

d) By using only historical data (과거 데이터만 사용)

28. Which aspect of AI ethics addresses the potential misuse of AI technologies?
28. AI 윤리의 어떤 측면이 AI 기술의 잠재적 오용을 다루는가?

a) Transparency (투명성)

b) Security (보안)

c) Fairness (공정성)

d) Accountability (책임성)

29. What should organizations do to ensure the ongoing ethical management of AI systems?
29. AI 시스템의 윤리적 관리를 지속하기 위해 조직은 무엇을 해야 하는가?

a) Regularly review and update ethical guidelines and practices (윤리적 지침과 관행을 정기적으로 검토하고 업데이트함)

b) Avoid updating AI systems (AI 시스템 업데이트를 피함)

c) Limit the number of people involved in AI management (AI 관리에 참여하는 사람의 수를 제한함)

d) Focus solely on technical performance (기술적 성과에만 집중함)

30. Why is it important to assess the social impact of AI systems?
30. AI 시스템의 사회적 영향을 평가하는 것이 중요한가?

a) To increase development costs (개발 비용을 증가시키기)

b) To understand and address potential societal consequences and ensure positive outcomes (잠재적인 사회적 결과를 이해하고 해결하여 긍정적인 결과를 보장하기)

c) To reduce the complexity of AI systems (AI 시스템의 복잡성을 줄이기)

d) To limit stakeholder engagement (이해관계자의 참여를 제한하기)

27번 정답: b   28번 정답: d   29번 정답: a   30번 정답: b

31. What is a key factor in ensuring the robustness of AI systems?
31. AI 시스템의 견고성을 보장하기 위한 주요 요소는 무엇인가?

a) Designing systems with minimal error handling (최소한의 오류 처리로 시스템 설계)

b) Implementing comprehensive testing and validation procedures (포괄적인 테스트 및 검증 절차 구현)

c) Reducing the frequency of system updates (시스템 업데이트 빈도 줄이기)

d) Minimizing the amount of data used (데이터 사용량 최소화)

32. What should be done to ensure that AI systems are ethically aligned with organizational values?
32. AI 시스템이 조직의 가치와 윤리적으로 일치하도록 하기 위해 무엇을 해야 하는가?

a) Avoiding alignment with organizational values (조직적 가치와의 일치를 피함)

b) Integrating ethical considerations into all stages of AI development and deployment (윤리적 고려 사항을 AI 개발 및 배포의 모든 단계에 통합함)

c) Reducing the involvement of ethical experts (윤리적 전문가의 참여를 줄임)

d) Focusing solely on technical performance (기술적 성과에 집중)

33. How can organizations manage the ethical risks associated with AI-driven decision-making?
33. AI 주도의 의사결정에서 윤리적 위험을 관리하는 방법은 무엇인가?

a) Ignoring potential risks (잠재적 위험을 무시함)

b) Implementing oversight and accountability mechanisms and regularly reviewing AI decisions (감시와 책임 메커니즘을 구현하고 AI 결정을 정기적으로 검토함)

c) Using only automated decision-making processes (자동화된 의사결정 프로세스만 사용함)

d) Limiting the scope of AI applications (AI 애플리케이션의 범위를 제한함)

34. What does the principle of inclusivity in AI development emphasize?
34. AI 개발에서 포괄성 원칙이 강조하는 것은 무엇인가?

a) Using only a single demographic for training data (단일 인구 통계를 훈련 데이터로만 사용함)

b) Ensuring diverse perspectives and needs are considered and represented in AI systems (다양한 관점과 요구를 고려하여 AI 시스템에 반영함)

c) Limiting the range of applications (애플리케이션 범위를 제한함)

d) Reducing stakeholder involvement (이해관계자 참여를 줄임)

31번 정답: b   32번 정답: b   33번 정답: b   34번 정답: b

35. Why is it important to include ethical considerations in AI system design?
35. AI 시스템 설계에서 윤리적 고려를 포함하는 것이 중요한가?

a) To make the AI system more complex (AI 시스템을 더 복잡하게 만들기 위해)

b) To ensure that the AI system operates in a manner that aligns with societal values and norms (AI 시스템이 사회적 가치와 규범에 맞게 운영되도록 보장하기 위해)

c) To minimize the system's performance (시스템의 성능을 최소화하기 위해)

d) To reduce development time (개발 시간을 줄이기 위해)

36. What is a benefit of having a clear AI ethics policy?
36. 명확한 AI 윤리 정책의 이점은 무엇인가?

a) It makes AI systems less transparent (AI 시스템의 투명성을 감소시킴)

b) It provides a framework for making ethical decisions and managing risks associated with AI (윤리적 의사 결정 및 AI 관련 위험 관리의 프레임워크 제공)

c) It limits stakeholder engagement (이해관계자 참여 제한)

d) It reduces the need for human oversight (인간 감독의 필요성을 줄임)

37. How can AI systems be made more transparent?
37. AI 시스템을 더 투명하게 만들 수 있는 방법은 무엇인가?

a) By hiding the decision-making process (의사결정 과정을 숨김)

b) By providing clear documentation and explanations of how decisions are made (의사 결정이 어떻게 이루어지는지에 대한 명확한 문서와 설명을 제공함)

c) By using complex algorithms without explanation (설명 없이 복잡한 알고리즘 사용)

d) By limiting access to system outputs (시스템 출력에 대한 접근 제한)

38. What is an example of a practice that supports responsible AI deployment?
38. 책임 있는 AI 배포를 지원하는 관행의 예는 무엇인가?

a) Ignoring user feedback (사용자 피드백을 무시함)

b) Incorporating user feedback and adjusting the system based on real-world use (사용자 피드백을 통합하고 실제 사용을 기반으로 시스템 조정함)

c) Using outdated technologies (구식 기술을 사용함)

d) Reducing the frequency of updates (업데이트 빈도를 줄임)

35번 정답: b   36번 정답: b   37번 정답: b   38번 정답: b

39. Which of the following is a responsibility of AI developers?
39. AI 개발자의 책임 중 하나는 무엇인가?

a) Ignoring ethical guidelines (윤리적 지침을 무시)

b) Ensuring that AI systems are developed and deployed in a manner that is ethical and aligns with societal values (AI 시스템을 사회적 가치와 윤리적 일치에 따라 개발하고 배포를 보장)

c) Using only pre-built models without modification (수정 없이 미리 제작된 모델만 사용)

d) Limiting the diversity of date sources (날짜 출처의 다양성 제한)

40. What is an essential aspect of ensuring that AI systems are accountable?
40. AI 시스템이 책임을 지도록 보장하기 위한 필수 측면은 무엇인가?

a) Reducing human oversight (인간 감독 줄이기)

b) Implementing mechanisms for tracking and addressing issues that arise from AI system use (AI 시스템 사용에서 발생하는 문제를 추적하고 해결하기 위한 메커니즘 구현)

c) Minimizing the transparency of the system (시스템의 투명성을 최소화)

d) Limiting the scope of AI applications (AI 애플리케이션의 범위를 제한)

41. How can organizations ensure that AI systems are secure?
41. 조직이 AI 시스템의 보안을 보장하려면 어떻게 해야 하는가?

a) By implementing robust security measures and regularly updating them (견고한 보안 조치를 구현하고 정기적으로 업데이트)

b) By using outdated security practices (구식 보안 관행 사용)

c) By reducing the frequency of security audits (보안 감사의 빈도를 줄임)

d) By ignoring potential vulnerabilities (잠재적 취약점을 무시함)

42. Why is stakeholder engagement important in AI development?
42. AI 개발에서 이해관계자의 참여가 왜 중요한가?

a) To speed up the development process (개발 프로세스를 가속화하기)

b) To ensure that diverse perspectives are considered and that the AI system meets the needs of all stakeholders (다양한 관점을 보장하고 AI 시스템이 모든 이해관계자의 요구를 충족하도록 보장하기)

c) To reduce development costs (개발 비용을 줄이기)

d) To limit the number of features in the AI system (AI 시스템의 기능 수를 제한하기)

39번 정답: b   40번 정답: b   41번 정답: a   42번 정답: b

43. Which principle ensures that AI systems do not inadvertently harm individuals or groups?

43. AI 시스템이 개인이나 그룹에 의도치 않은 피해를 주지 않도록 보장하는 원칙은 무엇인가?

a) Transparency (투명성)
b) Security (보안)
c) Fairness (공정성)
d) Safety (안전)

44. What should organizations do to address potential ethical issues with AI systems?

44. 조직은 AI 시스템과 관련된 잠재적인 윤리적 문제를 해결하기 위해 무엇을 해야 하는가?

a) Avoid discussing ethical issues (윤리적 문제 논의를 피함)
b) Proactively identify and address potential ethical issues throughout the AI lifecycle (AI 생애 주기 전반에 걸쳐 잠재적인 윤리적 문제를 적극적으로 식별하고 해결)
c) Limit the involvement of ethicists (윤리 전문가의 참여를 제한)
d) Focus solely on technical performance (기술적 성과에만 집중)

45. Which practice helps ensure that AI systems respect user privacy?

45. AI 시스템이 사용자 프라이버시를 존중하도록 보장하는 관행은 무엇인가?

a) Collecting and storing extensive personal data (광범위한 개인 데이터를 수집 및 저장)
b) Implementing privacy-preserving techniques and minimizing data collection (프라이버시 보호 기법을 구현하고 데이터 수집을 최소화)
c) Using unencrypted data storage (암호화되지 않은 데이터 저장소 사용)
d) Ignoring data protection regulations (데이터 보호 규정을 무시)

46. What role does human oversight play in the responsible use of AI?

46. AI의 책임 있는 사용에서 인간의 감독이 하는 역할은 무엇인가?

a) It is optional for low-risk applications (저위험 애플리케이션에서는 선택 사항)
b) It is crucial for ensuring that AI systems operate ethically and can be adjusted as needed (AI 시스템이 윤리적으로 운영되고 필요에 따라 조정될 수 있도록 보장하는 데 중요)
c) It complicates the AI development process (AI 개발 과정을 복잡하게 만듦)
d) It is only necessary for AI systems used in high-risk areas (고위험 분야에서 사용되는 AI 시스템에만 필요)

43번 정답: d   44번 정답: b   45번 정답: b   46번 정답: b

47. What is an important factor in evaluating the fairness of an AI system?
47. AI 시스템의 공정성을 평가하는 데 중요한 요소는 무엇인가?

a) The speed of model training (모델 훈련 속도)

b) The representativeness of the training data and the fairness of the model's predictions (훈련 데이터의 대표성과 모델 예측의 공정성)

c) The cost of developing the AI system (AI 시스템 개발 비용)

d) The complexity of the algorithms used (사용된 알고리즘의 복잡성)

48. How can organizations ensure the ethical deployment of AI systems?
48. 조직이 AI 시스템의 윤리적 배포를 보장하려면 어떻게 해야 하는가?

a) By minimizing transparency and accountability (투명성과 책임을 최소화)

b) By implementing ethical guidelines and monitoring systems to ensure responsible use (책임 있는 사용을 보장하기 위해 윤리적 지침과 모니터링 시스템을 구현)

c) By ignoring potential ethical issues (잠재적인 윤리적 문제를 무시)

d) By limiting stakeholder engagement (이해관계자 참여를 제한)

49. What is the benefit of conducting regular audits of AI systems?
49. AI 시스템의 정기 감사 수행의 이점은 무엇인가?

a) To reduce the accuracy of the models (모델의 정확도를 줄이기)

b) To identify and address any issues related to performance, fairness, and ethics (성능, 공정성, 윤리와 관련된 문제를 식별하고 해결하기)

c) To increase the development costs (개발 비용을 증가시키기)

d) To limit user feedback (사용자 피드백을 제한하기)

50. What should be done to ensure AI systems are robust and resilient?
50. AI 시스템이 견고하고 회복력이 있도록 하기 위해 무엇이 이루어져야 하는가?

a) Relying solely on untested models (검증되지 않은 모델에만 의존하기)

b) Conducting extensive testing and incorporating feedback to improve the system's robustness (시스템의 견고성을 높이기 위해 광범위한 테스트와 피드백 반영하기)

c) Ignoring performance metrics (성능 지표 무시하기)

d) Reducing the amount of data used (사용되는 데이터 양 줄이기)

47번 정답: b   48번 정답: b   49번 정답: b   50번 정답: b

51. Which of the following is a key consideration for responsible AI development?
51. 책임 있는 AI 개발을 위한 주요 고려 사항은 무엇인가?

a) Minimizing transparency and documentation (투명성 및 문서화 최소화)

b) Ensuring that AI systems align with ethical standards and societal values (윤리적 기준 및 사회적 가치에 맞춤)

c) Using outdated algorithms (구식 알고리즘 사용)

d) Reducing the involvement of domain experts (전문가 참여 축소)

52. How can organizations support the fair and ethical use of AI technologies?
52. 조직이 AI 기술의 공정하고 윤리적인 사용을 지원할 수 있는 방법은 무엇인가?

a) By focusing solely on technical performance (기술 성능에만 집중)

b) By implementing policies and practices that address ethical concerns and promote fairness (윤리 및 공정성 관련 정책 실행)

c) By avoiding transparency (투명성 피함)

d) By limiting the scope of AI applications (AI 적용 범위 제한)

53. What is the purpose of establishing clear guidelines for AI ethics?
53. AI 윤리에 대한 명확한 지침을 설정하는 목적은 무엇인가?

a) To streamline the development process (개발 과정 단순화)

b) To provide a framework for making responsible decisions and managing ethical risks (책임 있는 결정과 윤리적 위험 관리의 틀 제공)

c) To reduce development costs (개발 비용 절감)

d) To limit the number of features in the AI system (AI 시스템의 기능 수 제한)

54. Which practice helps ensure that AI systems are designed with fairness in mind?
54. AI 시스템이 공정성을 염두에 두고 설계되도록 돕는 실천 방안은 무엇인가?

a) Using only historical data (역사적 데이터만 사용)

b) Implementing fairness-aware algorithms and continuously evaluating for bias (공정성 알고리즘 사용 및 지속적 편향 평가)

c) Reducing the diversity of data sources (데이터 출처 다양성 축소)

d) Minimizing the use of validation data (검증 데이터 사용 최소화)

51번 정답: b   52번 정답: b   53번 정답: b   54번 정답: b

55. How can organizations address the challenges of AI system interpretability?
55. 조직이 AI 시스템 해석 가능성의 문제를 해결할 수 있는 방법은 무엇인가?

a) By using complex, opaque models (복잡하고 불투명한 모델 사용)

b) By developing tools and techniques that enhance the interpretability of AI systems (AI 시스템 해석 가능성을 높이는 도구 및 기술 개발)

c) By ignoring the need for interpretability (해석 필요성 무시)

d) By focusing solely on model accuracy (모델 정확도에만 집중)

56. What is a key consideration for ensuring the security of AI systems?
56. AI 시스템 보안을 보장하기 위한 주요 고려 사항은 무엇인가?

a) Implementing robust access controls and encryption measures (강력한 접근 제어 및 암호화 조치 실행)

b) Using outdated security practices (구식 보안 관행 사용)

c) Reducing the frequency of security updates (보안 업데이트 빈도 감소)

d) Ignoring potential vulnerabilities (잠재적 취약점 무시)

57. Why is it important to include diverse perspectives in AI development?
57. AI 개발에 다양한 관점을 포함하는 것이 중요한 이유는 무엇인가?

a) To speed up the development process (개발 과정 가속화)

b) To ensure that AI systems are inclusive and address the needs of various stakeholders (포용성을 갖추고 다양한 이해관계자의 요구를 충족하기 위함)

c) To reduce the number of features in the system (시스템의 기능 수를 줄이기 위함)

d) To limit stakeholder engagement (이해관계자의 참여를 제한하기 위함)

58. What role does transparency play in responsible AI deployment?
58. 책임 있는 AI 배포에서 투명성의 역할은 무엇인가?

a) It complicates the system's use (시스템 사용을 복잡하게 함)

b) It helps stakeholders understand and trust the decision-making process of AI systems (이해관계자가 AI 시스템의 의사결정 과정을 이해하고 신뢰하도록 도움)

c) It reduces system performance (시스템 성능을 저하)

d) It limits the development of new features (새로운 기능 개발을 제한)

55번 정답: b   56번 정답: a   57번 정답: b   58번 정답: b

59. What is an important practice for managing ethical risks in AI systems?
59. AI 시스템에서 윤리적 위험을 관리하기 위한 중요한 실천은 무엇인가?

a) Ignoring feedback from users (사용자 피드백 무시)

b) Regularly reviewing and updating ethical guidelines and practices (윤리 지침과 실천 방안을 정기적으로 검토하고 업데이트)

c) Limiting the scope of the AI system (AI 시스템의 범위 제한)

d) Reducing transparency (투명성 축소)

60. How can organizations ensure AI systems align with societal values?
60. 조직이 AI 시스템을 사회적 가치에 맞추도록 보장할 수 있는 방법은 무엇인가?

a) By focusing only on technical performance (기술 성능에만 집중)

b) By incorporating ethical considerations into all stages of development and deployment (개발과 배포의 모든 단계에 윤리적 고려사항 포함)

c) By limiting stakeholder involvement (이해관계자 참여 제한)

d) By ignoring potential ethical issues (잠재적 윤리 문제 무시)

61. What is a benefit of integrating ethical considerations into AI system design?
61. AI 시스템 설계에 윤리적 고려사항을 통합하는 이점은 무엇인가?

a) Increased development time (개발 시간 증가)

b) Ensured alignment with societal values and reduced risk of negative impacts (사회적 가치와의 일치 보장 및 부정적 영향 위험 감소)

c) Reduced system performance (시스템 성능 저하)

d) Limiting the scope of applications (응용 범위 제한)

62. Which approach helps ensure the fairness of AI systems?
62. AI 시스템의 공정성을 보장하는 접근 방식은 무엇인가?

a) Using biased data (편향된 데이터 사용)

b) Implementing techniques to detect and mitigate biases in data and algorithms (데이터 및 알고리즘의 편향을 탐지하고 완화하는 기술 구현)

c) Reducing the diversity of data sources (데이터 출처의 다양성 축소)

d) Ignoring fairness considerations (공정성 고려 무시)

59번 정답: b   60번 정답: b   61번 정답: b   62번 정답: b

63. How can AI systems be made more interpretable?
63. AI 시스템의 해석 가능성을 높이는 방법은 무엇인가?

a) By using only black-box models (블랙박스 모델만 사용)

b) By applying techniques that provide insights into how decisions are made (의사결정 과정에 대한 통찰을 제공하는 기술 적용)

c) By limiting the amount of data used (사용 데이터 양 제한)

d) By ignoring interpretability (해석 가능성 무시)

64. What is a key principle of responsible AI deployment?
64. 책임 있는 AI 배포의 핵심 원칙은 무엇인가?

a) Ignoring user feedback (사용자 피드백 무시)

b) Ensuring that AI systems are designed and used in ways that are ethical and aligned with societal values (AI 시스템이 윤리적이고 사회적 가치에 부합하도록 설계 및 사용 보장)

c) Reducing transparency (투명성 축소)

d) Minimizing stakeholder engagement (이해관계자 참여 최소화)

65. Why is it essential to review AI systems regularly?
65. AI 시스템을 정기적으로 검토해야 하는 이유는 무엇인가?

a) To increase system complexity (시스템 복잡성 증가)

b) To identify and address issues related to performance, ethics, and fairness (성능, 윤리, 공정성 관련 문제를 식별하고 해결하기)

c) To reduce the accuracy of the models (모델 정확도 저하)

d) To limit user feedback (사용자 피드백 제한)

66. What should organizations focus on to manage the ethical risks of AI systems?
66. 조직이 AI 시스템의 윤리적 위험을 관리하기 위해 집중해야 할 것은 무엇인가?

a) Ignoring potential risks (잠재적 위험 무시)

b) Implementing risk management strategies and ensuring transparency and accountability (위험 관리 전략을 시행하고 투명성과 책임성 보장)

c) Using outdated technologies (구식 기술 사용)

d) Reducing the number of features in the system (시스템 기능 수 감소)

63번 정답: b   64번 정답: b   65번 정답: b   66번 정답: b

67. What is the purpose of including diverse perspectives in AI system design?
67. AI 시스템 설계에 다양한 관점을 포함하는 목적은 무엇인가?

a) To speed up the development process (개발 과정 가속화)

b) To ensure that the system is inclusive and meets the needs of various stakeholders (시스템이 포용적이고 다양한 이해관계자의 요구를 충족하기 위함)

c) To reduce the number of features (기능 수 감소)

d) To limit stakeholder engagement (이해관계자 참여 제한)

68. What is an effective practice for ensuring the security of AI systems?
68. AI 시스템의 보안을 보장하기 위한 효과적인 실천 방안은 무엇인가?

a) Ignoring potential vulnerabilities (잠재적 취약점 무시)

b) Using outdated security practices (구식 보안 관행 사용)

c) Implementing robust security measures and conducting regular security audits (강력한 보안 조치 시행 및 정기적인 보안 감사 실시)

d) Reducing the frequency of security updates (보안 업데이트 빈도 감소)

69. How can organizations ensure AI systems are fair and unbiased?
69. 조직이 AI 시스템이 공정하고 편향되지 않도록 보장할 수 있는 방법은 무엇인가?

a) Using biased data (편향된 데이터 사용)

b) Applying fairness-aware algorithms and regularly evaluating for bias (공정성 인식 알고리즘 적용 및 편향 정기 평가)

c) Limiting the diversity of data sources (데이터 출처 다양성 제한)

d) Ignoring fairness considerations (공정성 고려 무시)

70. What role does ethical oversight play in AI system development?
70. AI 시스템 개발에서 윤리적 감독의 역할은 무엇인가?

a) It is optional for low-risk applications (저위험 응용에 선택적임)

b) It is crucial for ensuring that AI systems are developed and deployed responsibly (AI 시스템이 책임 있게 개발되고 배포되도록 보장하는 데 중요)

c) It complicates the development process (개발 과정을 복잡하게 함)

d) It is only necessary for high-risk applications (고위험 응용에만 필요)

67번 정답: b   68번 정답: c   69번 정답: b   70번 정답: b

71. How can organizations manage the social impact of AI systems?
71. 조직이 AI 시스템의 사회적 영향을 관리하는 방법은 무엇인가?

a) Ignoring potential societal consequences (잠재적 사회적 결과 무시)

b) Assessing and addressing the potential social impacts and ensuring positive outcomes (잠재적 사회적 영향을 평가하고 긍정적 결과 보장)

c) Reducing the complexity of the system (시스템 복잡성 감소)

d) Limiting stakeholder engagement (이해관계자 참여 제한)

72. What is a key aspect of responsible AI deployment?
72. 책임 있는 AI 배포의 핵심 측면은 무엇인가?

a) Ignoring ethical considerations (윤리적 고려 무시)

b) Integrating ethical guidelines and practices throughout the AI lifecycle (AI 수명 주기 전반에 걸쳐 윤리 지침과 실천 방안 통합)

c) Reducing the number of features (기능 수 감소)

d) Minimizing transparency (투명성 최소화)

73. Why is it important to conduct regular audits of AI systems?
73. AI 시스템의 정기 감사가 중요한 이유는 무엇인가?

a) To reduce development costs (개발 비용 절감)

b) To identify and address issues related to performance, ethics, and fairness (성능, 윤리, 공정성 관련 문제를 식별하고 해결)

c) To limit user feedback (사용자 피드백 제한)

d) To increase system complexity (시스템 복잡성 증가)

74. What should be considered to ensure AI systems are inclusive?
74. AI 시스템이 포용적이도록 보장하기 위해 고려해야 할 것은 무엇인가?

a) Using data from a single demographic (단일 인구 집단의 데이터 사용)

b) Ignoring fairness considerations (공정성 고려 무시)

c) Reducing stakeholder involvement (이해관계자 참여 축소)

d) Ensuring diverse perspectives and needs are represented and considered in AI systems (AI 시스템에 다양한 관점과 필요를 반영하고 고려)

71번 정답: b   72번 정답: b   73번 정답: b   74번 정답: d

75. How can organizations promote transparency in AI systems?
75. 조직이 AI 시스템에서 투명성을 증진하는 방법은 무엇인가?

a) By hiding the decision-making process (의사 결정 과정을 숨기기)

b) By providing clear documentation and explanations of how AI systems operate and make decisions (AI 시스템이 작동하고 결정하는 방식을 명확하게 문서화하고 설명 제공)

c) By limiting access to system outputs (시스템 출력에 대한 접근 제한)

d) By using complex algorithms without explanation (설명 없이 복잡한 알고리즘 사용)

76. What practice helps ensure AI systems are ethically aligned with societal values?
76. AI 시스템이 윤리적으로 사회적 가치와 일치하도록 보장하는 실천은 무엇인가?

a) Ignoring ethical guidelines (윤리 지침 무시)

b) Integrating ethical considerations into all stages of AI development and deployment (AI 개발 및 배포의 모든 단계에 윤리적 고려 포함)

c) Reducing the scope of applications (응용 범위 축소)

d) Limiting stakeholder engagement (이해관계자 참여 제한)

77. Why is it important to evaluate the fairness of AI systems?
77. AI 시스템의 공정성을 평가하는 것이 중요한 이유는 무엇인가?

a) To reduce the complexity of models (모델의 복잡성 감소)

b) To ensure that the AI system's outcomes are fair and do not disproportionately impact any group (AI 시스템의 결과가 공정하고 특정 그룹에 불균형적으로 영향을 미치지 않도록 보장)

c) To limit the number of features (기능 수 제한)

d) To increase development time (개발 시간 증가)

78. What is a benefit of having a clear AI ethics policy?
78. 명확한 AI 윤리 정책을 갖는 이점은 무엇인가?

a) It limits stakeholder engagement (이해관계자 참여 제한)

b) It provides a framework for making ethical decisions and managing risks associated with AI (윤리적 결정을 내리고 AI 관련 위험을 관리하는 틀 제공)

c) It reduces system performance (시스템 성능 저하)

d) It simplifies the development process (개발 과정 단순화)

75번 정답: b   76번 정답: b   77번 정답: b   78번 정답: b

79. How can AI systems be designed to be more accountable?
79. AI 시스템을 더 책임감 있게 설계하는 방법은 무엇인가?

a) By limiting human oversight (인간의 감독 제한)

b) By implementing mechanisms for tracking and addressing issues that arise from AI system use (AI 시스템 사용으로 발생하는 문제를 추적하고 해결하는 메커니즘 구현)

c) By ignoring performance metrics (성능 지표 무시)

d) By reducing the frequency of updates (업데이트 빈도 감소)

80. What should organizations do to ensure the ethical management of AI systems?
80. 조직이 AI 시스템의 윤리적 관리를 보장하기 위해 해야 할 일은 무엇인가?

a) Avoid updating AI systems (AI 시스템 업데이트 회피)

b) Regularly review and update ethical guidelines and practices (윤리 지침과 실천 방안을 정기적으로 검토하고 업데이트)

c) Limit the number of people involved in AI management (AI 관리에 참여하는 인원 제한)

d) Focus solely on technical performance (기술 성능에만 집중)

81. What role does human oversight play in responsible AI deployment?
81. 책임 있는 AI 배포에서 인간 감독의 역할은 무엇인가?

a) It is optional for low-risk applications (저위험 응용에 선택적임)

b) It is essential for ensuring ethical operation and addressing issues as they arise (윤리적 운영과 문제 발생 시 해결을 보장하는 데 필수적임)

c) It complicates the development process (개발 과정을 복잡하게 함)

d) It is only necessary for high-risk applications (고위험 응용에만 필요함)

82. How can organizations manage potential ethical risks associated with AI systems?
82. 조직이 AI 시스템과 관련된 잠재적 윤리적 위험을 관리하는 방법은 무엇인가?

a) Ignoring potential risks (잠재적 위험 무시)

b) Proactively identifying and addressing ethical risks throughout the AI lifecycle (AI 수명 주기 전반에 걸쳐 윤리적 위험을 능동적으로 식별하고 해결)

c) Limiting the number of features (기능 수 제한)

d) Reducing transparency (투명성 감소)

79번 정답: b   80번 정답: b   81번 정답: b   82번 정답: b

83. What is a key factor in ensuring AI systems are robust?

83. AI 시스템이 견고하도록 보장하는 핵심 요소는 무엇인가?

a) Relying solely on untested models (테스트되지 않은 모델에만 의존)

b) Conducting comprehensive testing and incorporating feedback to improve robustness (포괄적인 테스트 수행 및 피드백 반영을 통한 견고성 향상)

c) Ignoring performance metrics (성능 지표 무시)

d) Reducing the amount of data used (사용 데이터 양 축소)

84. Why is it important to include diverse perspectives in AI development?

84. AI 개발에 다양한 관점을 포함하는 것이 중요한 이유는 무엇인가?

a) To reduce the complexity of models (모델 복잡성 감소)

b) To ensure that the AI system is inclusive and meets the needs of various stakeholders (AI 시스템이 포용적이고 다양한 이해관계자의 요구를 충족하기 위함)

c) To limit stakeholder engagement (이해관계자 참여 제한)

d) To reduce development costs (개발 비용 절감)

85. How can organizations ensure that AI systems respect user privacy?

85. 조직이 AI 시스템이 사용자 프라이버시를 존중하도록 보장하는 방법은 무엇인가?

a) Collecting and storing extensive personal data (광범위한 개인 데이터 수집 및 저장)

b) Implementing privacy-preserving techniques and minimizing data collection (프라이버시 보호 기술 구현 및 데이터 수집 최소화)

c) Using unencrypted data storage (암호화되지 않은 데이터 저장소 사용)

d) Ignoring data protection regulations (데이터 보호 규정 무시)

86. What is an effective way to address potential ethical issues with AI systems?

86. AI 시스템과 관련된 잠재적 윤리 문제를 해결하는 효과적인 방법은 무엇인가?

a) Avoid discussing ethical issues (윤리 문제 논의 회피)

b) Proactively identify and address potential ethical issues throughout the AI lifecycle (AI 수명 주기 전반에 걸쳐 잠재적 윤리 문제를 능동적으로 식별하고 해결)

c) Limit the involvement of ethicists (윤리학자의 참여 제한)

d) Focus solely on technical performance (기술 성능에만 집중)

83번 정답: b   84번 정답: b   85번 정답: b   86번 정답: b

87. How can organizations promote inclusivity in AI systems?
87. 조직이 AI 시스템에서 포용성을 증진할 수 있는 방법은 무엇인가?

a) Using data from a single demographic (단일 인구 집단의 데이터 사용)

b) Ensuring diverse perspectives and needs are represented and considered in AI systems (AI 시스템에 다양한 관점과 요구를 반영하고 고려)

c) Limiting stakeholder involvement (이해관계자 참여 제한)

d) Ignoring fairness considerations (공정성 고려 무시)

88. What is a key consideration for managing the performance of AI systems?
88. AI 시스템의 성능을 관리하기 위한 주요 고려 사항은 무엇인가?

a) Ignoring performance metrics (성능 지표 무시)

b) Regularly monitoring and evaluating system performance and making necessary adjustments (시스템 성능을 정기적으로 모니터링하고 평가하며 필요한 조정 수행)

c) Reducing the complexity of models (모델 복잡성 축소)

d) Limiting the amount of data used (사용 데이터 양 제한)

89. How can organizations ensure AI systems are secure?
89. 조직이 AI 시스템의 보안을 보장할 수 있는 방법은 무엇인가?

a) Ignoring potential vulnerabilities (잠재적 취약점 무시)

b) Implementing robust security measures and conducting regular security audits (강력한 보안 조치를 시행하고 정기적인 보안 감사를 수행)

c) Using outdated security practices (구식 보안 관행 사용)

d) Reducing the frequency of security updates (보안 업데이트 빈도 감소)

90. Why is it important to address fairness in AI systems?
90. AI 시스템에서 공정성을 다루는 것이 중요한 이유는 무엇인가?

a) To increase the complexity of models (모델의 복잡성 증가)

b) To ensure that AI systems provide equitable outcomes and do not disproportionately affect any group (AI 시스템이 공정한 결과를 제공하고 특정 그룹에 불균형적 영향을 미치지 않도록 보장)

c) To limit stakeholder engagement (이해관계자 참여 제한)

d) To reduce system performance (시스템 성능 저하)

87번 정답: b   88번 정답: b   89번 정답: b   90번 정답: b

91. What should organizations focus on to ensure ethical AI deployment?
91. 조직이 윤리적 AI 배포를 보장하기 위해 집중해야 할 것은 무엇인가?

a) Integrating ethical considerations into all stages of AI system development and deployment (AI 시스템 개발 및 배포의 모든 단계에 윤리적 고려 포함)

b) Ignoring ethical guidelines (윤리 지침 무시)

c) Reducing the number of features (기능 수 감소)

d) Minimizing transparency (투명성 최소화)

92. How can AI systems be made more transparent?
92. AI 시스템의 투명성을 높이는 방법은 무엇인가?

a) By hiding the decision-making process (의사 결정 과정을 숨기기)

b) By providing clear explanations of how decisions are made and ensuring accessibility of information (의사 결정 과정에 대한 명확한 설명 제공 및 정보 접근성 보장)

c) By using complex algorithms without explanation (설명 없이 복잡한 알고리즘 사용)

d) By limiting access to system outputs (시스템 출력 접근 제한)

93. What role does regular review play in responsible AI management?
93. 책임 있는 AI 관리를 위해 정기적인 검토가 하는 역할은 무엇인가?

a) It complicates the development process (개발 과정을 복잡하게 함)

b) It helps identify and address issues related to performance, ethics, and fairness (성능, 윤리, 공정성 관련 문제를 식별하고 해결하는 데 도움)

c) It reduces system accuracy (시스템 정확도 감소)

d) It limits stakeholder engagement (이해관계자 참여 제한)

94. How can organizations ensure AI systems are accountable?
94. 조직이 AI 시스템의 책임성을 보장할 수 있는 방법은 무엇인가?

a) By limiting human oversight (인간 감독 제한)

b) By implementing mechanisms for tracking, auditing, and addressing issues that arise (문제 발생 시 추적, 감사, 해결을 위한 메커니즘 구현)

c) By ignoring performance metrics (성능 지표 무시)

d) By reducing the frequency of updates (업데이트 빈도 축소)

91번 정답: a   92번 정답: b   93번 정답: b   94번 정답: b

95. Why is it important to involve stakeholders in AI system development?
95. AI 시스템 개발에 이해관계자를 참여시키는 것이 중요한 이유는 무엇인가?

a) To increase the complexity of the system (시스템 복잡성 증가)

b) To ensure the system meets the needs and expectations of various groups and considers diverse perspectives (시스템이 다양한 그룹의 요구와 기대를 충족하고 다양한 관점을 반영하도록 하기 위함)

c) To limit stakeholder engagement (이해관계자 참여 제한)

d) To reduce system performance (시스템 성능 저하)

96. What is a benefit of having clear ethical guidelines for AI systems?
96. AI 시스템에 명확한 윤리 지침을 갖는 이점은 무엇인가?

a) It complicates the development process (개발 과정을 복잡하게 함)

b) It provides a framework for making responsible decisions and managing risks (책임 있는 결정을 내리고 위험을 관리하는 틀 제공)

c) It reduces system performance (시스템 성능 저하)

d) It limits stakeholder engagement (이해관계자 참여 제한)

97. How can organizations ensure AI systems are developed responsibly?
97. 조직이 AI 시스템을 책임감 있게 개발하도록 보장할 수 있는 방법은 무엇인가?

a) By focusing solely on technical performance (기술 성능에만 집중)

b) By integrating ethical considerations into all stages of AI development and deployment (AI 개발 및 배포의 모든 단계에 윤리적 고려 포함)

c) By reducing the number of features (기능 수 감소)

d) By ignoring potential ethical issues (잠재적 윤리 문제 무시)

98. Why is it crucial to conduct regular audits of AI systems?
98. AI 시스템의 정기 감사를 수행하는 것이 중요한 이유는 무엇인가?

a) To increase development costs (개발 비용 증가)

b) To identify and address issues related to performance, ethics, and fairness (성능, 윤리, 공정성 관련 문제를 식별하고 해결)

c) To limit stakeholder involvement (이해관계자 참여 제한)

d) To reduce system complexity (시스템 복잡성 감소)

95번 정답: b   96번 정답: b   97번 정답: b   98번 정답: b

99. What is a key practice for ensuring the ethical management of AI systems?

99. AI 시스템의 윤리적 관리를 보장하기 위한 주요 실천은 무엇인가?

a) Ignoring ethical risks (윤리적 위험 무시)

b) Proactively addressing potential ethical risks and integrating ethical guidelines (잠재적 윤리적 위험을 능동적으로 해결하고 윤리 지침 통합)

c) Limiting stakeholder engagement (이해관계자 참여 제한)

d) Reducing transparency (투명성 축소)

100. How can organizations ensure AI systems are inclusive and meet societal needs?

100. 조직이 AI 시스템이 포용적이고 사회적 요구를 충족하도록 보장할 수 있는 방법은 무엇인가?

a) By using data from a single demographic (단일 인구 집단의 데이터 사용)

b) By incorporating diverse perspectives and ensuring inclusivity in AI design and deployment (AI 설계와 배포에서 다양한 관점을 포함하고 포용성 보장)

c) By limiting stakeholder involvement (이해관계자 참여 제한)

d) By ignoring fairness considerations (공정성 고려 무시)

99번 정답: b   100번 정답: b

도메인 5: AI 솔루션을 위한 보안, 규정 준수 및 거버넌스

AI/ML 워크로드에 대한 AWS의 보안 모범 사례(IAM, KMS, 네트워크 보안 등), 규정 준수 요구사항(GDPR, HIPAA 등), 거버넌스 프레임워크의 구현 방법을 평가하며, 특히 Amazon SageMaker의 보안 기능들(프라이빗 VPC, 암호화, 권한 관리 등)과 모델 모니터링 도구들의 활용법, 그리고 데이터 라이프사이클 전반에 걸친 보안 통제 구현 능력을 테스트하므로, AWS의 공동 책임 모델을 기반으로 AI 워크로드의 보안, 규정 준수, 거버넌스를 통합적으로 구현하는 방법과 AWS 서비스들의 구성 방법 및 모범 사례들을 체계적으로 학습하는 것이 중요하다.

1. Which AWS service provides a centralized way to manage permissions and policies for AWS resources?

1. AWS 리소스의 권한과 정책을 중앙에서 관리할 수 있는 AWS 서비스는 무엇인가?

a) Amazon S3 (아마존 S3)

b) AWS IAM

c) AWS Lambda (AWS 람다)

d) Amazon RDS (아마존 RDS)

2. What is the primary purpose of AWS KMS (Key Management Service)?

2. AWS KMS (키 관리 서비스)의 주요 목적은 무엇인가?

a) To manage AWS resources (AWS 리소스 관리)

b) To encrypt data at rest and in transit (저장 및 전송 중 데이터 암호화)

c) To monitor resource usage (리소스 사용 모니터링)

d) To automate deployment tasks (배포 작업 자동화)

1번 정답: b   2번 정답: b

3. Which AWS service helps you to detect and respond to security threats in real-time?

3. 실시간으로 보안 위협을 감지하고 대응하는 데 도움을 주는 AWS 서비스는 무엇인가?

a) AWS Shield (AWS 실드)
b) AWS WAF (웹 애플리케이션 방화벽)
c) AWS GuardDuty (AWS 가드듀티)
d) AWS CloudTrail (AWS 클라우드트레일)

4. What does AWS Config do?

4. AWS Config는 무엇을 하는가?

a) Manages network traffic (네트워크 트래픽 관리)
b) Monitors and records AWS resource configurations (AWS 리소스 구성 모니터링 및 기록)
c) Encrypts data in S3 (S3 데이터 암호화)
d) Automates server provisioning (서버 프로비저닝 자동화)

5. Which AWS service is designed to provide continuous security monitoring and compliance auditing?

5. 지속적인 보안 모니터링 및 컴플라이언스 감사를 제공하도록 설계된 AWS 서비스는 무엇인가?

a) AWS Security Hub (AWS 시큐리티 허브)
b) Amazon CloudWatch (아마존 클라우드와치)
c) AWS X-Ray (AWS 엑스레이)
d) AWS CodePipeline (AWS 코드파이프라인)

6. What is the purpose of AWS IAM roles?

6. AWS IAM 역할의 목적은 무엇인가?

a) To assign permissions to users (사용자에게 권한 할당)
b) To automate backups (백업 자동화)
c) To provide access to AWS services (AWS 서비스에 대한 접근 제공)
d) To manage networking settings (네트워크 설정 관리)

3번 정답: c   4번 정답: b   5번 정답: a   6번 정답: c

7. Which AWS service provides a firewall for controlling incoming and outgoing traffic to your AWS resources?

7. AWS 리소스에 대한 인바운드 및 아웃바운드 트래픽을 제어하는 방화벽을 제공하는 AWS 서비스는 무엇인가?

a) AWS Network ACL (AWS 네트워크 ACL)

b) AWS Shield (AWS 실드)

c) AWS WAF (웹 애플리케이션 방화벽)

d) AWS Config (AWS 콘피그)

8. What is AWS Shield used for?

8. AWS Shield는 무엇을 위해 사용되는가?

a) Data encryption (데이터 암호화)

b) Distributed Denial of Service (DDoS) protection (분산 서비스 거부(DDoS) 보호)

c) Access management (접근 관리)

d) Resource monitoring (리소스 모니터링)

9. Which service helps you audit and log API activity in your AWS account?

9. AWS 계정에서 API 활동을 감사하고 로그를 기록하는 데 도움을 주는 서비스는 무엇인가?

a) AWS CloudTrail (AWS 클라우드트레일)

b) AWS Config (AWS 콘피그)

c) AWS GuardDuty (AWS 가드듀티)

d) AWS WAF (웹 애플리케이션 방화벽)

10. What does AWS Artifact provide?

10. AWS Artifact는 무엇을 제공하는가?

a) Automated compliance reports (자동화된 컴플라이언스 보고서)

b) Real-time threat detection (실시간 위협 감지)

c) Encryption key management (암호화 키 관리)

d) Resource provisioning (리소스 프로비저닝)

7번 정답: a   8번 정답: b   9번 정답: a   10번 정답: a

11. Which AWS service helps in the management of security groups and network ACLs?
11. 보안 그룹과 네트워크 ACL 관리를 돕는 AWS 서비스는 무엇인가?

a) Amazon VPC (아마존 VPC)
b) AWS IAM
c) AWS CloudFormation (AWS 클라우드포메이션)
d) AWS Config (AWS 콘피그)

12. What is the purpose of AWS CloudTrail?
12. AWS CloudTrail의 목적은 무엇인가?

a) To monitor network traffic (네트워크 트래픽 모니터링)
b) To record API calls and activity (API 호출 및 활동 기록)
c) To manage encryption keys (암호화 키 관리)
d) To provide DDoS protection (DDoS 보호 제공)

13. Which AWS service allows you to set up compliance reports for regulations like GDPR and HIPAA?
13. GDPR 및 HIPAA와 같은 규정을 위한 컴플라이언스 보고서를 설정할 수 있는 AWS 서비스는 무엇인가?

a) AWS Config (AWS 콘피그)
b) AWS Shield (AWS 실드)
c) AWS WAF (웹 애플리케이션 방화벽)
d) AWS KMS (AWS 키관리서비스)

14. What is the AWS Well-Architected Framework primarily used for?
14. AWS Well-Architected Framework의 주요 사용 목적은 무엇인가?

a) Designing scalable applications (확장 가능한 애플리케이션 설계)
b) Ensuring security and compliance best practices (보안 및 컴플라이언스 모범 사례 보장)
c) Automating backups (백업 자동화)
d) Managing API usage (API 사용 관리)

11번 정답: a   12번 정답: b   13번 정답: a   14번 정답: b

15. Which AWS service provides a centralized view of security and compliance findings across AWS accounts?

15. AWS 계정 전반의 보안 및 컴플라이언스 결과를 중앙에서 볼 수 있는 AWS 서비스는 무엇인가?

a) AWS Security Hub (AWS 시큐리티 허브)
b) AWS Config (AWS 콘피그)
c) AWS GuardDuty (AWS 가드듀티)
d) AWS Inspector (AWS 인스펙터)

16. What does AWS Secrets Manager help manage?

16. AWS Secrets Manager는 무엇을 관리하는 데 도움을 주는가?

a) Security groups (보안 그룹)
b) IAM policies (IAM 정책)
c) Encryption keys (암호화 키)
d) Secrets and credentials (비밀 정보와 자격 증명)

17. Which AWS service helps you to automate compliance checks and security assessments?

17. 컴플라이언스 검사와 보안 평가를 자동화하는 데 도움을 주는 AWS 서비스는 무엇인가?

a) AWS Inspector (AWS 인스펙터)
b) AWS CodeDeploy (AWS 코드디플로이)
c) AWS X-Ray (AWS 엑스레이)
d) AWS CloudFormation (AWS 클라우드포메이션)

18. What does AWS Macie help with?

18. AWS Macie는 무엇을 돕는가?

a) Detecting and protecting sensitive data (민감 데이터 탐지 및 보호)
b) Managing API access (API 접근 관리)
c) Monitoring network traffic (네트워크 트래픽 모니터링)
d) Automating security policies (보안 정책 자동화)

15번 정답: a   16번 정답: d   17번 정답: a   18번 정답: a

19. Which AWS service provides a managed, scalable firewall to protect applications from common web exploits?

19. 일반적인 웹 공격으로부터 애플리케이션을 보호하기 위한 관리형 확장 가능한 방화벽 AWS 서비스는 무엇인가?

a) AWS Shield (AWS 실드)

b) AWS WAF (웹 애플리케이션 방화벽)

c) AWS Config (AWS 콘피그)

d) AWS GuardDuty (AWS 가드듀티)

20. What is the function of AWS Security Groups?

20. AWS Security Groups의 기능은 무엇인가?

a) Encrypt data (데이터 암호화)

b) Control inbound and outbound traffic to instances (인스턴스에 대한 인바운드 및 아웃바운드 트래픽 제어)

c) Monitor application performance (애플리케이션 성능 모니터링)

d) Automate database backups (데이터베이스 백업 자동화)

21. Which AWS service can be used to implement identity federation?

21. 신원 연합 구현에 사용할 수 있는 AWS 서비스는 무엇인가?

a) AWS IAM

b) AWS SSO

c) AWS Shield (AWS 실드)

d) AWS KMS (AWS 키관리서비스)

22. What does AWS Key Management Service (KMS) primarily do?

22. AWS Key Management Service (KMS)의 주요 역할은 무엇인가?

a) Monitors network traffic (네트워크 트래픽 모니터링)

b) Manages cryptographic keys (암호화 키 관리)

c) Provides web application firewall rules (웹 애플리케이션 방화벽 규칙 제공)

d) Automates server scaling (서버 스케일링 자동화)

19번 정답: b   20번 정답: b   21번 정답: b   22번 정답: b

23. Which AWS service can help you detect unexpected changes to your AWS resources?
23. AWS 리소스의 예상치 못한 변경 사항을 감지하는 데 도움을 주는 AWS 서비스는 무엇인가?

a) AWS CloudTrail (AWS 클라우드트레일)
b) AWS Security Hub (AWS 시큐리티 허브)
c) AWS Config (AWS 콘피그)
d) AWS X-Ray (AWS 엑스레이)

24. What is AWS GuardDuty used for?
24. AWS GuardDuty는 무엇을 위해 사용되는가?

a) Monitoring and responding to security threats (보안 위협 모니터링 및 대응)
b) Managing resource scaling (리소스 스케일링 관리)
c) Automating code deployments (코드 배포 자동화)
d) Controlling network traffic (네트워크 트래픽 제어)

25. Which AWS service provides data encryption capabilities to protect sensitive information?
25. 민감한 정보를 보호하기 위해 데이터 암호화 기능을 제공하는 AWS 서비스는 무엇인가?

a) AWS KMS (AWS 키관리서비스)
b) AWS WAF (웹 애플리케이션 방화벽)
c) AWS Shield (AWS 실드)
d) AWS Config (AWS 콘피그)

26. Which AWS service helps in detecting potential misconfigurations in your AWS environment?
26. AWS 환경에서 잠재적 구성 오류를 감지하는 데 도움을 주는 AWS 서비스는 무엇인가?

a) AWS CloudFormation (AWS 클라우드포메이션)
b) AWS Config (AWS 콘피그)
c) AWS GuardDuty (AWS 가드듀티)
d) AWS X-Ray (AWS 엑스레이)

23번 정답: c   24번 정답: a   25번 정답: a   26번 정답: b

27. What does AWS WAF protect against?

27. AWS WAF는 무엇으로부터 보호하는가?

a) Network intrusion (네트워크 침입)
b) Web application exploits (웹 애플리케이션 공격)
c) Data loss (데이터 손실)
d) DDoS attacks (DDoS 공격)

28. Which AWS service can be used to manage and rotate credentials securely?

28. 자격 증명을 안전하게 관리하고 순환하는 데 사용할 수 있는 AWS 서비스는 무엇인가?

a) AWS Secrets Manager (AWS 시크릿 매니저)
b) AWS KMS (AWS 키관리서비스)
c) AWS IAM
d) AWS GuardDuty (AWS 가드듀티)

29. What is AWS Shield Advanced used for?

29. AWS Shield Advanced는 무엇을 위해 사용되는가?

a) Basic network protection (기본 네트워크 보호)
b) Advanced DDoS protection (고급 DDoS 보호)
c) Database encryption (데이터베이스 암호화)
d) Network performance optimization (네트워크 성능 최적화)

30. What does AWS CloudTrail help you with in terms of security?

30. 보안 측면에서 AWS CloudTrail이 제공하는 도움은 무엇인가?

a) Encrypting data (데이터 암호화)
b) Logging API calls (API 호출 기록)
c) Managing network traffic (네트워크 트래픽 관리)
d) Automating deployments (배포 자동화)

27번 정답: b   28번 정답: a   29번 정답: b   30번 정답: b

31. Which AWS service provides a visual tool to inspect and audit AWS CloudFormation templates for security issues?

31. 보안 문제에 대해 AWS CloudFormation 템플릿을 검사하고 감사할 수 있는 시각적 도구를 제공하는 AWS 서비스는 무엇인가?

a) AWS Config (AWS 콘피그)

b) AWS Security Hub (AWS 시큐리티 허브)

c) AWS CloudFormation Guard

d) AWS Shield (AWS 실드)

32. Which AWS service provides security recommendations and compliance checks for AWS resources?

32. AWS 리소스에 대한 보안 권장 사항과 컴플라이언스 검사를 제공하는 AWS 서비스는 무엇인가?

a) AWS Security Hub (AWS 시큐리티 허브)

b) AWS WAF (웹 애플리케이션 방화벽)

c) AWS Config (AWS 콘피그)

d) AWS CloudTrail (AWS 클라우드트레일)

33. What type of information does AWS Macie classify and protect?

33. AWS Macie가 분류하고 보호하는 정보의 유형은 무엇인가?

a) Application performance data (애플리케이션 성능 데이터)

b) Web traffic patterns (웹 트래픽 패턴)

c) Sensitive and personal data (민감 정보 및 개인 정보)

d) Network configurations (네트워크 구성)

34. Which AWS service would you use to detect unusual API activity?

34. 비정상적인 API 활동을 감지하기 위해 사용할 AWS 서비스는 무엇인가?

a) AWS GuardDuty (AWS 가드듀티)

b) AWS Config (AWS 콘피그)

c) AWS Macie (AWS 메이시)

d) AWS WAF (웹 애플리케이션 방화벽)

31번 정답: c   32번 정답: a   33번 정답: c   34번 정답: a

35. Which AWS service helps to ensure that data is encrypted both in transit and at rest?

35. 데이터가 전송 중이거나 저장 중일 때 암호화되도록 보장하는 AWS 서비스는 무엇인가?

a) AWS KMS (AWS 키관리서비스)
b) AWS Secrets Manager (AWS 시크릿 매니저)
c) AWS WAF (웹 애플리케이션 방화벽)
d) AWS Config (AWS 콘피그)

36. Which AWS service provides insights into security-related events and configuration changes?

36. 보안 관련 이벤트 및 구성 변경에 대한 인사이트를 제공하는 AWS 서비스는 무엇인가?

a) AWS CloudTrail (AWS 클라우드트레일)
b) AWS Security Hub (AWS 시큐리티 허브)
c) AWS Config (AWS 콘피그)
d) AWS GuardDuty (AWS 가드듀티)

37. Which AWS service is designed to provide detailed security assessments for your EC2 instances?

37. EC2 인스턴스에 대한 상세한 보안 평가를 제공하도록 설계된 AWS 서비스는 무엇인가?

a) AWS Inspector (AWS 인스펙터)
b) AWS GuardDuty (AWS 가드듀티)
c) AWS Shield (AWS 실드)
d) AWS Config (AWS 콘피그)

38. Which AWS service can help with compliance requirements by providing security-related findings from AWS security services?

38. AWS 보안 서비스의 보안 관련 결과를 제공하여 컴플라이언스 요구 사항을 지원하는 AWS 서비스는 무엇인가?

a) AWS Security Hub (AWS 시큐리티 허브)
b) AWS CloudTrail (AWS 클라우드트레일)
c) AWS Inspector (AWS 인스펙터)
d) AWS Macie (AWS 메이시)

35번 정답: a   36번 정답: a   37번 정답: a   38번 정답: a

39. Which AWS service provides network security for your web applications by filtering malicious traffic?

39. 악성 트래픽을 필터링하여 웹 애플리케이션에 네트워크 보안을 제공하는 AWS 서비스는 무엇인가?

a) AWS WAF (웹 애플리케이션 방화벽)

b) AWS Shield (AWS 실드)

c) AWS Config (AWS 콘피그)

d) AWS KMS (AWS 키관리서비스)

40. Which AWS service provides a dashboard for security posture and compliance status across your AWS accounts?

40. AWS 계정 전반에 걸쳐 보안 상태와 컴플라이언스 상태를 위한 대시보드를 제공하는 AWS 서비스는 무엇인가?

a) AWS Security Hub (AWS 시큐리티 허브)

b) AWS Config (AWS 콘피그)

c) AWS GuardDuty (AWS 가드듀티)

d) AWS CloudTrail (AWS 클라우드트레일)

41. What does AWS Secrets Manager do with sensitive information?

41. AWS Secrets Manager는 민감한 정보를 어떻게 처리하는가?

a) Automates deployment (배포 자동화)

b) Rotates and manages secrets (비밀 정보 회전 및 관리)

c) Monitors network traffic (네트워크 트래픽 모니터링)

d) Encrypts data at rest (데이터 암호화)

42. Which AWS service allows you to review your cloud infrastructure and identify compliance issues?

42. 클라우드 인프라를 검토하고 컴플라이언스 문제를 식별할 수 있는 AWS 서비스는 무엇인가?

a) AWS Config (AWS 콘피그)

b) AWS Security Hub (AWS 시큐리티 허브)

c) AWS GuardDuty (AWS 가드듀티)

d) AWS Inspector (AWS 인스펙터)

39번 정답: a   40번 정답: a   41번 정답: b   42번 정답: a

43. What type of data does AWS GuardDuty analyze to detect potential security threats?

43. 잠재적인 보안 위협을 감지하기 위해 AWS GuardDuty가 분석하는 데이터 유형은 무엇인가?

a) Log data (로그 데이터)
b) Network data (네트워크 데이터)
c) User activity (사용자 활동)
d) Configuration data (구성 데이터)

44. Which AWS service offers DDoS protection at both the network and application layers?

44. 네트워크 및 애플리케이션 계층에서 DDoS 보호를 제공하는 AWS 서비스는 무엇인가?

a) AWS Shield (AWS 실드)
b) AWS WAF (AWS 키관리서비스)
c) AWS Config (AWS 콘피그)
d) AWS Inspector (AWS 인스펙터)

45. What does AWS Config help you manage and audit?

45. AWS Config는 무엇을 관리하고 감사하는 데 도움을 주는가?

a) Network traffic (네트워크 트래픽)
b) Resource configurations (리소스 구성)
c) API usage (API 사용)
d) Application performance (애플리케이션 성능)

46. Which AWS service provides a suite of tools for managing the security of your AWS account?

46. AWS 계정의 보안을 관리하기 위한 도구 모음을 제공하는 AWS 서비스는 무엇인가?

a) AWS Security Hub (AWS 시큐리티 허브)
b) AWS Config (AWS 콘피그)
c) AWS CloudTrail (AWS 클라우드트레일)
d) AWS KMS (AWS 키관리서비스)

43번 정답: a   44번 정답: a   45번 정답: b   46번 정답: a

47. Which AWS service offers encryption key management with integrated access control policies?

47. 통합된 접근 제어 정책을 갖춘 암호화 키 관리를 제공하는 AWS 서비스는 무엇인가?

a) AWS KMS (AWS 키 관리 서비스)
b) AWS Secrets Manager (AWS 시크릿 매니저)
c) AWS WAF (웹 애플리케이션 방화벽)
d) AWS Config (AWS 콘피그)

48. What does AWS X-Ray help you analyze?

48. AWS X-Ray는 무엇을 분석하는 데 도움을 주는가?

a) Security threats (보안 위협)
b) Application performance (애플리케이션 성능)
c) Network traffic (네트워크 트래픽)
d) Compliance issues (컴플라이언스 문제)

49. What is the role of AWS WAF in protecting web applications?

49. AWS WAF가 웹 애플리케이션 보호에서 하는 역할은 무엇인가?

a) Encrypts data (데이터 암호화)
b) Manages secrets (비밀 관리)
c) Filters HTTP/S requests (HTTP/S 요청 필터링)
d) Controls network traffic (네트워크 트래픽 제어)

50. Which AWS service is designed to provide security findings and compliance statuses for your AWS environment?

50. AWS 환경에 대한 보안 결과와 컴플라이언스 상태를 제공하도록 설계된 AWS 서비스는 무엇인가?

a) AWS Security Hub (AWS 시큐리티 허브)
b) AWS Config (AWS 콘피그)
c) AWS CloudTrail (AWS 클라우드트레일)
d) AWS GuardDuty (AWS 가드듀티)

47번 정답: a   48번 정답: b   49번 정답: c   50번 정답: a

51. What does AWS CloudTrail primarily monitor?

51. AWS CloudTrail이 주로 모니터링하는 것은 무엇인가?

a) API activity (API 활동)
b) Network traffic (네트워크 트래픽)
c) Data encryption (데이터 암호화)
d) Application performance (애플리케이션 성능)

52. Which AWS service provides a managed service for data encryption and key management?

52. 데이터 암호화 및 키 관리를 위한 관리형 서비스를 제공하는 AWS 서비스는 무엇인가?

a) AWS KMS (AWS 키관리서비스)
b) AWS Secrets Manager (AWS 시크릿 매니저)
c) AWS Shield (AWS 실드)
d) AWS Config (AWS 콘피그)

53. What does AWS Macie primarily focus on?

53. AWS Macie의 주요 초점은 무엇인가?

a) Application performance monitoring (애플리케이션 성능 모니터링)
b) Sensitive data discovery and protection (민감 데이터 발견 및 보호)
c) Network traffic analysis (네트워크 트래픽 분석)
d) Resource provisioning (리소스 프로비저닝)

54. Which AWS service helps in detecting and responding to potential security misconfigurations?

54. 잠재적인 보안 구성 오류를 감지하고 대응하는 데 도움을 주는 AWS 서비스는 무엇인가?

a) AWS Config (AWS 콘피그)
b) AWS Inspector (AWS 인스펙터)
c) AWS GuardDuty (AWS 가드듀티)
d) AWS X-Ray (AWS 엑스레이)

51번 정답: a   52번 정답: a   53번 정답: b   54번 정답: a

55. Which AWS service would you use to implement policies for controlling access to AWS resources?

55. AWS 리소스에 대한 접근을 제어하는 정책을 구현하기 위해 사용할 AWS 서비스는 무엇인가?

a) AWS IAM
b) AWS Secrets Manager (AWS 시크릿 매니저)
c) AWS WAF (웹 애플리케이션 방화벽)
d) AWS KMS (AWS 키관리서비스)

56. What kind of protection does AWS Shield provide?

56. AWS Shield가 제공하는 보호 유형은 무엇인가?

a) Basic DDoS protection (기본 DDoS 보호)
b) Advanced DDoS protection (고급 DDoS 보호)
c) Data encryption (데이터 암호화)
d) Network performance optimization (네트워크 성능 최적화)

57. What does AWS Security Hub integrate with to provide a comprehensive security view?

57. AWS Security Hub는 포괄적인 보안 뷰를 제공하기 위해 무엇과 통합되는가?

a) AWS CloudTrail (AWS 클라우드트레일)
b) AWS GuardDuty (AWS 가드듀티)
c) AWS Config (AWS 콘피그)
d) All of the above (위의 모든 것)

58. Which AWS service provides data visibility and security through machine learning models?

58. 기계 학습 모델을 통해 데이터 가시성과 보안을 제공하는 AWS 서비스는 무엇인가?

a) AWS Macie (AWS 메이시)
b) AWS X-Ray (AWS 엑스레이)
c) AWS CloudWatch (AWS 클라우드와치)
d) AWS Inspector (AWS 인스펙터)

55번 정답: a   56번 정답: b   57번 정답: d   58번 정답: a

59. Which AWS service provides insights into network security and protects applications from common web exploits?

59. 네트워크 보안에 대한 인사이트를 제공하고 일반적인 웹 공격으로부터 애플리케이션을 보호하는 AWS 서비스는 무엇인가?

a) AWS WAF (웹 애플리케이션 방화벽)

b) AWS Shield (AWS 실드)

c) AWS Config (AWS 콘피그)

d) AWS KMS (AWS 키관리서비스)

60. What does AWS CloudFormation Guard help you with?

60. AWS CloudFormation Guard는 무엇을 돕는가?

a) Security assessments (보안 평가)

b) Resource deployment (리소스 배포)

c) Policy compliance for CloudFormation templates (CloudFormation 템플릿의 정책 준수)

d) Data encryption (데이터 암호화)

61. Which AWS service provides automated compliance checks and reports?

61. 자동화된 컴플라이언스 검사와 보고서를 제공하는 AWS 서비스는 무엇인가?

a) AWS Config (AWS 콘피그)

b) AWS Security Hub (AWS 시큐리티 허브)

c) AWS GuardDuty (AWS 가드듀티)

d) AWS Macie (AWS 메이시)

62. Which AWS service provides advanced threat detection by analyzing AWS CloudTrail logs?

62. AWS CloudTrail 로그를 분석하여 고급 위협 탐지를 제공하는 AWS 서비스는 무엇인가?

a) AWS GuardDuty (AWS 가드듀티)

b) AWS Config (AWS 콘피그)

c) AWS Inspector (AWS 인스펙터)

d) AWS Shield (AWS 실드)

59번 정답: a   60번 정답: c   61번 정답: a   62번 정답: a

63. What is the purpose of AWS Secrets Manager?

63. AWS Secrets Manager의 목적은 무엇인가?

a) Network traffic monitoring (네트워크 트래픽 모니터링)

b) Credential and secrets management (자격 증명 및 비밀 관리)

c) Resource provisioning (리소스 프로비저닝)

d) Application performance optimization (애플리케이션 성능 최적화)

64. Which AWS service would you use to review and ensure compliance with security best practices for AWS resources?

64. AWS 리소스에 대한 보안 모범 사례 준수를 검토하고 보장하기 위해 사용할 AWS 서비스는 무엇인가?

a) AWS Security Hub (AWS 시큐리티 허브)

b) AWS CloudFormation

c) AWS Inspector (AWS 인스펙터)

d) AWS Config (AWS 콘피그)

65. What does AWS GuardDuty analyze to identify potential security threats?

65. 잠재적인 보안 위협을 식별하기 위해 AWS GuardDuty가 분석하는 것은 무엇인가?

a) User data (사용자 데이터)

b) API calls (API 호출)

c) Network and DNS logs (네트워크 및 DNS 로그)

d) Application code (애플리케이션 코드)

66. Which AWS service is designed to protect your web applications from common threats like SQL injection and XSS?

66. SQL 인젝션 및 XSS와 같은 일반적인 위협으로부터 웹 애플리케이션을 보호하기 위해 설계된 AWS 서비스는 무엇인가?

a) AWS WAF (웹 애플리케이션 방화벽)

b) AWS Shield (AWS 실드)

c) AWS Config (AWS 콘피그)

d) AWS KMS (AWS 키관리서비스)

63번 정답: b   64번 정답: a   65번 정답: c   66번 정답: a

67. What is the purpose of AWS CloudTrail?
67. AWS CloudTrail의 목적은 무엇인가?

a) Network monitoring (네트워크 모니터링)
b) API activity logging (API 활동 로깅)
c) Encryption key management (암호화 키 관리)
d) Threat detection (위협 감지)

68. Which AWS service helps to manage and rotate encryption keys securely?
68. 암호화 키를 안전하게 관리하고 순환하는 데 도움을 주는 AWS 서비스는 무엇인가?

a) AWS KMS (웹 애플리케이션 방화벽)
b) AWS Secrets Manager (AWS 시크릿 매니저)
c) AWS Config (AWS 콘피그)
d) AWS WAF (AWS 키관리서비스)

69. What type of data does AWS Macie classify?
69. AWS Macie가 분류하는 데이터 유형은 무엇인가?

a) Personal and sensitive data (개인 및 민감 데이터)
b) Network traffic data (네트워크 트래픽 데이터)
c) Application logs (애플리케이션 로그)
d) Resource configurations (리소스 구성)

70. Which AWS service provides a unified view of security alerts and compliance status?
70. 보안 경고와 컴플라이언스 상태에 대한 통합 뷰를 제공하는 AWS 서비스는 무엇인가?

a) AWS Security Hub (AWS 시큐리티 허브)
b) AWS Config (AWS 콘피그)
c) AWS GuardDuty (AWS 가드듀티)
d) AWS CloudTrail (AWS 클라우드트레일)

67번 정답: b   68번 정답: a   69번 정답: a   70번 정답: a

71. What does AWS Inspector assess in your AWS environment?

71. AWS Inspector는 AWS 환경에서 무엇을 평가하는가?

a) Security vulnerabilities (보안 취약점)
b) Network traffic patterns (네트워크 트래픽 패턴)
c) Data encryption settings (데이터 암호화 설정)
d) API usage (API 사용)

72. Which AWS service helps you protect your applications against DDoS attacks?

72. DDoS 공격으로부터 애플리케이션을 보호하는 데 도움을 주는 AWS 서비스는 무엇인가?

a) AWS Shield (AWS 실드)
b) AWS WAF (웹 애플리케이션 방화벽)
c) AWS Config (AWS 콘피그)
d) AWS CloudTrail (AWS 클라우드트레일)

73. What is the purpose of AWS WAF?

73. AWS WAF의 목적은 무엇인가?

a) Monitoring network traffic (네트워크 트래픽 모니터링)
b) Protecting web applications from common web exploits (일반적인 웹 공격으로부터 웹 애플리케이션 보호)
c) Managing encryption keys (암호화 키 관리)
d) Automating backups (백업 자동화)

74. Which AWS service is used to enforce compliance with security standards across AWS resources?

74. AWS 리소스 전반에 걸쳐 보안 표준 준수를 강제하는 데 사용되는 AWS 서비스는 무엇인가?

a) AWS Config (AWS 콘피그)
b) AWS Security Hub (AWS 시큐리티 허브)
c) AWS GuardDuty (AWS 가드듀티)
d) AWS Inspector (AWS 인스펙터)

71번 정답: a   72번 정답: a   73번 정답: b   74번 정답: a

75. Which AWS service helps you analyze and respond to security incidents by providing actionable insights?

75. 실행 가능한 인사이트를 제공하여 보안 사고를 분석하고 대응하는 데 도움을 주는 AWS 서비스는 무엇인가?

a) AWS Security Hub (AWS 시큐리티 허브)

b) AWS Inspector (AWS 인스펙터)

c) AWS Macie (AWS 메이시)

d) AWS X-Ray (AWS 엑스레이)

76. What kind of threats does AWS GuardDuty detect?

76. AWS GuardDuty가 탐지하는 위협의 종류는 무엇인가?

a) Infrastructure threats (인프라 위협)

b) Network threats (네트워크 위협)

c) Data threats (데이터 위협)

d) Application threats (애플리케이션 위협)

77. Which AWS service provides a way to centrally manage access to multiple AWS accounts and services?

77. 여러 AWS 계정 및 서비스에 대한 접근을 중앙에서 관리할 수 있는 방법을 제공하는 AWS 서비스는 무엇인가?

a) AWS IAM

b) AWS Secrets Manager (AWS 시크릿 매니저)

c) AWS CloudFormation (AWS 클라우드포메이션)

d) AWS Config (AWS 콘피그)

78. What feature does AWS Config provide for evaluating AWS resource configurations?

78. AWS Config가 AWS 리소스 구성을 평가하기 위해 제공하는 기능은 무엇인가?

a) Security vulnerability assessment (보안 취약점 평가)

b) Compliance monitoring (컴플라이언스 모니터링)

c) Network performance monitoring (네트워크 성능 모니터링)

d) Data encryption (데이터 암호화)

75번 정답: a   76번 정답: b   77번 정답: a   78번 정답: b

79. Which AWS service is designed to handle web application firewall functionality?

79. 웹 애플리케이션 방화벽 기능을 처리하도록 설계된 AWS 서비스는 무엇인가?

a) AWS WAF (웹 애플리케이션 방화벽)
b) AWS Shield (AWS 실드)
c) AWS GuardDuty (AWS 가드듀티)
d) AWS KMS (AWS 키관리서비스)

80. What does AWS CloudTrail record?

80. AWS CloudTrail은 무엇을 기록하는가?

a) Network traffic logs (네트워크 트래픽 로그)
b) API activity logs (API 활동 로그)
c) Application performance data (애플리케이션 성능 데이터)
d) Data encryption logs (데이터 암호화 로그)

81. Which AWS service is used for analyzing logs and generating security findings?

81. 로그를 분석하고 보안 결과를 생성하는 데 사용되는 AWS 서비스는 무엇인가?

a) AWS GuardDuty (AWS 가드듀티)
b) AWS Config (AWS 콘피그)
c) AWS Macie (AWS 메이시)
d) AWS Shield (AWS 실드)

82. What is AWS Security Hub's primary function?

82. AWS Security Hub의 주요 기능은 무엇인가?

a) Centralizing security findings (보안 결과 중앙화)
b) Managing encryption keys (암호화 키 관리)
c) Monitoring network traffic (네트워크 트래픽 모니터링)
d) Automating deployment (배포 자동화)

79번 정답: a   80번 정답: b   81번 정답: a   82번 정답: a

83. Which AWS service helps detect and mitigate potential security vulnerabilities in your environment?

83. 환경 내 잠재적인 보안 취약점을 감지하고 완화하는 데 도움을 주는 AWS 서비스는 무엇인가?

a) AWS Inspector (AWS 인스펙터)

b) AWS Config (AWS 콘피그)

c) AWS CloudTrail (AWS 클라우드트레일)

d) AWS Macie (AWS 메이시)

84. What is the role of AWS Secrets Manager in handling sensitive information?

84. 민감한 정보를 처리하는 데 있어 AWS Secrets Manager의 역할은 무엇인가?

a) Encrypting data (데이터 암호화)

b) Managing and rotating secrets (비밀 관리 및 순환)

c) Monitoring API activity (API 활동 모니터링)

d) Detecting network threats (네트워크 위협 감지)

85. Which AWS service is designed to help with threat detection using machine learning algorithms?

85. 머신러닝 알고리즘을 사용하여 위협 감지를 돕도록 설계된 AWS 서비스는 무엇인가?

a) AWS GuardDuty (AWS 가드듀티)

b) AWS Inspector (AWS 인스펙터)

c) AWS Security Hub (AWS 시큐리티 허브)

d) AWS WAF (웹 애플리케이션 방화벽)

86. Which AWS service allows for the auditing of compliance and security configurations in real-time?

86. 실시간으로 컴플라이언스 및 보안 구성을 감사할 수 있는 AWS 서비스는 무엇인가?

a) AWS Config (AWS 콘피그)

b) AWS CloudTrail (AWS 클라우드트레일)

c) AWS Shield (AWS 실드)

d) AWS KMS (AWS 키관리서비스)

83번 정답: a   84번 정답: b   85번 정답: a   86번 정답: a

87. What does AWS Shield Advanced offer in terms of DDoS protection?
87. DDoS 보호 측면에서 AWS Shield Advanced가 제공하는 기능은 무엇인가?

a) Basic DDoS protection (기본 DDoS 보호)

b) Advanced and proactive DDoS protection (고급 및 사전 예방적 DDoS 보호)

c) Network traffic monitoring (네트워크 트래픽 모니터링)

d) Application performance optimization (애플리케이션 성능 최적화)

88. Which AWS service provides visibility into security and compliance status by aggregating findings from other AWS services?
88. 다른 AWS 서비스의 결과를 통합하여 보안 및 컴플라이언스 상태에 대한 가시성을 제공하는 AWS 서비스는 무엇인가?

a) AWS Security Hub (AWS 시큐리티 허브)

b) AWS Config (AWS 콘피그)

c) AWS Inspector (AWS 인스펙터)

d) AWS Macie (AWS 메이시)

89. What kind of data does AWS Macie primarily focus on protecting?
89. AWS Macie가 주로 보호하는 데이터 유형은 무엇인가?

a) Network data (네트워크 데이터)

b) Personal and sensitive data (개인 및 민감 데이터)

c) Application performance data (애플리케이션 성능 데이터)

d) API activity logs (API 활동 로그)

90. Which AWS service offers comprehensive security assessment tools for your EC2 instances?
90. EC2 인스턴스를 위한 종합적인 보안 평가 도구를 제공하는 AWS 서비스는 무엇인가?

a) AWS Inspector (AWS 인스펙터)

b) AWS WAF (웹 애플리케이션 방화벽)

c) AWS GuardDuty (AWS 가드듀티)

d) AWS CloudTrail (AWS 클라우드트레일)

87번 정답: b   88번 정답: a   89번 정답: b   90번 정답: a

91. What feature of AWS KMS helps with compliance?
91. AWS KMS의 어떤 기능이 컴플라이언스에 도움이 되는가?

a) Key rotation and management (키 회전 및 관리)
b) Network traffic analysis (네트워크 트래픽 분석)
c) Security posture monitoring (보안 상태 모니터링)
d) Application performance tracking (애플리케이션 성능 추적)

92. Which AWS service provides the capability to monitor and control access to AWS resources?
92. 어떤 AWS 서비스가 AWS 리소스에 대한 모니터링 및 접근 제어 기능을 제공하나?

a) AWS IAM (AWS 아이엠)
b) AWS Config (AWS 콘피그)
c) AWS CloudTrail (AWS 클라우드트레일)
d) AWS Inspector (AWS 인스펙터)

93. What is AWS Config primarily used for?
93. 어떤 AWS 서비스가 AWS 리소스에 대한 모니터링 및 접근 제어 기능을 제공하나?

a) Analyzing security threats (보안 위협 분석)
b) Configuring network security (네트워크 보안 구성)
c) Tracking resource configurations and compliance (리소스 구성 및 준수 추적)
d) Encrypting sensitive data (민감 데이터 암호화)

94. Which AWS service provides integrated threat intelligence for security threat detection?
94. AWS에서 보안 위협 감지를 위한 통합 위협 인텔리전스를 제공하는 서비스는 무엇인가?

a) AWS GuardDuty (AWS 가드듀티)
b) AWS Inspector (AWS 인스펙터)
c) AWS Security Hub (AWS 시큐리티 허브)
d) AWS Shield (AWS 쉴드)

91번 정답: a   92번 정답: a   93번 정답: c   94번 정답: a

95. What does AWS Security Hub aggregate?
95. AWS Security Hub (AWS 시큐리티 허브)은 무엇을 집계하는가?

a) Security findings from various AWS services (다양한 AWS 서비스의 보안 결과)
b) Resource usage data (리소스 사용 데이터)
c) Application logs (애플리케이션 로그)
d) Encryption key metrics (암호화 키 메트릭)

96. Which AWS service helps in the discovery and protection of sensitive data within your AWS environment?
96. AWS 환경 내에서 민감 데이터를 발견하고 보호하는 데 도움이 되는 서비스는 무엇인가?

a) AWS Macie (AWS 메이시)
b) AWS KMS (AWS KMS)
c) AWS Config (AWS 콘피그)
d) AWS WAF (웹 애플리케이션 방화벽)

97. Which AWS service is designed to help protect your web applications from common internet threats?
97. 일반적인 인터넷 위협으로부터 웹 애플리케이션을 보호하도록 설계된 AWS 서비스는 무엇인가?

a) AWS WAF (웹 애플리케이션 방화벽)
b) AWS Shield (AWS 쉴드)
c) AWS GuardDuty (AWS 가드듀티)
d) AWS Config (AWS 콘피그)

98. Which AWS service helps you manage security policies and compliance across multiple AWS accounts?
98. 여러 AWS 계정에서 보안 정책 및 준수를 관리하는 데 도움이 되는 AWS 서비스는 무엇인가?

a) AWS Security Hub (AWS 시큐리티 허브)
b) AWS Config (AWS 콘피그)
c) AWS Inspector (AWS 인스펙터)
d) AWS KMS (AWS KMS)

95번 정답: a   96번 정답: a   97번 정답: a   98번 정답: a

99. What kind of compliance does AWS Config focus on?

99. AWS Config (AWS 콘피그)이 집중하는 준수 사항은 무엇인가?

a) Data encryption (데이터 암호화)
b) Resource configuration and auditing (리소스 구성 및 감사)
c) API monitoring (API 모니터링)
d) Application performance (애플리케이션 성능)

100. What does AWS GuardDuty use to provide threat detection?

100. AWS GuardDuty (AWS 가드듀티)는 위협 감지를 위해 무엇을 사용하나?

a) Machine learning (머신 러닝)
b) Manual reviews (수동 검토)
c) Automated backups (자동 백업)
d) Data encryption (데이터 암호화)

99번 정답: b   100번 정답: a

적중문제

$$\frac{300}{0}$$

1. Which of the following algorithms is used for supervised learning?

1. 다음 중 지도 학습 알고리즘은 무엇인가?

a) Amazon Forecast (아마존 포캐스트)

b) Principal component analysis (주성분 분석)

c) Decision tree (의사 결정 트리)

d) Association rule mining (연관 규칙 분석)

2. Which AWS service is mainly utilized for tasks involving natural language processing?

2. 자연어 처리 작업에 주로 사용되는 AWS 서비스는 무엇인가?

a) Amazon SageMaker (아마존 세이지메이커)

b) Amazon Comprehend (아마존 컴프리핸드)

c) Amazon Rekognition (아마존 레코그니션)

d) K-means clustering (K-평균 클러스터링)

3. Which AWS service is used for building and training custom machine learning models at scale?

3. 맞춤형 머신 러닝 모델을 대규모로 구축하고 학습하는 데 사용되는 AWS 서비스는 무엇인가?

a) Amazon Rekognition (아마존 레코그니션)

b) Amazon SageMaker (아마존 세이지메이커)

c) Amazon Polly (아마존 폴리)

d) Amazon Forecast (아마존 포캐스트)

4. Which option best explains how AI, Machine Learning (ML), and Deep Learning (DL) are related to each other?

4. 다음 중 AI, 머신 러닝(ML), 딥 러닝(DL) 간 관계를 가장 잘 설명하는 것은 무엇인가?

a) AI is a subset of ML, and ML is a subset of DL (AI는 ML의 하위 집합이고, ML은 DL의 하위 집합이다)

b) DL is a subset of AI, while AI and ML are distinct fields (DL은 AI의 하위 집합이며, AI와 ML은 별개의 분야이다)

c) AI is the broadest field, and DL is a subset of ML, which is itself a subset of AI (AI가 가장 넓은 분야이고, DL은 ML의 하위 집합이며, ML은 AI의 하위 집합이다)

d) AI, ML, and DL are three independent fields with no overlap (AI, ML, DL은 서로 겹치지 않는 독립적인 세 분야이다)

5. What is the role of a feature engineering pipeline in an AI project?

5. AI 프로젝트에서 특징 엔지니어링 파이프라인의 역할은 무엇인가?

a) To collect and store data (데이터 수집 및 저장)

b) To train and deploy machine learning models (머신 러닝 모델 학습 및 배포)

c) To create new features from existing data (기존 데이터에서 새로운 특징 생성)

d) To evaluate the performance of machine learning models (머신 러닝 모델 성능 평가)

6. Which of the following is a type of neural network architecture commonly used for image recognition?
6. 다음 중 이미지 인식에 일반적으로 사용되는 신경망 아키텍처 유형은 무엇인가?

a) Recurrent Neural Network (RNN) (순환 신경망)

b) Convolutional Neural Network (CNN) (합성곱 신경망)

c) Long Short-Term Memory (LSTM) (장단기 메모리)

d) Generative Adversarial Network (GAN) (생성적 적대 신경망)

7. What is the purpose of explainable AI (XAI)?
7. 설명 가능한 인공지능(XAI)의 목적은 무엇인가?

a) To make AI models more accurate (AI 모델을 더 정확하게)

b) To make AI models more efficient (AI 모델을 더 효율적으로)

c) To make AI models more understandable (AI 모델을 더 이해하기 쉽게)

d) To make AI models more scalable (AI 모델을 더 확장 가능하게)

8. Which of the following is the main objective of explainable AI (XAI)?
8. 다음 중 설명 가능한 인공지능(XAI)의 목적은 무엇인가?

a) Enhancing the interpretability of AI models (AI 모델의 해석 가능성 향상)

b) Improving the efficiency of AI models (AI 모델의 효율성 향상)

c) Increasing the accuracy of AI models (AI 모델의 정확성 향상)

d) Making AI models more scalable (AI 모델의 확장성 향상)

9. What is the primary difference between a generative model and a discriminative model?
9. 생성 모델과 판별 모델의 주요 차이점은 무엇인가?

a) Generative models learn to generate new data, while discriminative models learn to classify existing data. (생성 모델은 새로운 데이터를 생성하고, 판별 모델은 기존 데이터를 분류함)

b) Generative models are used for supervised learning, while discriminative models are used for unsupervised learning. (생성 모델은 지도 학습에, 판별 모델은 비지도 학습에 사용됨)

c) Generative models are more accurate than discriminative models. (생성 모델이 판별 모델보다 더 정확함)

d) Generative models are easier to train than discriminative models (생성 모델이 판별 모델보다 학습이 더 쉬움)

10. What is the role of a hyperparameter tuning pipeline in a machine learning project?
10. 머신 러닝 프로젝트에서 하이퍼파라미터 튜닝 파이프라인의 역할은 무엇인가?

a) To select the best algorithm for a given problem (주어진 문제에 가장 적합한 알고리즘 선택)

b) To optimize the performance of a machine learning model (머신 러닝 모델 성능 최적화)

c) To preprocess the data before training the model (모델 학습 전 데이터 전처리)

d) To evaluate the accuracy of the model (모델 정확도 평가)

11. Which of the following is a type of neural network architecture commonly used for sequence data (e.g., text, time series)?
11. 다음 중 시퀀스 데이터(예: 텍스트, 시계열)에 일반적으로 사용되는 신경망 아키텍처는 무엇인가?

a) Convolutional Neural Network (CNN) (합성곱 신경망)

b) Recurrent Neural Network (RNN) (순환 신경망)

c) Generative Adversarial Network (GAN) (생성적 적대 신경망)

d) Decision Tree (의사 결정 트리)

12. Which AWS service is used for building and training custom machine learning models at scale?
12. 맞춤형 머신 러닝 모델을 대규모로 구축하고 학습하는 데 사용되는 AWS 서비스는 무엇인가?

a) Amazon Rekognition (아마존 레코그니션)

b) Amazon SageMaker (아마존 세이지메이커)

c) Amazon Polly (아마존 폴리)

d) Amazon Forecast (아마존 포캐스트)

13. What is the purpose of explainable AI (XAI)?
13. 설명 가능한 인공지능(XAI)의 목적은 무엇인가?

a) To make AI models more accurate (AI 모델을 더 정확하게)

b) To make AI models more efficient (AI 모델을 더 효율적으로)

c) To make AI models more understandable (AI 모델을 더 이해하기 쉽게)

d) To make AI models more scalable (AI 모델을 더 확장 가능하게)

14. What is the primary difference between a generative model and a discriminative model?

14. 생성 모델과 판별 모델의 주요 차이점은 무엇인가?

a) Generative models learn to generate new data, while discriminative models learn to classify existing data (생성 모델은 새로운 데이터를 생성하고, 판별 모델은 기존 데이터를 분류)

b) Generative models are used for supervised learning, while discriminative models are used for unsupervised learning (생성 모델은 지도 학습에, 판별 모델은 비지도 학습에 사용)

c) Generative models are more accurate than discriminative models (생성 모델이 판별 모델보다 더 정확)

d) Generative models are easier to train than discriminative models (생성 모델이 판별 모델보다 학습이 더 쉬움)

15. What is the role of a hyperparameter tuning pipeline in a machine learning project?

15. 머신 러닝 프로젝트에서 하이퍼파라미터 튜닝 파이프라인의 역할은 무엇인가?

a) To select the best algorithm for a given problem (주어진 문제에 가장 적합한 알고리즘 선택)

b) To optimize the performance of a machine learning model (머신 러닝 모델 성능 최적화)

c) To preprocess the data before training the model (모델 학습 전 데이터 전처리)

d) To evaluate the accuracy of the model (모델 정확도 평가)

16. What is the key difference between batch inferencing and real-time inferencing in AI systems?

16. AI 시스템에서 배치 추론과 실시간 추론의 주요 차이점은 무엇인가?

a) Batch inferencing requires labeled data, while real-time inferencing can use both labeled and unlabeled data (배치 추론은 라벨이 지정된 데이터가 필요하며, 실시간 추론은 라벨이 지정된 데이터와 지정되지 않은 데이터 모두 사용 가능)

b) Batch inferencing processes large volumes of data at once, while real-time inferencing processes data as it arrives (배치 추론은 대량 데이터를 한 번에 처리하고, 실시간 추론은 데이터가 도착하는 대로 처리)

c) Real-time inferencing is used for unsupervised learning, while batch inferencing is used for supervised learning (실시간 추론은 비지도 학습에 사용되며, 배치 추론은 지도 학습에 사용됨)

d) Real-time inferencing is slower and less accurate compared to batch inferencing (실시간 추론은 배치 추론보다 느리고 정확도가 낮음)

17. Which of the following data types is best suited for supervised learning?

17. 다음 중 지도 학습에 가장 적합한 데이터 유형은 무엇인가?

a) Unlabeled data (라벨이 지정되지 않은 데이터)

b) Structured data (구조화된 데이터)

c) Labeled data (라벨이 지정된 데이터)

d) Unstructured data (비구조화 데이터)

18. In the context of AI, what is the purpose of training a model?
18. AI에서 모델을 학습시키는 목적은 무엇인가?

a) To preprocess the data before feeding it into an algorithm (알고리즘에 입력하기 전에 데이터 전처리)

b) To enable the model to make accurate predictions or decisions based on new data (모델이 새로운 데이터를 기반으로 정확한 예측 또는 결정을 내릴 수 있도록 함)

c) To clean and structure the data for better algorithm performance (더 나은 알고리즘 성능을 위해 데이터를 정리하고 구조화)

d) To identify which algorithm performs best on raw data (원시 데이터에서 최상의 성능을 내는 알고리즘 식별)

19. Which of the following best describes the function of reinforcement learning in AI?
19. AI에서 강화 학습의 기능을 가장 잘 설명하는 것은 무엇인가?

a) It is a type of learning where the model is trained with labeled data (라벨이 지정된 데이터로 모델을 학습시키는 유형)

b) It involves learning by interacting with an environment and receiving rewards or penalties for actions (환경과 상호 작용하며 행동에 대해 보상 또는 페널티를 받으며 학습함)

c) It focuses on unsupervised learning to discover hidden patterns in data (데이터의 숨겨진 패턴을 발견하기 위한 비지도 학습에 중점)

d) It requires batch inferencing to adjust predictions based on user feedback (사용자 피드백을 기반으로 예측을 조정하기 위해 배치 추론이 필요함)

20. Which of the following describes the key characteristics of deep learning models compared to traditional machine learning models?
20. 다음 중 전통적인 머신 러닝 모델과 비교하여 딥 러닝 모델의 주요 특징을 설명하는 것은 무엇인가?

a) Deep learning models require a vast amount of labeled data, while traditional ML models only work with unlabeled data (딥 러닝 모델은 대량의 라벨이 지정된 데이터를 필요로 하며, 전통적인 머신 러닝 모델은 라벨이 없는 데이터로만 작동함)

b) Deep learning models use neural networks with multiple layers to automatically extract features, while traditional ML models require manual feature extraction (딥 러닝 모델은 다층 신경망을 사용해 자동으로 특징을 추출하며, 전통적인 머신 러닝 모델은 수동으로 특징을 추출해야 함)

c) Traditional machine learning models can only handle structured data, while deep learning models are limited to image and video data (전통적인 머신 러닝 모델은 구조화된 데이터만 처리 가능하고, 딥 러닝 모델은 이미지와 비디오 데이터에 제한됨)

d) Deep learning models are used exclusively for unsupervised learning tasks, while traditional ML models handle supervised learning (딥 러닝 모델은 비지도 학습에만 사용되며, 전통적인 머신 러닝 모델은 지도 학습을 처리함)

21. What is the primary characteristic of labeled data in AI models?

21. AI 모델에서 라벨이 지정된 데이터의 주요 특성은 무엇인가?

a) Data with explicit output labels used for training supervised learning models (지도 학습 모델 학습을 위한 명확한 출력 라벨이 지정된 데이터)

b) Data without predefined categories are used for clustering algorithms (사전 정의된 범주가 없는 데이터는 클러스터링 알고리즘에 사용됨)

c) Data that requires deep learning techniques to process (딥 러닝 기술을 사용해야 처리할 수 있는 데이터)

d) Data that consists of unstructured information like text and images (텍스트와 이미지 같은 비구조화 정보로 구성된 데이터)

22. In AI, what does bias in machine learning models pose the main challenge?

22. AI에서 머신 러닝 모델의 편향이 주요 문제를 일으키는 이유는 무엇인가?

a) It makes the model too sensitive to variance in the training data, leading to overfitting (모델이 학습 데이터의 분산에 너무 민감해져서 과적합이 발생함)

b) It causes systematic errors that can lead to unfair or inaccurate predictions across different groups (다른 그룹에 대해 불공평하거나 부정확한 예측을 초래하는 체계적인 오류를 발생시킴)

c) It restricts the model from learning from unlabeled data (모델이 라벨이 없는 데이터를 학습하지 못하게 제한함)

d) It increases the complexity of neural network models, leading to slower inferencing times (신경망 모델의 복잡성을 증가시켜 추론 시간이 느려짐)

23. Which type of learning involves using a dataset with no predefined output labels to find hidden structures or patterns?

23. 미리 정의된 출력 라벨이 없는 데이터셋을 사용하여 숨겨진 구조나 패턴을 찾는 학습 유형은 무엇인가?

a) Supervised learning (지도 학습)

b) Unsupervised learning (비지도 학습)

c) Reinforcement learning (강화 학습)

d) Semi-supervised learning (반지도 학습)

24. Which of the following best describes the use of large language models (LLMs) in AI?

24. 다음 중 대형 언어 모델(LLM)의 AI 활용을 가장 잘 설명하는 것은 무엇인가?

a) LLMs are AI models designed to process numerical data for regression tasks (LLM은 회귀 작업을 위해 수치 데이터를 처리하도록 설계된 AI 모델임)

b) LLMs are used to generate, understand, and respond to natural language by training on vast amounts of text data (LLM은 대량의 텍스트 데이터를 학습하여 자연어를 생성, 이해 및 응답하는 데 사용됨)

c) LLMs are used exclusively for batch inferencing due to the size and complexity of the models (LLM은 모델

의 크기와 복잡성 때문에 배치 추론에만 사용됨)

d) LLMs require reinforcement learning to train effectively (LLM은 효과적인 학습을 위해 강화 학습을 필요로 함)

25. What distinguishes supervised learning from unsupervised learning?
25. 지도 학습과 비지도 학습의 차이점은 무엇인가?

a) Supervised learning uses unlabeled data, while unsupervised learning uses labeled data (지도 학습은 라벨이 없는 데이터를 사용하고, 비지도 학습은 라벨이 있는 데이터를 사용함)

b) Supervised learning is focused on prediction tasks, while unsupervised learning aims to discover patterns or structures in data (지도 학습은 예측 작업에 중점을 두고, 비지도 학습은 데이터 내 패턴이나 구조를 발견하는 것을 목표로 함)

c) Unsupervised learning requires continuous feedback to improve the model, while supervised learning does not (비지도 학습은 모델을 개선하기 위해 지속적인 피드백이 필요하고, 지도 학습은 그렇지 않음)

d) Supervised learning is only used for text data, while unsupervised learning is used for image data (지도 학습은 텍스트 데이터에만 사용되고, 비지도 학습은 이미지 데이터에 사용됨)

26. Which of the following best explains the difference between structured and unstructured data in AI models?
26. AI 모델에서 구조화된 데이터와 비구조화 데이터의 차이를 가장 잘 설명하는 것은 무엇인가?

a) Structured data includes labeled information, while unstructured data is always unlabeled (구조화된 데이터는 라벨이 포함된 정보를 포함하고, 비구조화 데이터는 항상 라벨이 없음)

b) Structured data is organized into a defined format (like a table), while unstructured data lacks a predefined structure (like text or images) (구조화된 데이터는 정해진 형식(예: 테이블)으로 구성되고, 비구조화 데이터는 정해진 구조가 없음 (예: 텍스트 또는 이미지))

c) Unstructured data can only be used for unsupervised learning, while structured data is for supervised learning (비구조화 데이터는 비지도 학습에만 사용 가능하며, 구조화된 데이터는 지도 학습에 사용됨)

d) Structured data is limited to numerical values, while unstructured data is only used for text-based models (구조화된 데이터는 숫자 값으로 제한되고, 비구조화 데이터는 텍스트 기반 모델에만 사용됨)

27. Your company is considering implementing an AI solution to enhance customer service by automating responses to common customer inquiries. The primary goals are to reduce response times and handle a high volume of queries efficiently. Which AWS service would be most appropriate for building a chatbot to achieve these objectives, and what key capabilities should you focus on?
27. 귀사는 고객 문의에 자동으로 응답하는 AI 솔루션을 도입하여 고객 서비스를 개선하려고 합니다. 주요 목표는 응답 시간을 줄이고 대량의 문의를 효율적으로 처리하는 것입니다. 이러한 목표를 달성하기 위해 챗봇을 구축할 때 가장 적합한 AWS 서비스는 무엇이며, 집중해야 할 주요 기능은 무엇인가?

a) Amazon Lex for natural language understanding and chatbot interactions (자연어 이해 및 챗봇 상호 작용을 위한 Amazon Lex)

b) Amazon Polly for text-to-speech conversion (텍스트 음성 변환을 위한 Amazon Polly)

c) Amazon Rekognition for visual analysis of customer interactions (고객 상호 작용의 시각적 분석을 위한 Amazon Rekognition)

d) Amazon Transcribe for converting audio to text (오디오를 텍스트로 변환하기 위한 Amazon Transcribe)

28. You are tasked with developing a predictive maintenance system for industrial machinery. The system needs to predict potential equipment failures based on historical sensor data to prevent downtime. Which type of machine learning technique is most appropriate for this use case, and why?

28. 산업 기계에 대한 예측 유지 관리 시스템을 개발해야 합니다. 이 시스템은 과거 센서 데이터를 기반으로 잠재적인 장비 고장을 예측하여 가동 중단을 방지해야 합니다. 이 사용 사례에 가장 적합한 머신 러닝 기술은 무엇이며, 그 이유는 무엇인가?

a) Classification because you need to categorize equipment into failure and non-failure classes (장비를 고장 및 비고장 클래스로 분류해야 하기 때문에 분류 사용)

b) Regression because you need to predict the time until a potential failure occurs (잠재적 고장이 발생할 때까지의 시간을 예측해야 하기 때문에 회귀 사용)

c) Clustering because you need to group similar types of failures (유사한 유형의 고장을 그룹화해야 하기 때문에 군집화 사용)

d) Dimensionality Reduction, because you need to simplify the sensor data (센서 데이터를 단순화해야 하기 때문에 차원 축소 사용)

29. A retail company wants to implement a recommendation system to suggest products to customers based on their browsing history and past purchases. The goal is to personalize the shopping experience and increase sales. Which AWS service should the company use, and what primary benefit does this service provide?

29. 한 소매업체가 고객의 검색 기록과 이전 구매를 기반으로 제품을 추천하는 추천 시스템을 구현하려고 합니다. 목표는 쇼핑 경험을 개인화하고 매출을 증대하는 것입니다. 이 회사가 사용해야 할 AWS 서비스는 무엇이며, 이 서비스의 주요 이점은 무엇인가?

a) Amazon Comprehend for sentiment analysis of customer reviews (고객 리뷰의 감성 분석을 위한 Amazon Comprehend)

b) Amazon Personalize for generating personalized product recommendations (개인 맞춤형 제품 추천 생성을 위한 Amazon Personalize)

c) Amazon Translate for translating product descriptions into multiple languages (제품 설명을 여러 언어로 번역하기 위한 Amazon Translate)

d) Amazon Rekognition for identifying products in customer images (고객 이미지에서 제품을 식별하기 위한 Amazon Rekognition)

30. Your organization needs to implement a solution that automates the extraction of data from forms and invoices. This solution should handle various formats and provide structured data for further processing. Which AWS service would be most appropriate for this task, and what feature does it offer?

30. 귀 조직은 양식과 송장에서 데이터를 자동으로 추출하는 솔루션을 구현해야 합니다. 이 솔루션은 다양한 형식을 처리하

고 추가 처리를 위한 구조화된 데이터를 제공해야 합니다. 이 작업에 가장 적합한 AWS 서비스와 해당 기능은 무엇인가?

a) Amazon Textract for extracting text and structured data from forms and invoices (양식과 송장에서 텍스트 및 구조화된 데이터를 추출하는 Amazon Textract)

b) Amazon Rekognition for detecting objects in scanned images (스캔된 이미지에서 객체를 감지하는 Amazon Rekognition)

c) Amazon Polly for converting text data into speech (텍스트 데이터를 음성으로 변환하는 Amazon Polly)

d) Amazon Lex for processing natural language input from forms (양식에서 자연어 입력을 처리하는 Amazon Lex)

31. You need to analyze customer feedback from various sources, including social media posts, reviews, and support tickets, to identify common themes and sentiments. Which AWS service would help you perform sentiment analysis and extract key phrases from this unstructured text data?

31. 소셜 미디어 게시물, 리뷰, 지원 티켓 등 다양한 출처의 고객 피드백을 분석하여 공통 주제와 감정을 식별해야 합니다. 비구조화된 텍스트 데이터에서 감성 분석과 주요 구문 추출을 돕는 AWS 서비스는 무엇인가?

a) Amazon Comprehend for natural language processing and sentiment analysis (자연어 처리 및 감정 분석을 위한 Amazon Comprehend)

b) Amazon SageMaker for building and training custom machine learning models (맞춤형 머신 러닝 모델을 구축하고 학습하기 위한 Amazon SageMaker)

c) Amazon Translate for translating feedback into English (피드백을 영어로 번역하기 위한 Amazon Translate)

d) Amazon Polly for converting feedback into spoken audio (피드백을 음성으로 변환하기 위한 Amazon Polly)

32. Your project involves building a real-time speech-to-text application that can transcribe customer support calls for further analysis. Which AWS service should you use, and what capability is essential for this application?

32. 실시간 음성-텍스트 변환 애플리케이션을 구축하여 고객 지원 통화를 기록하고 추가 분석을 수행해야 합니다. 이 애플리케이션에 적합한 AWS 서비스와 필요한 주요 기능은 무엇인가?

a) Amazon Transcribe for converting speech to text in real-time (실시간으로 음성을 텍스트로 변환하기 위한 Amazon Transcribe)

b) Amazon Lex for building a conversational interface (대화형 인터페이스 구축을 위한 Amazon Lex)

c) Amazon Polly for generating speech from text (텍스트를 음성으로 생성하기 위한 Amazon Polly)

d) Amazon Rekognition for analyzing video content (비디오 콘텐츠 분석을 위한 Amazon Rekognition)

33. In a recent analysis, you discovered that using AI/ML for a specific project does not provide sufficient cost benefits compared to traditional methods. What factors should you consider to determine if AI/ML is appropriate for your use case?

33. 최근 분석에서 특정 프로젝트에 AI/ML을 사용하는 것이 전통적인 방법에 비해 충분한 비용 절감 효과를 제공하지 않는다는 사실을 발견했습니다. AI/ML이 사용 사례에 적합한지 판단하기 위해 고려해야 할 요소는 무엇인가?

a) The complexity of the problem and the need for automation or predictive capabilities (문제의 복잡성과 자동화 또는 예측 기능의 필요성)

b) The availability of free AI/ML tools and services (무료 AI/ML 도구 및 서비스의 가용성)

c) The ease of implementing AI/ML solutions without specialized knowledge (전문 지식 없이 AI/ML 솔루션을 구현하기 쉬운지 여부)

d) The specific outcome requirements and predictability of the results (특정 결과 요구사항과 결과의 예측 가능성)

34. Your company is evaluating different machine-learning techniques for customer segmentation based on purchase behavior. The goal is to group customers with similar purchasing patterns. Which machine learning technique would be best suited for this task, and why?
34. 귀 회사는 구매 행동에 기반한 고객 세분화를 위해 다양한 머신 러닝 기법을 평가하고 있습니다. 목표는 유사한 구매 패턴을 가진 고객을 그룹화하는 것입니다. 이 작업에 가장 적합한 머신 러닝 기법과 그 이유는 무엇인가?

a) Classification, to categorize customers into predefined segments (사전에 정의된 세그먼트로 고객을 분류하기 위한 분류)

b) Regression, to predict future purchase amounts (미래 구매 금액을 예측하기 위한 회귀)

c) Clustering, to group customers with similar purchasing behavior (유사한 구매 행동을 가진 고객을 그룹화하기 위한 군집화)

d) Time Series Analysis, to forecast future purchasing trends (미래 구매 트렌드를 예측하기 위한 시계열 분석)

35. Which of the following is not a suitable scenario for implementing AI/ML solutions?
35. 다음 중 AI/ML 솔루션을 구현하기에 적절하지 않은 시나리오는 무엇인가?

a) Predicting customer churn in a subscription-based business (구독 기반 비즈니스에서 고객 이탈 예측)

b) Automating fraud detection in financial transactions (금융 거래에서 사기 탐지 자동화)

c) Running a cost-benefit analysis on a fixed investment project (고정 투자 프로젝트에 대한 비용-편익 분석 수행)

d) Personalizing recommendations for an e-commerce website (전자상거래 사이트에서 맞춤형 추천 제공)

36. Which machine learning technique is best suited for predicting a continuous value, such as the future price of a stock?
36. 주식의 미래 가격과 같은 연속값을 예측하는 데 가장 적합한 머신 러닝 기법은 무엇인가?

a) Classification (분류)

b) Clustering (군집화)

c) Regression (회귀)

d) Natural Language Processing (NLP) (자연어 처리)

37. Which of the following is an example of an AI/ML application where computer vision is used?
37. 다음 중 컴퓨터 비전이 사용되는 AI/ML 애플리케이션의 예는 무엇인가?

a) Speech-to-text transcription for meeting notes (회의 기록을 위한 음성-텍스트 변환)

b) Fraud detection in credit card transactions (신용 카드 거래에서의 사기 탐지)

c) Image recognition for product defect detection in manufacturing (제조업에서 제품 결함 감지를 위한 이미지 인식)

d) Predicting customer lifetime value for a subscription service (구독 서비스에서 고객 생애 가치를 예측)

38. Which AWS service would you use to automatically convert spoken language into text?
38. 음성 언어를 자동으로 텍스트로 변환하는 데 사용할 수 있는 AWS 서비스는 무엇인가?

a) Amazon Transcribe (아마존 트랜스크라이브)

b) Amazon Polly (아마존 폴리)

c) Amazon Comprehend (아마존 컴프리헨드)

d) Amazon Lex (아마존 렉스)

39. What is a key consideration when deciding whether to implement an AI/ML solution for a business problem?
39. 비즈니스 문제에 AI/ML 솔루션을 도입할지 결정할 때 고려해야 할 주요 요소는 무엇인가?

a) The total number of employees in the company (회사의 총 직원 수)

b) The amount of data available and the complexity of the problem (사용 가능한 데이터 양과 문제의 복잡성)

c) Whether a competitor has already solved the problem (경쟁사가 이미 문제를 해결했는지 여부)

d) The number of software licenses required (필요한 소프트웨어 라이선스 수)

40. Which machine learning technique is appropriate for predicting whether a transaction is fraudulent or not, based on historical transaction data?
40. 과거 거래 데이터를 기반으로 거래가 사기인지 아닌지 예측하는 데 적합한 머신 러닝 기법은 무엇인가?

a) Clustering (군집화)

b) Regression (회귀)

c) Classification (분류)

d) Reinforcement learning (강화 학습)

41. Which AWS AI/ML service can be used to detect and interpret text in images?
41. 이미지 내 텍스트를 감지하고 해석하는 데 사용할 수 있는 AWS AI/ML 서비스는 무엇인가?

a) Amazon Polly (아마존 폴리)

b) Amazon Rekognition (아마존 레코그니션)

c) Amazon Comprehend (아마존 컴프리헨드)

d) Amazon Translate (아마존 트랜슬레이트)

42. What is a potential drawback of using AI/ML solutions for business decision-making?
42. 비즈니스 의사 결정에 AI/ML 솔루션을 사용하는 잠재적 단점은 무엇인가?

a) AI/ML solutions are deterministic and always produce specific results (AI/ML 솔루션은 결정론적이며 항상 특정 결과를 생성함)

b) AI/ML models can be expensive to develop and require large datasets to be effective (AI/ML 모델 개발 비용이 높고 효과적이려면 대규모 데이터셋이 필요함)

c) AI/ML eliminates the need for human oversight in decision-making processes (AI/ML이 의사 결정 과정에서 인간의 감독 필요성을 제거함)

d) AI/ML models can only be applied to structured data, limiting their use (AI/ML 모델은 구조화된 데이터에만 적용 가능하여 사용이 제한됨)

43. What type of machine learning problem is a recommendation system (such as those used by e-commerce platforms) trying to solve?
43. 추천 시스템(전자 상거래 플랫폼에서 사용하는)은 어떤 유형의 머신 러닝 문제를 해결하려고 하는가?

a) Clustering (군집화)

b) Classification (분류)

c) Regression (회귀)

d) Collaborative filtering (협업 필터링)

44. You have been tasked with using a pre-trained language model to build a sentiment analysis application. The model needs to be deployed to handle real-time queries from users. How would you approach this task, and which AWS service would be most appropriate for deployment and scaling?
44. 사전 학습된 언어 모델을 사용하여 감정 분석 애플리케이션을 구축해야 합니다. 이 모델은 사용자로부터 실시간 쿼리를 처리할 수 있도록 배포해야 합니다. 이 작업에 적합한 접근 방식과 배포 및 확장에 가장 적합한 AWS 서비스는 무엇인가?

a) Use an open-source pre-trained model and deploy it using a self-hosted API on an EC2 instance (오픈 소스 사전 학습 모델을 사용하고 EC2 인스턴스에서 자체 호스팅 API로 배포)

b) Use a pre-trained model from Amazon SageMaker JumpStart and deploy it using Amazon SageMaker Endpoints (Amazon SageMaker JumpStart의 사전 학습 모델을 사용하고 Amazon SageMaker Endpoints로 배포)

c) Use a pre-trained model from Amazon Comprehend and deploy it using AWS Lambda (Amazon Comprehend의 사전 학습 모델을 사용하고 AWS Lambda로 배포)

d) Use a custom-trained model and deploy it on AWS Elastic Beanstalk (맞춤형 학습 모델을 사용하고 AWS Elastic Beanstalk에 배포)

45. A company wants to build a recommendation system that utilizes both structured customer data and unstructured product reviews. The data pipeline needs to handle data collection, feature extraction, and model training. Which AWS services should you use for data collection and feature engineering, and how would you integrate these services into the pipeline?

45. 한 회사가 구조화된 고객 데이터와 비구조화된 제품 리뷰를 활용하는 추천 시스템을 구축하려고 한다. 데이터 파이프라인은 데이터 수집, 특징 추출 및 모델 학습을 처리해야 합니다. 데이터 수집과 특징 엔지니어링에 적합한 AWS 서비스와 이를 파이프라인에 통합하는 방법은 무엇인가?

a) Considerations: Model accuracy, training time, and resource availability. AWS Service: Amazon SageMaker Model Evaluation

b) Considerations: Model size, deployment complexity, and licensing costs. AWS Service: Amazon SageMaker Data Wrangler

c) Considerations: Data quantity, data quality, and computational resources. AWS Service: Amazon SageMaker Hyperparameter Tuning Jobs

d) Considerations: Model interpretability, explainability, and training data format. AWS Service: Amazon SageMaker Model Monitor

46. You are implementing an ML pipeline for an e-commerce application where you need to predict product demand based on historical sales data. After training the model, you want to deploy it for real-time predictions and need to ensure that the model performs well over time. Which AWS services would you use for deployment and monitoring, and why?

46. 전자 상거래 애플리케이션용 ML 파이프라인을 구현하여 과거 판매 데이터를 기반으로 제품 수요를 예측해야 합니다. 모델 학습 후 실시간 예측을 위해 배포하고 시간이 지나도 성능이 유지되도록 해야 합니다. 배포 및 모니터링을 위해 사용할 AWS 서비스와 그 이유는 무엇인가?

a) Deployment: Amazon SageMaker Endpoints, Monitoring: Amazon CloudWatch

b) Deployment: AWS Lambda, Monitoring: Amazon SageMaker Model Monitor

c) Deployment: Amazon Elastic Beanstalk, Monitoring: Amazon CloudWatch

d) Deployment: Amazon API Gateway, Monitoring: Amazon S3

47. A data scientist is exploring the use of different ML models for a classification task. They have access to several open-source pre-trained models but are considering whether to fine-tune these models or train a new model from scratch. What factors should be considered in deciding between using a pre-trained model or training a custom model, and which AWS service can facilitate this decision?

47. 데이터 과학자가 분류 작업을 위해 다양한 ML 모델을 탐색하고 있습니다. 여러 오픈 소스 사전 학습 모델에 접근할 수 있지만, 이 모델을 미세 조정할지 아니면 새로운 모델을 처음부터 학습할지 고려 중입니다. 사전 학습 모델 사용과 맞춤형 모델 학습 간 결정 시 고려해야 할 요소와 이를 지원하는 AWS 서비스는 무엇인가?

a) Considerations: Model accuracy, training time, and resource availability. AWS Service: Amazon SageMaker Model Evaluation

b) Considerations: Model size, deployment complexity, and licensing costs. AWS Service: Amazon SageMaker Data Wrangler

c) Considerations: Data quantity, data quality, and computational resources. AWS Service: Amazon SageMaker Hyperparameter Tuning Jobs

d) Considerations: Model interpretability, explainability, and training data format. AWS Service: Amazon SageMaker Model Monitor

48. Which component of an ML pipeline is responsible for handling missing values, scaling features, and encoding categorical variables?
48. ML 파이프라인의 구성 요소 중 결측값 처리, 특징 스케일링, 범주형 변수 인코딩을 담당하는 것은 무엇인가?

a) Model training (모델 학습)
b) Hyperparameter tuning (하이퍼파라미터 튜닝)
c) Data preprocessing (데이터 전처리)
d) Deployment (배포)

49. Which stage of the ML pipeline involves selecting features that improve model performance and discarding irrelevant ones?
49. ML 파이프라인의 단계 중 모델 성능을 향상시키는 특징을 선택하고 불필요한 특징을 제외하는 단계는 무엇인가?

a) Feature engineering (특징 엔지니어링)
)b) Exploratory data analysis (EDA) (탐색적 데이터 분석)
c) Hyperparameter tuning (하이퍼파라미터 튜닝)
d) Model evaluation (모델 평가)

50. Which AWS service can be used for data preparation and exploration before feeding data into an ML model?
50. 데이터를 ML 모델에 입력하기 전에 데이터 준비와 탐색에 사용할 수 있는 AWS 서비스는 무엇인가?

a) Amazon SageMaker Data Wrangler (아마존 세이지메이커 데이터 랭글러)
b) Amazon SageMaker Model Monitor (아마존 세이지메이커 모델 모니터)
c) AWS Lambda (AWS 람다)
d) Amazon Comprehend (아마존 컴프리헨드)

51. When using a pre-trained open-source model, what is the most important step to ensure the model performs well on your specific task?
51. 사전 학습된 오픈 소스 모델을 사용할 때, 모델이 특정 작업에서 잘 작동하도록 보장하는 가장 중요한 단계는 무엇인가?

a) Hyperparameter tuning (하이퍼파라미터 튜닝)

b) Model evaluation on a test dataset (테스트 데이터셋에서 모델 평가)

c) Feature engineering (특징 엔지니어링)

d) Transfer learning (전이 학습)

52. Which AWS service allows you to monitor the performance of a machine learning model in production and detect data drift?

52. 프로덕션 환경에서 머신 러닝 모델의 성능을 모니터링하고 데이터 드리프트를 감지할 수 있는 AWS 서비스는 무엇인가?

a) Amazon SageMaker Feature Store (아마존 세이지메이커 피처 스토어)

b) Amazon SageMaker Model Monitor (아마존 세이지메이커 모델 모니터)

c) AWS Lambda (AWS 람다)

d) Amazon SageMaker Ground Truth (아마존 세이지메이커 그라운드 트루스)

53. Which method allows you to deploy a machine learning model as an API that applications in production can call?

53. 프로덕션 환경의 애플리케이션이 호출할 수 있는 API로 머신 러닝 모델을 배포할 수 있는 방법은 무엇인가?

a) Hyperparameter tuning (하이퍼파라미터 튜닝)

b) Managed API service (관리형 API 서비스)

c) Model training (모델 학습)

d) Feature engineering (특징 엔지니어링)

54. Which component of the ML pipeline includes initial data exploration, generating descriptive statistics, and identifying patterns?

54. ML 파이프라인의 구성 요소 중 초기 데이터 탐색, 설명 통계 생성, 패턴 식별을 포함하는 것은 무엇인가?

a) Feature engineering (특징 엔지니어링)

b) Exploratory Data Analysis (EDA) (탐색적 데이터 분석)

c) Model training (모델 학습)

d) Hyperparameter tuning (하이퍼파라미터 튜닝)

55. Which AWS service can be used to automate the process of hyperparameter tuning for machine learning models?

55. 머신 러닝 모델의 하이퍼파라미터 튜닝 과정을 자동화하는 데 사용할 수 있는 AWS 서비스는 무엇인가?

a) Amazon SageMaker Autopilot (아마존 세이지메이커 오토파일럿)

b) Amazon SageMaker Ground Truth (아마존 세이지메이커 그라운드 트루스)

c) Amazon SageMaker Hyperparameter Tuning (아마존 세이지메이커 하이퍼파라미터 튜닝)

d) AWS Batch (AWS 배치)

56. Which of the following is the correct order of stages in a typical machine learning pipeline?
56. 다음 중 일반적인 머신 러닝 파이프라인의 올바른 단계 순서는 무엇인가?

a) Data collection -> Model training -> Feature engineering -> Evaluation -> Deployment (데이터 수집 -> 모델 학습 -> 특징 엔지니어링 -> 평가 -> 배포)
b) Data preprocessing -> Model training -> Feature engineering -> Evaluation -> Deployment (데이터 전처리 -> 모델 학습 -> 특징 엔지니어링 -> 평가 -> 배포)
c) Data collection -> Data preprocessing -> Feature engineering -> Model training -> Evaluation -> Deployment (데이터 수집 -> 데이터 전처리 -> 특징 엔지니어링 -> 모델 학습 -> 평가 -> 배포)
d) Data collection -> Hyperparameter tuning -> Feature engineering -> Model training -> Deployment (데이터 수집 -> 하이퍼파라미터 튜닝 -> 특징 엔지니어링 -> 모델 학습 -> 배포)

57. What is the primary goal of using feature engineering in an ML pipeline?
57. ML 파이프라인에서 특징 엔지니어링을 사용하는 주요 목적은 무엇인가?

a) To reduce the dimensionality of the dataset (데이터셋의 차원을 축소하기 위해)
b) To improve model interpretability (모델의 해석 가능성을 높이기 위해)
c) To enhance the predictive power of the model (모델의 예측력을 강화하기 위해)
d) To automate data collection (데이터 수집을 자동화하기 위해)

58. Which AWS service is designed to help with labeling and annotating large datasets for supervised learning models?
58. 지도 학습 모델을 위한 대규모 데이터셋 라벨링과 주석을 돕는 AWS 서비스는 무엇인가?

a) Amazon SageMaker Ground Truth (아마존 세이지메이커 그라운드 트루스)
b) Amazon SageMaker Data Wrangler (아마존 세이지메이커 데이터 랭글러)
c) Amazon Polly (아마존 폴리)
d) AWS Lambda (AWS 람다)

59. Which method would you use if you want to host a machine learning model on your infrastructure and manage the API service manually?
59. 인프라에 머신 러닝 모델을 호스팅하고 API 서비스를 수동으로 관리하려면 어떤 방법을 사용해야 하는가?

a) Managed API service (관리형 API 서비스)
b) Self-hosted API (자체 호스팅 API)
c) Transfer learning (전이 학습)
d) Hyperparameter tuning (하이퍼파라미터 튜닝)

60. Which AWS service would you use to deploy a machine learning model to a fully managed endpoint for real-time inferencing?
60. 실시간 추론을 위해 머신 러닝 모델을 완전 관리형 엔드포인트에 배포하는 데 사용할 수 있는 AWS 서비스는 무엇인가?

a) Amazon SageMaker Endpoint (아마존 세이지메이커 엔드포인트)

b) Amazon SageMaker Feature Store (아마존 세이지메이커 피처 스토어)

c) Amazon Elastic Compute Cloud (EC2) (아마존 Ec2)

d) AWS Lambda (AWS 람다)

61. What is the primary role of Amazon SageMaker Model Monitor in the ML pipeline?
61. ML 파이프라인에서 Amazon SageMaker Model Monitor의 주요 역할은 무엇인가?

a) To train machine learning models (머신 러닝 모델을 학습시키기 위해)

b) To preprocess and clean data (데이터를 전처리하고 정제하기 위해)

c) To monitor models in production and detect anomalies (프로덕션 환경에서 모델을 모니터링하고 이상을 감지하기 위해)

d) To store features for reuse across different models (다른 모델에서 재사용할 수 있도록 특징을 저장하기 위해)

62. Which of the following best describes the primary goal of MLOps (Machine Learning Operations)?
62. 다음 중 MLOps(머신 러닝 운영)의 주요 목표를 가장 잘 설명하는 것은 무엇인가?

a) To automate model training (모델 학습을 자동화하기 위해)

b) To manage technical debt and ensure repeatability in machine learning workflows (기술 부채를 관리하고 머신 러닝 워크플로우의 반복성을 보장하기 위해)

c) To replace data scientists with automated tools (데이터 과학자를 자동화된 도구로 대체하기 위해)

d) To improve the user interface of machine learning models (머신 러닝 모델의 사용자 인터페이스를 개선하기 위해)

63. Which AWS service is designed to simplify and automate MLOps processes, such as model deployment, monitoring, and retraining?
63. 모델 배포, 모니터링, 재학습과 같은 MLOps 프로세스를 간소화하고 자동화하도록 설계된 AWS 서비스는 무엇인가?

a) Amazon SageMaker Studio (아마존 세이지메이커 스튜디오)

b) Amazon Comprehend (아마존 컴프리헨드)

c) Amazon Polly (아마존 폴리)

d) AWS CloudFormation (AWS 클라우드포메이션)

64. Which metric would you prioritize when assessing the overall balance between precision and recall for a binary classification problem?
64. 이진 분류 문제에서 정밀도와 재현율 간의 균형을 평가할 때 우선적으로 고려할 메트릭은 무엇인가?

a) Accuracy (정확도)
b) F1 Score (F1 점수)
c) AUC (Area Under the ROC Curve) (ROC 곡선 아래 면적)
d) Precision (정밀도)

65. In the context of MLOps, which of the following is a primary reason for implementing automated model retraining?
65. MLOps의 맥락에서 자동화된 모델 재학습을 구현하는 주요 이유는 무엇인가?

a) To reduce infrastructure costs (인프라 비용 절감)
b) To update the user interface for end-users (최종 사용자를 위한 사용자 인터페이스 업데이트)
c) To mitigate model drift over time (시간에 따른 모델 드리프트 완화)
d) To improve data collection processes (데이터 수집 프로세스 개선)

66. Which of the following metrics is most relevant for measuring the production performance of a machine learning model from a business perspective?
66. 비즈니스 관점에서 머신 러닝 모델의 프로덕션 성능을 측정하는 데 가장 관련성이 높은 메트릭은 무엇인가?

a) F1 Score (F1 점수)
b) Accuracy (정확도)
c) Return on Investment (ROI) (투자 수익률)
d) Area Under the ROC Curve (AUC) (ROC 곡선 아래 면적)

67. Which stage of MLOps focuses on minimizing technical debt related to the deployment and maintenance of machine learning models?
67. MLOps의 단계 중 머신 러닝 모델 배포 및 유지 관리와 관련된 기술 부채를 최소화하는 데 중점을 두는 단계는 무엇인가?

a) Experimentation (실험)
b) Model monitoring (모델 모니터링)
c) Model retraining (모델 재학습)
d) Production readiness (프로덕션 준비)

68. What is the key difference between accuracy and AUC (Area Under the ROC Curve) when evaluating machine learning models?
68. 머신 러닝 모델을 평가할 때 정확도와 AUC(ROC 곡선 아래 면적) 간의 주요 차이점은 무엇인가?

a) Accuracy measures how well a model predicts across all classes, while AUC focuses only on binary classification problems (정확도는 모델이 모든 클래스에 대해 얼마나 잘 예측하는지를 측정하며, AUC는 이진 분류 문제에만 중점을 둠)

b) Accuracy considers true positives and false positives, while AUC measures the trade-off between true positives and false positives (정확도는 진양성과 위양성을 고려하고, AUC는 진양성과 위양성 간의 균형을 측정함)

c) AUC considers class imbalance, while accuracy does not (AUC는 클래스 불균형을 고려하지만, 정확도는 고려하지 않음)

d) Accuracy and AUC are the same metrics but used in different contexts (정확도와 AUC는 동일한 메트릭이지만 다른 상황에서 사용됨)

69. Which process in MLOps involves capturing the results of experiments in a repeatable and trackable way, ensuring that model improvements are transparent and reproducible?
69. MLOps의 과정 중 실험 결과를 반복 가능하고 추적 가능한 방식으로 기록하여 모델 개선이 투명하고 재현 가능하도록 하는 과정은 무엇인가?

a) Experimentation (실험)

b) Model retraining (모델 재학습)

c) Deployment (배포)

d) Monitoring (모니터링)

70. What is the purpose of model monitoring in an MLOps pipeline?
70. MLOps 파이프라인에서 모델 모니터링의 목적은 무엇인가?

a) To automate model retraining (모델 재학습 자동화)

b) To identify and alert when model performance degrades over time (시간이 지남에 따라 모델 성능이 저하될 때 경고)

c) To update hyperparameters in real-time (실시간으로 하이퍼파라미터 업데이트)

d) To adjust feature engineering processes (특징 엔지니어링 프로세스 조정)

71. Which of the following is an example of a business metric used to assess the success of a machine learning model in a production environment?
71. 프로덕션 환경에서 머신 러닝 모델의 성공을 평가하는 데 사용되는 비즈니스 메트릭의 예는 무엇인가?

a) Precision (정밀도)

b) Recall (재현율)

c) Cost per user (사용자당 비용)

d) Accuracy (정확도)

72. In MLOps, which scenario would most likely require you to implement scalable systems?

72. MLOps에서 확장 가능한 시스템을 구현해야 할 가능성이 높은 시나리오는 무엇인가?

a) Training a model on a small dataset with limited features (제한된 특징을 가진 작은 데이터셋으로 모델 학습)

b) Deploying a model for inference on a high-traffic web application (고트래픽 웹 애플리케이션에 추론을 위한 모델 배포)

c) Conducting a one-time analysis on a static dataset (정적 데이터셋에 대한 일회성 분석 수행)

d) Performing manual data labeling for supervised learning (지도 학습을 위한 데이터 수동 라벨링 수행)

73. Which model performance metric would you use to evaluate how well a model separates positive and negative classes across varying thresholds?
73. 모델이 다양한 임계값에서 양성과 음성 클래스를 얼마나 잘 분리하는지 평가하기 위한 모델 성능 메트릭은 무엇인가?

a) Accuracy (정확도)

b) AUC (Area Under the ROC Curve) (ROC 곡선 아래 면적)

c) Precision (정밀도)

d) F1 Score (F1 점수)

74. In MLOps, what is the primary benefit of using repeatable processes during model experimentation?
74. MLOps에서 모델 실험 중 반복 가능한 프로세스를 사용하는 주요 이점은 무엇인가?

a) It improves model accuracy (모델 정확도 향상)

b) It reduces the time spent on data preprocessing (데이터 전처리 시간 단축)

c) It ensures that any improvements made to the model can be easily reproduced and validated (모델에 적용된 모든 개선 사항이 쉽게 재현되고 검증될 수 있도록 보장함)

d) It automates feature selection (특징 선택 자동화)

75. Which of the following best describes "technical debt" in the context of MLOps?
75. MLOps의 맥락에서 "기술 부채"를 가장 잘 설명하는 것은 무엇인가?

a) The cost of running machine learning models in production (프로덕션에서 머신 러닝 모델을 실행하는 비용)

b) The infrastructure costs of deploying models at scale (대규모 모델 배포의 인프라 비용)

c) The accumulated complexity from short-term fixes in code, data pipelines, or deployment processes that make future changes harder (코드, 데이터 파이프라인, 배포 프로세스에서의 단기 수정으로 인한 복잡성 누적이 미래 변경을 어렵게 만듦)

d) The overhead from using open-source models (오픈 소스 모델 사용으로 인한 오버헤드)

76. What is the primary purpose of model retraining in an MLOps workflow?
76. MLOps 워크플로우에서 모델 재학습의 주요 목적은 무엇인가?

a) To optimize hyperparameters (하이퍼파라미터 최적화)

b) To ensure models remain accurate over time as new data becomes available (새로운 데이터가 제공됨에 따라 모델의 정확성을 유지하기 위해)

c) To improve data collection efficiency (데이터 수집 효율성 향상)

d) To reduce the number of features in a dataset (데이터셋의 특징 수를 줄이기 위해)

77. Which AWS service would be most appropriate for managing and deploying a machine learning model as a production API endpoint?
77. 머신 러닝 모델을 프로덕션 API 엔드포인트로 관리 및 배포하는 데 가장 적합한 AWS 서비스는 무엇인가?

a) AWS Lambda (AWS 람다)

b) Amazon SageMaker Endpoint (아마존 세이지메이커 엔드포인트)

c) Amazon DynamoDB (아마존 다이나모DB)

d) AWS Fargate (AWS 파게이트)

78. Which of the following is not a key component of transformer-based large language models (LLMs)?
78. 다음 중 트랜스포머 기반 대형 언어 모델(LLM)의 주요 구성 요소가 아닌 것은 무엇인가?

a) Self-attention mechanism (자기 주의 메커니즘)

b) Recurrence layers (순환 레이어)

c) Token embeddings (토큰 임베딩)

d) Positional encoding (위치 인코딩)

79. What is the primary purpose of embeddings in generative AI models?
79. 생성 AI 모델에서 임베딩의 주요 목적은 무엇인가?

a) To increase model speed by reducing the number of layers (레이어 수를 줄여 모델 속도를 높이기 위해)

b) To transform input data into fixed-size vectors for easier manipulation by neural networks (입력 데이터를 고정 크기 벡터로 변환하여 신경망이 더 쉽게 조작할 수 있도록 하기 위해)

c) To split large data sets into smaller chunks for faster processing (대규모 데이터 세트를 더 작은 조각으로 분할하여 빠른 처리 가능하게 하기 위해)

d) To implement token-based learning algorithms (토큰 기반 학습 알고리즘을 구현하기 위해)

80. Which of the following generative AI models is specifically designed for generating images by modeling the stepwise addition of noise to an image?

80. 다음 중 이미지에 단계적으로 노이즈를 추가하여 이미지를 생성하도록 설계된 생성 AI 모델은 무엇인가?

a) Transformer (트랜스포머)

b) Variational Autoencoder (VAE) (변분 오토인코더)

c) GAN (Generative Adversarial Network) (생성적 적대 신경망)

d) Diffusion model (확산 모델)

81. Which AWS service would be most appropriate for deploying and fine-tuning a pre-trained foundation model for natural language processing tasks?
81. 자연어 처리 작업을 위한 사전 학습된 기초 모델을 배포하고 미세 조정하는 데 가장 적합한 AWS 서비스는 무엇인가?

a) Amazon Polly (아마존 폴리)

b) Amazon SageMaker (아마존 세이지메이커)

c) AWS Glue (AWS 글루)

d) Amazon Rekognition (아마존 레코그니션)

82. In the foundation model lifecycle, which stage involves adjusting a pre-trained model to a specific task or domain using a smaller, task-specific dataset?
82. 기초 모델 수명 주기에서 사전 학습된 모델을 특정 작업이나 도메인에 맞추기 위해 더 작은, 작업 특화 데이터셋을 사용하는 단계는 무엇인가?

a) Pre-training (사전 학습)

b) Fine-tuning (미세 조정)

c) Evaluation (평가)

d) Deployment (배포)

83. What is the purpose of chunking in generative AI, especially in large language models (LLMs)?
83. 생성 AI, 특히 대형 언어 모델(LLM)에서 청킹(chunking)의 목적은 무엇인가?

a) To reduce the model's parameter size (모델의 매개변수 크기를 줄이기 위해)

b) To split large inputs into smaller pieces for efficient processing (대규모 입력을 더 작은 조각으로 나눠 효율적인 처리를 위해)

c) To convert input data into vectors (입력 데이터를 벡터로 변환하기 위해)

d) To generate embeddings for text (텍스트 임베딩을 생성하기 위해)

84. Which generative AI use case would most likely benefit from the application of a multi-modal model?
84. 다중 모달 모델의 적용으로 가장 큰 이점을 얻을 수 있는 생성 AI 사용 사례는 무엇인가?

a) Text summarization (텍스트 요약)

b) Image generation (이미지 생성)

c) Video captioning (비디오 캡션 생성)

d) Code generation (코드 생성)

85. Which foundational model lifecycle stage focuses on selecting the optimal dataset for training a model based on the domain and task requirements?
85. 기초 모델 수명 주기에서 도메인과 작업 요구사항에 따라 모델 학습을 위한 최적의 데이터셋을 선택하는 데 중점을 두는 단계는 무엇인가?

a) Model selection (모델 선택)

b) Data selection (데이터 선택)

c) Evaluation (평가)

d) Pre-training (사전 학습)

86. In prompt engineering for large language models, what is the primary goal of designing an effective prompt?
86. 대형 언어 모델을 위한 프롬프트 엔지니어링에서 효과적인 프롬프트를 설계하는 주요 목표는 무엇인가?

a) To maximize the model's computational efficiency (모델의 계산 효율성을 극대화하기 위해)

b) To fine-tune the model's parameters for better results (더 나은 결과를 위해 모델의 매개변수를 미세 조정하기 위해)

c) To guide the model in generating the most relevant and accurate output (모델이 가장 관련성 높고 정확한 출력을 생성하도록 안내하기 위해)

d) To reduce the training time required for the model (모델 학습에 필요한 시간을 줄이기 위해)

87. Which metric is typically used to evaluate the quality of text generated by a language model when compared to human-generated text?
87. 언어 모델이 생성한 텍스트의 품질을 인간이 생성한 텍스트와 비교하여 평가하는 데 일반적으로 사용되는 메트릭은 무엇인가?

a) BLEU (Bilingual Evaluation Understudy Score)

b) F1 Score (F1 점수)

c) AUC (Area Under the Curve)

d) MSE (Mean Squared Error)

88. Which AWS service allows developers to build and deploy conversational interfaces and chatbots using natural language processing capabilities?
88. 자연어 처리 기능을 사용하여 대화형 인터페이스와 챗봇을 구축하고 배포할 수 있는 AWS 서비스는 무엇인가?

a) Amazon Polly (아마존 폴리)

b) Amazon Lex (아마존 렉스)

c) Amazon Comprehend (아마존 컴프리헨드)

d) AWS Glue (AWS 글루)

89. What role does vector representation play in the context of embeddings for generative AI models?

89. 생성 AI 모델에서 임베딩의 벡터 표현은 어떤 역할을 하는가?

a) They speed up model training by reducing the number of neurons in a layer (레이어의 뉴런 수를 줄여 모델 학습 속도를 높임)

b) They allow models to represent words, sentences, or images in a dense numerical format that preserves relationships (단어, 문장, 이미지를 관계를 유지하는 밀집 숫자 형식으로 모델이 표현할 수 있도록 함)

c) They reduce the size of input data to improve memory usage (입력 데이터 크기를 줄여 메모리 사용을 개선함)

d) They serve as a metric for model evaluation (모델 평가의 메트릭으로 사용됨)

90. Which type of generative AI model is particularly suited for generating realistic human-like images or videos?

90. 현실감 있는 인간과 같은 이미지나 비디오를 생성하는 데 특히 적합한 생성 AI 모델 유형은 무엇인가?

a) Transformer models (트랜스포머 모델)

b) GANs (Generative Adversarial Networks) (생성적 적대 신경망)

c) LSTM (Long Short-Term Memory) networks (장단기 메모리 네트워크)

d) Decision Trees (결정 트리)

91. Which foundation model lifecycle stage focuses on evaluating model performance using metrics like accuracy, precision, or F1 score?

91. 정확도, 정밀도, F1 점수와 같은 메트릭을 사용하여 모델 성능을 평가하는 데 중점을 두는 기초 모델 수명 주기의 단계는 무엇인가?

a) Pre-training (사전 학습)

b) Model selection (모델 선택)

c) Fine-tuning (미세 조정)

d) Evaluation (평가)

92. Which generative AI concept refers to the process of representing input text or data in a format that a neural network can understand, often using numerical vectors?

92. 입력 텍스트나 데이터를 신경망이 이해할 수 있는 형식으로 표현하는 과정으로, 종종 숫자 벡터를 사용하는 생성 AI 개념은 무엇인가?

a) Tokens (토큰)

b) Chunking (청킹)

c) Embeddings (임베딩)

d) Diffusion (확산)

93. In the context of generative AI, what is the purpose of transformer-based models like GPT?
93. 생성 AI의 맥락에서 GPT와 같은 트랜스포머 기반 모델의 목적은 무엇인가?

a) To handle sequential data using recurrence layers (순환 레이어를 통해 순차 데이터를 처리하기 위해)

b) To perform image recognition and object detection (이미지 인식 및 객체 탐지를 수행하기 위해)

c) To generate human-like text or language predictions using attention mechanisms (주의 메커니즘을 사용해 인간과 유사한 텍스트나 언어 예측을 생성하기 위해)

d) To reduce computational complexity by using decision trees (결정 트리를 사용하여 계산 복잡성을 줄이기 위해)

94. Which technique is commonly used to generate new data by gradually transforming noise into a realistic sample in generative models?
94. 생성 모델에서 노이즈를 점진적으로 변형하여 현실적인 샘플을 생성하는 데 일반적으로 사용되는 기술은 무엇인가?

a) Variational Autoencoder (VAE) (변분 오토인코더)

b) Generative Adversarial Network (GAN) (생성적 적대 신경망)

c) Diffusion Model (확산 모델)

d) Reinforcement Learning (강화 학습)

95. What is the key advantage of using pre-trained foundation models in a production environment?
95. 프로덕션 환경에서 사전 학습된 기초 모델을 사용하는 주요 이점은 무엇인가?

a) They eliminate the need for large datasets during model training (모델 학습 시 대규모 데이터셋의 필요성 제거)

b) They guarantee 100% accuracy on all tasks (모든 작업에서 100% 정확도 보장)

c) They reduce the time and cost associated with training models from scratch (모델을 처음부터 학습하는 데 드는 시간과 비용 절감)

d) They automatically optimize model hyperparameters (모델의 하이퍼파라미터를 자동으로 최적화함)

96. What is the primary role of a "foundation model" in AI?
96. AI에서 "기초 모델"의 주요 역할은 무엇인가?

a) To provide a base for building specialized models with additional training (추가 학습을 통해 특화된 모델

을 구축할 수 있는 기반을 제공하기 위해)

b) To perform specific tasks with high accuracy without further training (추가 학습 없이 높은 정확도로 특정 작업 수행)

c) To replace all existing machine learning models (모든 기존 머신 러닝 모델을 대체하기 위해)

d) To reduce the computational resources needed for model training (모델 학습에 필요한 계산 자원을 줄이기 위해)

97. Which metric is used to evaluate the trade-off between true positive rate and false positive rate across different threshold values for a classification model?
97. 분류 모델에서 다양한 임계값에 따른 진양성 비율과 위양성 비율 간의 균형을 평가하는 데 사용되는 메트릭은 무엇인가?

a) Precision (정밀도)

b) Recall (재현율)

c) ROC Curve (ROC 곡선)

d) Mean Absolute Error (MAE) (평균 절대 오차)

98. Which type of data is typically used in supervised learning models to train the algorithm?
98. 알고리즘을 학습시키기 위해 지도 학습 모델에서 일반적으로 사용하는 데이터 유형은 무엇인가?

a) Unlabeled data (라벨이 없는 데이터)

b) Structured data (구조화된 데이터)

c) Time-series data (시계열 데이터)

d) Labeled data (라벨이 있는 데이터)

99. What does "model re-training" refer to in the context of ML operations (MLOps)?
99. ML 운영(MLOps)에서 "모델 재학습"이 의미하는 것은 무엇인가?

a) The initial training of a model from scratch (모델을 처음부터 학습하는 것)

b) Periodically updating a model with new data to maintain its accuracy and relevance (정확성과 관련성을 유지하기 위해 새로운 데이터로 모델을 주기적으로 업데이트하는 것)

c) Adjusting the architecture of a model to improve performance (성능 향상을 위해 모델 구조를 조정하는 것)

d) Re-evaluating the performance of a model after deployment (배포 후 모델 성능을 재평가하는 것)

100. Which concept describes the process of using a pre-trained model to adapt it to a new but related task?
100. 사전 학습된 모델을 사용하여 새로운 그러나 관련된 작업에 적응시키는 과정을 설명하는 개념은 무엇인가?

a) Transfer Learning (전이 학습)

b) Reinforcement Learning (강화 학습)

c) Hyperparameter Tuning (하이퍼파라미터 튜닝)

d) Data Augmentation (데이터 증강)

101. Which AWS service helps monitor the performance of deployed machine learning models, providing insights into their behavior and accuracy over time?

101. 배포된 머신 러닝 모델의 성능을 모니터링하여 시간 경과에 따른 동작과 정확도에 대한 통찰력을 제공하는 AWS 서비스는 무엇인가?

a) Amazon SageMaker Model Monitor (아마존 세이지메이커 모델 모니터)

b) AWS CloudWatch (AWS 클라우드와치)

c) Amazon Redshift (아마존 레드시프트)

d) AWS CodePipeline (AWS 코드파이프라인)

102. Which metric would be most appropriate to use when evaluating the success of a recommendation system?

102. 추천 시스템의 성공을 평가할 때 가장 적절한 메트릭은 무엇인가?

a) BLEU Score (BLEU 점수)

b) Mean Absolute Error (평균 절대 오차)

c) Click-Through Rate (클릭률)

d) F1 Score (F1 점수)

103. What is a significant advantage of generative AI models in terms of adaptability?

103. 적응성 측면에서 생성 AI 모델의 주요 이점은 무엇인가?

a) They always provide consistent outputs regardless of input changes (입력 변화와 관계없이 일관된 출력을 제공함)

b) They can rapidly adjust to new types of data and tasks without extensive re-training (광범위한 재학습 없이도 새로운 데이터 유형과 작업에 신속하게 적응할 수 있음)

c) They are immune to biases present in the training data (훈련 데이터에 존재하는 편향에 영향을 받지 않음)

d) They guarantee high accuracy across all types of tasks (모든 작업 유형에서 높은 정확도를 보장함)

104. Which of the following is a common disadvantage of generative AI models related to interpretability?

104. 생성 AI 모델의 해석 가능성과 관련된 일반적인 단점은 무엇인가?

a) They produce outputs that are easily understandable and explainable (쉽게 이해되고 설명 가능한 출력을 생성함)

b) Their decision-making process is transparent and straightforward (의사 결정 과정이 투명하고 간단함)

c) They often generate results whose reasoning process is opaque, making it difficult to interpret how conclusions are drawn (결론에 도달하는 이유가 불투명하여 결과 해석이 어려운 경우가 많음)

d) They provide clear explanations for the output generated (생성된 출력에 대한 명확한 설명을 제공함)

105. When selecting a generative AI model for a specific application, which factor is crucial for ensuring compliance with regulatory standards?
105. 특정 애플리케이션을 위한 생성 AI 모델을 선택할 때 규제 표준을 준수하기 위해 중요한 요소는 무엇인가?

a) Model Type (모델 유형)

b) Performance Requirements (성능 요구 사항)

c) Capabilities (기능)

d) Constraints (제약 조건)

106. Which metric would best evaluate the effectiveness of a generative AI model in generating personalized recommendations?
106. 개인화된 추천을 생성하는 생성 AI 모델의 효과를 평가하는 데 가장 적절한 메트릭은 무엇인가?

a) Average Revenue per User (사용자당 평균 수익)

b) Accuracy (정확도)

c) Conversion Rate (전환율)

d) Customer Lifetime Value (고객 생애 가치)

107. What is a common disadvantage of generative AI solutions related to inaccuracy?
107. 부정확성과 관련된 생성 AI 솔루션의 일반적인 단점은 무엇인가?

a) They always generate outputs that are perfectly accurate and reliable (항상 완벽히 정확하고 신뢰할 수 있는 출력을 생성함)

b) They may produce outputs that are sometimes incorrect or nonsensical, known as "hallucinations" (때때로 부정확하거나 말이 되지 않는 출력을 생성하는데, 이를 "환각"이라고 함)

)c) They eliminate all sources of error in data processing (데이터 처리에서 모든 오류의 원인을 제거함)

d) They provide consistent accuracy across all applications (모든 애플리케이션에서 일관된 정확도를 제공함)

108. When assessing the business value of a generative AI application, which metric is most relevant for measuring user engagement and satisfaction?
108. 생성 AI 애플리케이션의 비즈니스 가치를 평가할 때, 사용자 참여도와 만족도를 측정하는 데 가장 관련성이 높은 메트릭은 무엇인가?

a) Cross-Domain Performance (도메인 간 성능)

b) Efficiency (효율성)

c) Accuracy (정확도)

d) Customer Lifetime Value (고객 생애 가치)

109. Which of the following factors should be considered when selecting a generative AI model to ensure it meets performance requirements?

109. 성능 요구 사항을 충족하기 위해 생성 AI 모델을 선택할 때 고려해야 할 요소는 무엇인가?

a) Model Interpretability (모델 해석 가능성)

b) Model Type (모델 유형)

c) Data Privacy (데이터 프라이버시)

d) Cross-Domain Performance (도메인 간 성능)

110. What factor is essential for evaluating the efficiency of a generative AI solution in a production environment?

110. 프로덕션 환경에서 생성 AI 솔루션의 효율성을 평가하는 데 필수적인 요소는 무엇인가?

a) Model Size (모델 크기)

b) Compliance (준수 여부)

c) Model Complexity (모델 복잡성)

d) Average Revenue per User (사용자당 평균 수익)

111. What is a significant challenge of using generative AI models in terms of nondeterminism?

111. 비결정론성 측면에서 생성 AI 모델을 사용할 때 주요 과제는 무엇인가?

a) Models produce the same output for identical inputs every time (모델이 동일한 입력에 대해 항상 동일한 출력을 생성함)

b) Models always provide predictable and consistent results (모델이 항상 예측 가능하고 일관된 결과를 제공함)

c) Models can produce varying outputs for the same input, leading to unpredictability (모델이 동일한 입력에 대해 다양한 출력을 생성하여 예측 불가능성을 초래함)

d) Models are guaranteed to perform identically across different applications (모델이 다양한 애플리케이션에서 동일하게 작동함을 보장함)

112. To address the challenge of model "hallucinations," which approach is most effective in generative AI?

112. 생성 AI에서 모델의 "환각" 문제를 해결하는 데 가장 효과적인 접근 방식은 무엇인가?

a) Increasing model size indefinitely (모델 크기를 무한히 늘리기)

b) Regularly updating training data and incorporating feedback mechanisms (훈련 데이터를 정기적으로 업

데이트하고 피드백 메커니즘을 도입하기)

c) Limiting the model to a single domain (모델을 단일 도메인으로 제한하기)

d) Ignoring model performance metrics (모델 성능 메트릭 무시하기)

113. Which advantage of generative AI models significantly impacts their ability to handle complex tasks?

113. 생성 AI 모델의 어떤 이점이 복잡한 작업을 처리하는 능력에 크게 영향을 미치는가?

a) Low computational requirements (낮은 계산 요구 사항)

b) High adaptability to new domains (새로운 도메인에 대한 높은 적응성)

c) Predictable performance across all applications (모든 애플리케이션에서 예측 가능한 성능)

d) Consistent manual tuning requirements (일관된 수동 튜닝 요구 사항)

114. When selecting a generative AI model, which factor is critical for ensuring it meets business-specific capabilities?

114. 생성 AI 모델을 선택할 때 비즈니스 특화 기능을 충족하기 위해 중요한 요소는 무엇인가?

a) Model Size (모델 크기)

b) Training Data Diversity (훈련 데이터 다양성)

c) Model Interpretability (모델 해석 가능성)

d) Performance Benchmarks (성능 기준)

115. In the context of evaluating generative AI models, which metric is most relevant for assessing the cost-effectiveness of deploying the solution?

115. 생성 AI 모델을 평가할 때 솔루션 배포의 비용 효율성을 평가하는 데 가장 관련성이 높은 메트릭은 무엇인가?

a) Efficiency (효율성)

b) Accuracy (정확도)

c) Customer Lifetime Value (고객 생애 가치)

d) Average Revenue per User (사용자당 평균 수익)

116. Which factor is most crucial for ensuring a generative AI model's outputs align with desired user experiences?

116. 생성 AI 모델의 출력이 원하는 사용자 경험과 일치하도록 보장하기 위해 가장 중요한 요소는 무엇인가?

a) Model Complexity (모델 복잡성)

b) Data Privacy (데이터 프라이버시)

c) Prompt Engineering (프롬프트 엔지니어링)

d) Model Size (모델 크기)

117. This question asks which disadvantage of generative AI models is associated with their tendency to produce inconsistent outputs that lack predictability?
117. 생성 AI 모델의 일관된 출력을 생성하는 데 있어 예측 불가능성과 관련된 단점은 무엇인가?

a) Nondeterminism (비결정론성)

b) High interpretability (높은 해석 가능성)

c) Consistent accuracy (일관된 정확성)

d) Low complexity (낮은 복잡성)

118. What is a key consideration when selecting a generative AI model for compliance with data privacy regulations?
118. 데이터 프라이버시 규정을 준수하기 위해 생성 AI 모델을 선택할 때 중요한 고려 사항은 무엇인가?

a) Model Type (모델 유형)

b) Data Privacy Measures (데이터 프라이버시 조치)

)c) Cross-Domain Performance (도메인 간 성능)

d) Model Complexity (모델 복잡성)

119. To measure the success of a generative AI model in enhancing customer interactions, which business value metric is most relevant?
119. 고객 상호작용을 향상시키는 데 있어 생성 AI 모델의 성공을 측정하기 위한 가장 관련 있는 비즈니스 가치 메트릭은 무엇인가?

a) Conversion Rate (전환율)

b) Efficiency (효율성)

c) Accuracy (정확도)

d) Model Size (모델 크기)

120. Which factor is most important for managing technical debt in generative AI systems?
120. 생성 AI 시스템에서 기술 부채를 관리하는 데 있어 가장 중요한 요소는 무엇인가?

a) Regular model updates and maintenance (정기적인 모델 업데이트 및 유지보수)

b) Model Size (모델 크기)

c) Data Privacy (데이터 프라이버시)

d) Prompt Engineering (프롬프트 엔지니어링)

121. Which of the following is a key metric for evaluating a generative AI model's impact on long-term customer engagement?
121. 장기적인 고객 참여에 대한 생성 AI 모델의 영향을 평가하기 위한 주요 메트릭은 무엇인가?

a) Customer Lifetime Value (고객 생애 가치)

b) Cross-Domain Performance (도메인 간 성능)

c) Model Complexity (모델 복잡성)

d) Efficiency (효율성)

122. What is a key advantage of using AWS generative AI services in terms of speed to market?
122. 시장 진출 속도 측면에서 AWS 생성 AI 서비스를 사용할 때의 주요 이점은 무엇인가?

a) Extensive manual tuning of models (광범위한 모델 수동 조정)

b) Simplified integration with third-party tools (타사 도구와의 통합이 간단함)

c) Pre-trained models and managed infrastructure that accelerate development and deployment (개발과 배포를 가속화하는 사전 학습된 모델과 관리형 인프라)

d) Increased data preprocessing requirements (데이터 전처리 요구 사항 증가)

123. What is the primary disadvantage of generative AI models in terms of hallucinations?
123. 환각(hallucinations) 측면에서 생성 AI 모델의 주요 단점은 무엇인가?

a) They provide exact replicas of training data (훈련 데이터의 정확한 복제본을 제공함)

b) They can generate outputs that do not align with reality or context, leading to misleading or erroneous information (현실이나 문맥과 맞지 않는 출력을 생성하여 오해를 불러일으키거나 잘못된 정보를 제공할 수 있음)

c) They ensure complete consistency across all generated results (모든 생성된 결과에서 완전한 일관성을 보장함)

d) They eliminate the need for further validation (추가 검증의 필요성을 제거함)

124. How does Amazon Bedrock enhance the development of generative AI applications?
124. Amazon Bedrock은 생성 AI 애플리케이션 개발을 어떻게 향상시키는가?

a) By providing a local development environment (로컬 개발 환경 제공)

b) By offering a fully managed platform with a wide range of foundation models and APIs (다양한 기초 모델과 API를 갖춘 완전 관리형 플랫폼 제공)

c) By requiring extensive custom model training (광범위한 사용자 지정 모델 학습 요구)

d) By limiting access to pre-built models (사전 구축된 모델에 대한 접근을 제한)

125. Which benefit does AWS infrastructure provide for generative AI applications in terms of

security?

125. 보안 측면에서 AWS 인프라가 생성 AI 애플리케이션에 제공하는 이점은 무엇인가?

a) No compliance certifications (준수 인증 없음)

b) Limited access control features (제한된 접근 제어 기능)

c) Comprehensive security controls, including encryption and access management (암호화 및 접근 관리와 같은 종합적인 보안 통제 기능)

d) Increased risk of data breaches (데이터 유출 위험 증가)

126. What is a primary cost trade-off consideration when using AWS generative AI services?
126. AWS 생성 AI 서비스를 사용할 때 주요 비용 절충 고려사항은 무엇인가?

a) Fixed pricing for all services (모든 서비스에 대해 고정 가격 제공)

b) Token-based pricing models and provisioned throughput for cost management (비용 관리를 위한 토큰 기반 가격 모델 및 프로비저닝 처리량)

c) Unlimited free access to all AWS services (모든 AWS 서비스에 대한 무제한 무료 액세스)

d) No additional costs for regional coverage (지역 커버리지에 대한 추가 비용 없음)

127. What is the advantage of using AWS generative AI services in terms of cost-effectiveness?
127. 비용 효율성 측면에서 AWS 생성 AI 서비스를 사용하는 이점은 무엇인가?

a) High upfront costs with no scalable options (확장 가능 옵션이 없는 높은 선행 비용)

b) Pay-as-you-go pricing that scales with usage (사용량에 따라 확장되는 종량제 가격)

c) Fixed long-term contracts for all services (모든 서비스에 대한 장기 고정 계약)

d) Inability to adjust service levels (서비스 수준 조정 불가)

128. What is a key benefit of AWS infrastructure in terms of compliance for generative AI applications?
128. 생성 AI 애플리케이션에 대한 준수 측면에서 AWS 인프라의 주요 이점은 무엇인가?

a) Limited compliance with industry standards (업계 표준에 대한 제한된 준수)

b) Extensive compliance certifications and adherence to industry standards (광범위한 준수 인증과 업계 표준 준수)

c) No support for regulatory requirements (규제 요구사항에 대한 지원 없음)

d) Inconsistent safety measures (일관되지 않은 안전 조치)

129. When considering the performance of AWS generative AI services, which cost trade-off factor is crucial?
129. AWS 생성 AI 서비스의 성능을 고려할 때 중요한 비용 절충 요소는 무엇인가?

a) Service availability and redundancy (서비스 가용성 및 중복성)

b) Unlimited data throughput (무제한 데이터 처리량)

c) Free usage of all AWS regions (모든 AWS 리전의 무료 사용)

d) Fixed performance levels across all services (모든 서비스의 고정 성능 수준)

130. How does the use of Amazon Q contribute to generative AI applications?
130. Amazon Q 사용이 생성 AI 애플리케이션에 어떻게 기여하는가?

a) By providing a platform for manual data preprocessing (수동 데이터 전처리 플랫폼 제공)

b) By offering interactive tools and playgrounds for building and experimenting with generative models (생성 모델을 구축하고 실험하기 위한 대화형 도구와 실험 환경 제공)

c) By focusing only on data storage solutions (데이터 저장 솔루션에만 초점 맞추기)

d) By restricting access to foundational models (기초 모델에 대한 접근 제한)

131. How does AWS ensure compliance and security in generative AI applications?
131. AWS는 생성 AI 애플리케이션에서 어떻게 준수와 보안을 보장하는가?

a) By offering unrestricted access to all data (모든 데이터에 대한 무제한 접근 제공)

b) By providing automated compliance reporting and robust security controls (자동화된 준수 보고와 강력한 보안 통제 제공)

c) By limiting security features to specific services (특정 서비스에만 보안 기능 제한)

d) By relying on external security providers (외부 보안 공급업체에 의존)

132. What is a common cost trade-off when using AWS generative AI services for real-time applications?
132. 실시간 애플리케이션에서 AWS 생성 AI 서비스를 사용할 때의 일반적인 비용 절충 요소는 무엇인가?

a) High upfront capital expenditure (높은 선행 자본 지출)

b) Variable costs based on token usage and request frequency (토큰 사용량과 요청 빈도에 따른 가변 비용)

c) Free unlimited access to all generative models (모든 생성 모델에 대한 무제한 무료 액세스)

d) Fixed pricing, irrespective of usage (사용량과 관계없는 고정 가격)

133. What factor is most crucial when considering AWS generative AI services for applications with high security and compliance requirements?
133. 높은 보안과 규제 준수 요건이 있는 애플리케이션에 AWS 생성 AI 서비스를 고려할 때 가장 중요한 요소는 무엇인가?

a) Service cost (서비스 비용)

b) Token-based pricing (토큰 기반 가격)

c) Availability of security features and compliance certifications (보안 기능과 규제 준수 인증의 가용성)

d) Ease of model fine-tuning (모델 미세 조정의 용이성)

134. Which AWS service is specifically designed for experimenting with and exploring various generative AI models in a user-friendly environment?
134. 다양한 생성 AI 모델을 실험하고 탐구할 수 있는 사용자 친화적인 환경을 제공하도록 설계된 AWS 서비스는 무엇인가?

a) Amazon Bedrock Playground (아마존 베드락 플레이그라운드)

b) Amazon S3 (아마존 S3)

c) Amazon CloudWatch (아마존 클라우드와치)

d) Amazon RDS (아마존 RDS)

135. In terms of AWS generative AI services, what does the term "token-based pricing" refer to?
135. AWS 생성 AI 서비스에서 "토큰 기반 가격"이라는 용어는 무엇을 의미하는가?

a) Pricing based on the number of API calls (API 호출 수에 따른 가격)

b) Pricing based on the amount of data stored (저장된 데이터 양에 따른 가격)

c) Pricing based on the number of tokens processed or generated by the AI model (AI 모델이 처리하거나 생성하는 토큰 수에 따른 가격)

d) Fixed monthly fees for using the service (서비스 사용에 대한 고정 월 요금)

136. When deploying a generative AI application using AWS services, which benefit is provided by AWS's global infrastructure?
136. AWS 서비스를 사용하여 생성 AI 애플리케이션을 배포할 때 AWS의 글로벌 인프라가 제공하는 이점은 무엇인가?

a) Increased data storage costs (데이터 저장 비용 증가)

b) Limited access to regional resources (지역 자원에 대한 제한된 접근)

c) Enhanced performance and availability through regional coverage (지역 커버리지를 통한 성능 및 가용성 향상)

d) Decreased model training options (모델 학습 옵션 감소)

137. When selecting a pre-trained model for an AWS-based application, which criterion is crucial for applications requiring real-time interactions with minimal delay?
137. AWS 기반 애플리케이션에 적합한 사전 학습 모델을 선택할 때, 최소 지연으로 실시간 상호작용이 필요한 애플리케이션에 중요한 기준은 무엇인가?

a) Model size (모델 크기)

b) Latency (지연 시간)

c) Cost (비용)

d) Multi-lingual capabilities (다국어 지원 기능)

138. How does the temperature parameter affect the responses generated by a language model during inference?
138. 추론 중 온도 매개변수가 언어 모델이 생성하는 응답에 어떻게 영향을 미치는가?

a) It controls the amount of training data used (사용되는 학습 데이터의 양을 제어함)

b) It adjusts the randomness of the generated output (생성된 출력의 무작위성을 조정함)

c) It changes the model's training duration (모델의 학습 기간을 변경함)

d) It alters the model's input length (모델의 입력 길이를 변경함)

139. Which AWS service would you use to store embeddings in a vector database for a generative AI application that requires high search efficiency and scalability?
139. 높은 검색 효율성과 확장성을 요구하는 생성 AI 애플리케이션의 벡터 데이터베이스에 임베딩을 저장하기 위해 사용할 AWS 서비스는 무엇인가?

a) Amazon RDS for PostgreSQL (아마존 RDS 포스트그레SQL)

b) Amazon Aurora (아마존 오로라)

c) Amazon OpenSearch Service (아마존 오픈서치 서비스)

d) Amazon DocumentDB (with MongoDB compatibility) (아마존 도큐먼트DB, 몽고DB 호환)

140. What is Retrieval Augmented Generation (RAG), and how can it be used in business applications?
140. 검색 증강 생성(RAG)이란 무엇이며, 비즈니스 애플리케이션에서 어떻게 사용할 수 있는가?

a) A technique for enhancing model accuracy by increasing training data (훈련 데이터 증가를 통한 모델 정확성 향상 기술)

b) A method for combining pre-trained models with retrieval mechanisms to generate contextually relevant responses (사전 학습 모델과 검색 메커니즘을 결합하여 맥락에 맞는 응답을 생성하는 방법)

c) A service for storing large volumes of unstructured data (대량의 비정형 데이터를 저장하는 서비스)

d) A model type focused solely on image recognition (이미지 인식에만 초점을 맞춘 모델 유형)

141. When evaluating pre-trained models for a specific application, which factor is most important if the application requires extensive customization for domain-specific tasks?
141. 특정 애플리케이션을 위한 사전 학습 모델을 평가할 때, 도메인 특화 작업을 위해 광범위한 맞춤화가 필요한 경우 가장 중요한 요소는 무엇인가?

a) Model complexity (모델 복잡성)

b) Cost (비용)

c) Multi-lingual capabilities (다국어 지원 기능)

d) Input/output length (입출력 길이)

142. In the context of using pre-trained models, which criterion should be prioritized if the application needs to support multiple languages?
142. 사전 학습 모델을 사용할 때 애플리케이션이 다국어를 지원해야 하는 경우 우선시해야 할 기준은 무엇인가?

a) Input/output length (입출력 길이)

b) Multi-lingual capabilities (다국어 지원 기능)

c) Model size (모델 크기)

d) Customization (맞춤화)

143. Which AWS service is best suited for managing graph data and relationships, particularly useful for storing and querying embeddings in a vector-based format?
143. 그래프 데이터와 관계를 관리하는 데 적합하며, 특히 벡터 기반 형식으로 임베딩을 저장하고 쿼리하는 데 유용한 AWS 서비스는 무엇인가?

a) Amazon Neptune (아마존 넵튠)

b) Amazon Aurora (아마존 오로라)

c) Amazon RDS for PostgreSQL (아마존 RDS 포스트그레SQL)

d) Amazon OpenSearch Service (아마존 오픈서치 서비스)

144. What effect does adjusting the input/output length parameter have on the performance of a generative model?
144. 입력/출력 길이 매개변수를 조정하면 생성 모델의 성능에 어떤 영향을 미치는가?

a) It affects the model's training data (모델의 학습 데이터에 영향)

b) It influences the size and complexity of the generated response (생성된 응답의 크기와 복잡성에 영향)

c) It alters the model's learning rate (모델의 학습 속도를 변경)

d) It determines the number of training epochs (훈련 에포크 수를 결정)

145. Which AWS service would you use if you need a managed database that supports storing and querying document-based data, including embeddings?
145. 임베딩을 포함한 문서 기반 데이터를 저장하고 쿼리할 수 있는 관리형 데이터베이스가 필요한 경우 사용할 AWS 서비스는 무엇인가?

a) Amazon RDS for PostgreSQL (아마존 RDS 포스트그레SQL)

b) Amazon DocumentDB (with MongoDB compatibility) (아마존 도큐먼트DB, 몽고DB 호환)

c) Amazon Aurora (아마존 오로라)

d) Amazon OpenSearch Service (아마존 오픈서치 서비스)

146. When considering cost as a selection criterion for pre-trained models, which factor is typically the most impactful?
146. 사전 학습 모델을 선택할 때 비용을 기준으로 고려할 경우, 일반적으로 가장 큰 영향을 미치는 요소는 무엇인가?

a) Model customization options (모델 맞춤화 옵션)

b) Model complexity (모델 복잡성)

c) Latency (지연 시간)

d) Input/output length (입출력 길이)

147. Which AWS service provides an environment for experimenting with and fine-tuning generative AI models while leveraging pre-built templates?
147. 사전 구축된 템플릿을 활용하면서 생성 AI 모델을 실험하고 미세 조정할 수 있는 환경을 제공하는 AWS 서비스는 무엇인가?

a) Amazon SageMaker JumpStart (아마존 세이지메이커 점프스타트)

b) Amazon Comprehend (아마존 컴프리헨드)

c) Amazon Lex (아마존 렉스)

d) Amazon Polly (아마존 폴리)

148. When choosing a pre-trained model for an application requiring support for various document formats, which factor should be prioritized?
148. 다양한 문서 형식을 지원해야 하는 애플리케이션을 위한 사전 학습 모델을 선택할 때 우선시해야 할 요소는 무엇인가?

a) Input/output length (입출력 길이)

b) Model size (모델 크기)

c) Modality (모달리티)

d) Customization (맞춤화)

149. How does adjusting the "temperature" parameter affect the output of a generative AI model?
149. "온도" 매개변수를 조정하면 생성 AI 모델의 출력에 어떻게 영향을 미치는가?

a) It determines the model's accuracy (모델의 정확도를 결정함)

b) It controls the creativity and variability of the generated responses (생성된 응답의 창의성과 변동성을 조정함)

c) It changes the model's training duration (모델의 학습 기간을 변경함)

d) It modifies the model's data input size (모델의 데이터 입력 크기를 변경함)

150. In the context of generative AI, what is Retrieval Augmented Generation (RAG) primarily used for?

150. 생성 AI에서 검색 증강 생성(RAG)은 주로 무엇에 사용되는가?

a) Improving model training efficiency (모델 학습 효율성 향상)

b) Combining retrieval of external data with model generation to enhance response accuracy (응답 정확성을 높이기 위해 외부 데이터 검색과 모델 생성을 결합)

c) Reducing the complexity of model architecture (모델 아키텍처의 복잡성 감소)

d) Increasing the size of training datasets (훈련 데이터셋의 크기 증가)

151. Which AWS service offers vector search capabilities and is designed for high-performance querying of large volumes of vector embeddings?

151. 대량의 벡터 임베딩에 대한 고성능 쿼리를 위해 벡터 검색 기능을 제공하는 AWS 서비스는 무엇인가?

a) Amazon OpenSearch Service (아마존 오픈서치 서비스)

b) Amazon Neptune (아마존 넵튠)

c) Amazon Aurora (아마존 오로라)

d) Amazon RDS for PostgreSQL (아마존 RDS 포스트그레SQL)

152. What factor should be considered when choosing a pre-trained model for applications that need to generate text in multiple languages?

152. 다국어 텍스트를 생성해야 하는 애플리케이션을 위한 사전 학습 모델을 선택할 때 고려해야 할 요소는 무엇인가?

a) Model size (모델 크기)

b) Customization options (맞춤화 옵션)

c) Multi-lingual capabilities (다국어 지원 기능)

d) Latency (지연 시간)

153. Which AWS service is best for experimenting with different generative AI models and integrating them into applications using an easy-to-use interface?

153. 다양한 생성 AI 모델을 실험하고 이를 애플리케이션에 손쉽게 통합할 수 있는 인터페이스를 제공하는 AWS 서비스는 무엇인가?

a) Amazon SageMaker Studio (아마존 세이지메이커 스튜디오)

b) Amazon Lex (아마존 렉스)

c) Amazon Polly (아마존 폴리)

d) Amazon Comprehend (아마존 컴프리헨드)

154. What is a significant cost tradeoff when opting for fine-tuning a pre-trained foundation model compared to using in-context learning?

154. 사전 학습된 기초 모델을 세부 조정하는 것과 맥락 학습(in-context learning)을 사용하는 것 사이의 중요한 비용 절충은 무엇인가?

a) Fine-tuning often requires extensive computational resources and can be costly, but it allows for deeper customization specific to the task (세부 조정은 종종 많은 계산 자원을 필요로 하며 비용이 많이 들 수 있지만, 특정 작업에 대한 깊이 있는 맞춤화를 가능하게 함)

b) In-context learning is generally more expensive as it involves retraining the entire model from scratch (맥락 학습은 전체 모델을 처음부터 다시 학습해야 하므로 일반적으로 더 비용이 많이 듦)

c) Fine-tuning provides immediate results with no additional cost, while in-context learning requires significant setup time (세부 조정은 추가 비용 없이 즉각적인 결과를 제공하지만, 맥락 학습은 상당한 설정 시간이 필요함)

d) Fine-tuning does not involve any additional costs compared to in-context learning (세부 조정에는 맥락 학습에 비해 추가 비용이 들지 않음)

155. Which approach to foundation model customization typically incurs the lowest cost for adapting a model to new tasks or domains?
155. 기초 모델을 새로운 작업이나 도메인에 맞게 조정할 때 일반적으로 가장 낮은 비용이 드는 접근 방식은 무엇인가?

a) Pre-training (사전 학습)

b) Fine-tuning (미세 조정)

c) In-context learning (맥락 학습)

d) Retrieval Augmented Generation (RAG) (검색 증강 생성)

156. When implementing Retrieval Augmented Generation (RAG), what is a primary cost consideration?
156. 검색 증강 생성(RAG)을 구현할 때 주요 비용 고려 사항은 무엇인가?

a) Cost of retrieving and storing external data (외부 데이터를 검색하고 저장하는 비용)

b) Cost of model training from scratch (모델을 처음부터 학습하는 비용)

c) Cost of increasing the model's parameter size (모델의 매개변수 크기를 늘리는 비용)

d) Cost of fine-tuning the entire model (모델 전체를 미세 조정하는 비용)

157. What is one major advantage of using agents for multi-step tasks with Amazon Bedrock compared to traditional model training approaches?
157. Amazon Bedrock에서 다중 단계 작업을 위한 에이전트를 사용하는 것이 전통적인 모델 학습 방식에 비해 가지는 주요 이점은 무엇인가?

a) Agents for Amazon Bedrock require no computational resources (Amazon Bedrock용 에이전트는 계산 자원이 필요 없음)

b) Agents can automate complex workflows and manage multiple steps efficiently, reducing the need for custom model training (에이전트는 복잡한 워크플로를 자동화하고 여러 단계를 효율적으로 관리하여 맞춤형 모델 학습의 필요성을 줄임)

c) Agents do not need any form of integration with external systems (에이전트는 외부 시스템과의 통합이 필요 없음)

d) Agents eliminate the need for fine-tuning models (에이전트는 모델 미세 조정의 필요성을 제거함)

158. What is a key factor in evaluating the cost-effectiveness of pre-training a foundation model for a specific domain?
158. 특정 도메인에 맞춘 기초 모델의 사전 학습 비용 효율성을 평가할 때 중요한 요소는 무엇인가?

a) The availability of pre-trained models in the domain (해당 도메인에서 사전 학습된 모델의 가용성)

b) The computational resources and time required for pre-training the model from scratch (모델을 처음부터 사전 학습하는 데 필요한 계산 자원과 시간)

c) The complexity of the model architecture (모델 아키텍처의 복잡성)

d) The need for real-time inference capabilities (실시간 추론 기능의 필요성)

159. Which customization approach for foundation models is most suitable for scenarios where rapid adaptation to new tasks with minimal computational cost is required?
159. 최소한의 계산 비용으로 새로운 작업에 신속히 적응해야 하는 시나리오에 가장 적합한 기초 모델 커스터마이징 접근 방식은 무엇인가?

a) Pre-training (사전 학습)

b) Fine-tuning (미세 조정)

c) In-context learning (맥락 학습)

d) Retrieval Augmented Generation (RAG) (검색 증강 생성)

160. How does the use of agents for multi-step tasks impact the overall cost and efficiency of deploying generative AI solutions?
160. 다중 단계 작업에 에이전트를 사용하는 것이 생성 AI 솔루션의 전체 비용과 효율성에 어떻게 영향을 미치는가?

a) Agents increase costs significantly by requiring custom hardware and extensive training (에이전트는 맞춤형 하드웨어와 광범위한 학습을 요구하여 비용을 크게 증가시킴)

b) Agents can enhance efficiency and reduce overall costs by automating multi-step processes and minimizing the need for custom model development (에이전트는 다중 단계 프로세스를 자동화하고 맞춤형 모델 개발의 필요성을 최소화하여 효율성을 높이고 전체 비용을 줄일 수 있음)

c) Agents provide no cost benefits compared to traditional model approaches (에이전트는 전통적인 모델 접근 방식에 비해 비용 혜택을 제공하지 않음)

d) Agents only impact efficiency, with no effect on overall costs (에이전트는 효율성에만 영향을 미치며, 전체 비용에는 영향을 미치지 않음)

161. Which factor primarily influences the decision to use fine-tuning over in-context learning for foundation model customization?
161. 기초 모델 커스터마이징에서 맥락 학습 대신 미세 조정을 선택하는 결정에 주로 영향을 미치는 요소는 무엇인가?

a) The amount of domain-specific data available for adaptation (적응을 위한 도메인 특화 데이터의 양)

b) The cost of storing external data (외부 데이터 저장 비용)

c) The speed of model inference (모델 추론 속도)

d) The ease of integrating with existing systems (기존 시스템과의 통합 용이성)

162. What is a primary consideration when choosing Retrieval Augmented Generation (RAG) for a business application?
162. 비즈니스 애플리케이션에서 Retrieval Augmented Generation (RAG)을 선택할 때 주요 고려 사항은 무엇인가?

a) The cost of integrating retrieval mechanisms with the generative model (생성 모델과의 검색 메커니즘 통합 비용)

b) The need for extensive model retraining (광범위한 모델 재훈련의 필요성)

c) The computational power required for generating responses (응답 생성에 필요한 계산 능력)

d) The ability to handle real-time user interactions (실시간 사용자 상호작용을 처리할 수 있는 능력)

163. What benefit does Amazon Bedrock provide for managing complex multi-step tasks in generative AI applications?
163. Amazon Bedrock이 생성 AI 애플리케이션에서 복잡한 다단계 작업을 관리하는 데 제공하는 이점은 무엇인가?

a) It requires no training data (훈련 데이터가 필요 없음)

b) It automates the entire model training process (모델 훈련 과정을 자동화함)

c) It provides a framework for designing and deploying agents that handle multi-step tasks, improving operational efficiency (다단계 작업을 처리하는 프레임워크를 제공하여 운영 효율성을 높임)

d) It eliminates the need for any form of model evaluation (모든 형태의 모델 평가가 불필요함)

164. Which of the following best describes the role of "context" in prompt engineering?
164. 프롬프트 엔지니어링에서 "컨텍스트"의 역할을 가장 잘 설명하는 것은 무엇인가?

a) Context refers to the explicit instructions provided to the model to guide its responses (컨텍스트는 모델의 응답을 안내하기 위해 제공된 명확한 지침을 의미한다.)

b) Context involves the surrounding text or information that influences how the model interprets the prompt (컨텍스트는 모델이 프롬프트를 해석하는 데 영향을 미치는 주변 텍스트나 정보를 의미한다.)

c) Context is the model's ability to generate creative content based on minimal input (컨텍스트는 최소한의 입력으로 모델이 창의적인 콘텐츠를 생성하는 능력을 의미한다.)

d) Context is the initial setup required to train the model (컨텍스트는 모델을 훈련시키기 위해 필요한 초기 설정을 의미한다.)

165. Which technique in prompt engineering involves providing the model with a series of related prompts to guide its reasoning?

165. 프롬프트 엔지니어링에서 모델에게 일련의 관련된 프롬프트를 제공하여 논리적 추론을 유도하는 기술은 무엇인가?

a) Zero-shot (제로샷)
b) Few-shot (퓨샷)
c) Chain-of-thought (연쇄 사고)
d) Prompt templates (프롬프트 템플릿)

166. What is the primary benefit of using prompt templates in prompt engineering?
166. 프롬프트 엔지니어링에서 프롬프트 템플릿을 사용하는 주요 이점은 무엇인가?

a) They ensure the model's responses are always in a random format (모델의 응답이 항상 무작위 형식이 되도록 보장)
b) They simplify the prompt creation process by providing a structured format for consistent results (일관된 결과를 위한 구조화된 형식을 제공하여 프롬프트 작성 과정 단순화)
c) They increase the complexity of the prompts to enhance response creativity (응답의 창의성을 높이기 위해 프롬프트의 복잡성 증가)
d) They eliminate the need for context in generating responses (응답 생성에서 컨텍스트의 필요성을 제거)

167. What is a common practice to improve response quality in prompt engineering?
167. 프롬프트 엔지니어링에서 응답 품질을 향상시키기 위한 일반적인 방법은 무엇인가?

a) Using overly complex language in prompts (프롬프트에 지나치게 복잡한 언어를 사용하는 것)
b) Providing excessive information without relevance (관련 없는 과도한 정보를 제공하는 것)
c) Incorporating multiple comments and feedback loops (여러 개의 코멘트와 피드백 루프를 포함하는 것)
d) Ignoring the specific requirements of the task (작업의 구체적인 요구 사항을 무시하는 것)

168. Which of the following describes a "negative prompt" in prompt engineering?
168. 다음 중 프롬프트 엔지니어링에서 "부정적 프롬프트"를 설명하는 것은 무엇인가?

a) A prompt that contains errors and is likely to produce inaccurate responses (오류를 포함하고 부정확한 응답을 생성할 가능성이 있는 프롬프트)
b) A prompt that explicitly instructs the model to avoid certain topics or responses (특정 주제나 응답을 피하도록 명확히 지시하는 프롬프트)
c) A prompt that uses overly complex language to challenge the model (모델에 도전하도록 지나치게 복잡한 언어를 사용하는 프롬프트)
d) A prompt designed to generate creative and diverse outputs (창의적이고 다양한 출력을 생성하도록 설계된 프롬프트)

169. What is a potential risk of prompt engineering known as "jailbreaking"?
169. "탈옥"으로 알려진 프롬프트 엔지니어링의 잠재적 위험은 무엇인가?

a) It involves intentionally corrupting the training data to affect the model's performance (의도적으로 훈련 데이터를 손상시켜 모델의 성능에 영향을 미치는 것)

b) It refers to unauthorized manipulation of the model to produce responses that bypass safety measures and ethical guidelines (모델을 무단으로 조작하여 안전 조치와 윤리 지침을 우회하는 응답을 생성하게 하는 것)

c) It leads to the model generating random outputs due to lack of context (컨텍스트 부족으로 인해 모델이 무작위 출력을 생성하게 하는 것)

d) It is the use of prompt templates to ensure consistency in responses (응답의 일관성을 보장하기 위해 프롬프트 템플릿을 사용하는 것)

170. What is the main purpose of using "chain-of-thought" prompting in complex tasks?
170. 복잡한 작업에서 "연쇄 사고" 프롬프트를 사용하는 주요 목적은 무엇인가?

a) To generate responses based on previous outputs without additional context (추가 컨텍스트 없이 이전 출력에 기반하여 응답을 생성하기)

b) To guide the model through a sequence of logical steps to reach a final answer (모델이 최종 답변에 도달하도록 논리적 단계의 순서를 안내하기)

c) To produce random and creative outputs for brainstorming sessions (브레인스토밍 세션을 위해 무작위적이고 창의적인 출력을 생성하기)

d) To simplify the model's understanding of individual prompts (각각의 프롬프트에 대한 모델의 이해를 단순화하기)

171. Which prompt engineering technique involves providing a few examples of the desired input-output pairs to help the model understand the task?
171. 프롬프트 엔지니어링에서 원하는 입력-출력 쌍의 몇 가지 예시를 제공하여 모델이 작업을 이해하도록 돕는 기술은 무엇인가?

a) Zero-shot (제로샷)

b) Few-shot (퓨샷)

c) Single-shot (단일샷)

d) Chain-of-thought (연쇄 사고)

172. What is a key risk associated with "poisoning" in prompt engineering?
172. 프롬프트 엔지니어링에서 "포이즈닝"과 관련된 주요 위험은 무엇인가?

a) It refers to the model generating overly verbose responses (모델이 지나치게 장황한 응답을 생성하는 것을 의미한다)

b) It involves maliciously introducing biased or harmful data into the training process to negatively impact the model's behavior (모델의 행동에 부정적인 영향을 주기 위해 편향되거나 유해한 데이터를 악의적으로 훈련 과정에 도입하는 것)

c) It results in the model producing irrelevant outputs due to lack of context (컨텍스트 부족으로 인해 모델이 관련 없는 출력을 생성하게 되는 것)

d) It is the practice of using too many examples in prompt templates (프롬프트 템플릿에 너무 많은 예시를 사용하는 것)

173. What is a key advantage of using "prompt templates" in a production environment?
173. 프로덕션 환경에서 "프롬프트 템플릿"을 사용하는 주요 이점은 무엇인가?

a) They allow for more random and less predictable responses (더 랜덤하고 예측 불가능한 응답을 생성)

b) They ensure consistent and repeatable responses across similar prompts (유사한 프롬프트에 대해 일관되고 반복 가능한 응답을 보장)

c) They increase the model's creativity by varying prompt formats (프롬프트 형식을 다양하게 하여 모델의 창의성 향상)

d) They reduce the need for prompt optimization in different scenarios (다양한 시나리오에서 프롬프트 최적화의 필요성을 낮춤)

174. What is the primary function of "model latent space" in prompt engineering?
174. 프롬프트 엔지니어링에서 "모델 잠재공간"의 주요 기능은 무엇인가?

a) They allow for more random and less predictable responses (더 랜덤하고 예측 불가능한 응답을 생성)

b) They ensure consistent and repeatable responses across similar prompts (유사한 프롬프트에 대해 일관되고 반복 가능한 응답을 보장)

c) They increase the model's creativity by varying prompt formats (프롬프트 형식을 다양하게 하여 모델의 창의성 향상)

d) They reduce the need for prompt optimization in different scenarios (다양한 시나리오에서 프롬프트 최적화의 필요성을 낮춤)

175. In prompt engineering, what is the purpose of "zero-shot" prompting?
175. 프롬프트 엔지니어링에서 "제로샷" 프롬프트의 목적은 무엇인가?

a) To provide the model with multiple examples to learn from. (여러 학습 예시 제공)

b) To generate responses based on a prompt without any prior examples or additional context. (사전 예시나 추가 맥락 없이 응답 생성)

c) To iteratively refine prompts based on feedback. (피드백을 바탕으로 프롬프트 반복 개선)

d) To guide the model through a series of related prompts. (관련된 프롬프트 시리즈 안내)

176. How does "in-context learning" differ from traditional fine-tuning in prompt engineering?

176. 프롬프트 엔지니어링에서 "맥락 학습"은 기존의 미세 조정과 어떻게 다른가?

a) In-context learning involves training the model from scratch with new data while fine-tuning adjusts existing models (새 데이터로 처음부터 모델 훈련)

b) In-context learning adapts the model's responses based on prompt examples provided during inference while fine-tuning adjusts the model's weights through additional training (추론 시 제공된 프롬프트 예시로 모델 응답 조정)

c) In-context learning requires no additional data, while fine-tuning involves extensive data preparation (추가 데이터 없이 학습)

d) In-context learning and fine-tuning are identical in practice (실제로 동일하게 작동)

177. What is a significant risk associated with "hijacking" in prompt engineering?
177. 프롬프트 엔지니어링에서 "하이재킹"과 관련된 주요 위험은 무엇인가?

a) It involves the model producing overly verbose outputs (장황한 출력 생성)

b) It refers to unauthorized manipulation of the model to produce responses that bypass safety measures or produce inappropriate content (안전 조치 우회 및 부적절한 콘텐츠 생성)

c) It leads to the model generating random outputs due to lack of context (맥락 부족으로 무작위 출력 생성)

d) It is the use of prompt templates to ensure consistency in responses (일관성 보장용 프롬프트 템플릿 사용)

178. Which of the following is a best practice for ensuring high-quality responses in prompt engineering?
178. 프롬프트 엔지니어링에서 고품질 응답을 보장하기 위한 모범 사례는 무엇인가?

a) Using overly general prompts to maximize creativity (일반적인 프롬프트 사용)

b) Limiting the use of context to avoid confusion (맥락 사용 제한)

c) Experimenting with various prompt styles and structures to find the most effective approach (다양한 스타일 및 구조 실험)

d) Avoiding feedback loops to prevent model bias (피드백 루프 방지)

179. In the context of prompt engineering, what is "response quality improvement"?
179. 프롬프트 엔지니어링에서 "응답 품질 개선"이란 무엇인가?

a) Modifying the model's architecture to enhance performance (모델 구조 수정)

b) Adjusting the prompt to generate more accurate and relevant responses (정확하고 관련성 높은 응답 생성)

c) Increasing the model's training data to improve its capabilities (훈련 데이터 증가)

d) Applying advanced algorithms to refine the model's output (고급 알고리즘 적용)

180. What does "negative prompt engineering" aim to achieve?
180. "네거티브 프롬프트 엔지니어링"의 목표는 무엇인가?

a) To encourage the model to generate more creative outputs (창의적 출력 생성 유도)

b) To instruct the model to avoid generating certain types of content or responses (특정 콘텐츠나 응답 생성 방지)

c) To provide the model with additional context to enhance its understanding (이해력 향상 위한 추가 맥락 제공)

d) To generate responses based on minimal input (최소 입력 기반 응답 생성)

181. Which technique involves providing the model with a single example to improve response accuracy?
181. 모델의 응답 정확성을 높이기 위해 단일 예시를 제공하는 기술은 무엇인가?

a) Chain-of-thought (연쇄 사고)

b) Zero-shot (제로샷)

c) Single-shot (단일샷)

d) Few-shot (소수샷)

182. What is "prompt poisoning," and how does it impact the model?
182. "프롬프트 중독"이란 무엇이며, 모델에 어떤 영향을 미치는가?

a) It is the practice of using too many examples in prompt templates, which can overwhelm the model (과다한 예시 사용으로 모델 과부하)

b) It involves deliberately introducing misleading or biased prompts to corrupt the model's outputs and degrade its performance (오해의 소지가 있거나 편향된 프롬프트 도입으로 성능 저하)

c) It refers to using overly complex prompts to challenge the model's capabilities (복잡한 프롬프트 사용)

d) It is the process of removing context from prompts to simplify the responses (맥락 제거로 응답 단순화)

183. What is a key advantage of "few-shot" prompting over "zero-shot" prompting?
183. "제로샷" 프롬프트보다 "소수샷" 프롬프트의 주요 이점은 무엇인가?

a) Few-shot prompting provides no examples, making it more versatile (예시 없음으로 더 유연)

b) Few-shot prompting helps the model better understand the task by providing a few examples, improving accuracy compared to zero-shot prompting (소수 예시 제공으로 정확성 향상)

c) Few-shot prompting requires more training data than zero-shot prompting (더 많은 훈련 데이터 필요)

d) Few-shot prompting is less effective than zero-shot prompting in generating high-quality responses (고품질 응답 생성에 비효율적)

184. What is the primary purpose of "pre-training" a foundation model?
184. 기초 모델의 "사전 학습" 주요 목적은 무엇인가?

a) To adapt the model to specific domain requirements (모델을 특정 도메인 요구에 맞춤)

b) To provide the model with general knowledge and capabilities before fine-tuning specialized tasks (모델에 일반적인 지식과 능력을 제공하여 세부 작업을 위한 미세 조정 전 준비)

c) To optimize the model for real-time performance (실시간 성능 최적화)

d) To ensure the model can handle large-scale data sets (대규모 데이터 세트 처리 가능 보장)

185. In the context of fine-tuning foundation models, what does "instruction tuning" focus on?
185. 기초 모델의 미세 조정에서 "지시 튜닝"이 집중하는 것은 무엇인가?

a) Providing the model with examples of correct outputs for specific tasks (특정 작업에 대한 올바른 출력 예시 제공)

b) Adjusting the model to follow specific instructions or guidelines for task performance (작업 수행을 위한 특정 지시 또는 지침에 맞게 모델 조정)

c) Continuously training the model with new data from user interactions (사용자 상호작용의 새 데이터를 통한 모델 지속적 학습)

d) Adapting the model to handle a broader range of domains (더 넓은 범위의 도메인 처리에 모델 적응)

186. What is a key aspect of "continuous pre-training" for foundation models?
186. 기초 모델의 "지속적 사전 학습"에서 중요한 측면은 무엇인가?

a) Updating the model periodically with new data to keep it relevant and accurate (모델의 적절성과 정확성 유지를 위한 정기적 새 데이터 업데이트)

b) Adapting the model to new domains by applying transfer learning techniques (전이 학습 기법을 적용하여 새로운 도메인에 모델 적응)

c) Fine-tuning the model for specific tasks immediately after pre-training (사전 학습 후 특정 작업에 대해 모델 미세 조정)

d) Applying reinforcement learning to improve the model's responses (모델 응답 개선을 위한 강화 학습 적용)

187. Which data preparation step ensures that the data used for fine-tuning a foundation model is representative of the tasks the model will perform?
187. 기초 모델 미세 조정에 사용되는 데이터가 모델이 수행할 작업을 대표하도록 보장하는 데이터 준비 단계는 무엇인가?

a) Data curation (데이터 큐레이션)

b) Data labeling (데이터 라벨링)

c) Data governance (데이터 관리)

d) Data representativeness (데이터 대표성)

188. How does "reinforcement learning from human feedback" (RLHF) contribute to fine-tuning foundation models?
188. "인간 피드백을 통한 강화 학습"(RLHF)이 기초 모델의 미세 조정에 어떻게 기여하는가?

a) By generating synthetic data for training the model (모델 훈련을 위한 합성 데이터 생성)

b) By using human feedback to improve model responses and align them with user expectations (인간 피드백을 사용하여 모델 응답 개선 및 사용자 기대에 맞춤)

c) By applying transfer learning techniques to expand the model's domain coverage (모델의 도메인 적용 범위를 확장하기 위한 전이 학습 기법 적용)

d) By limiting model responses to avoid ethical issues (윤리적 문제를 피하기 위해 모델 응답 제한)

189. What role does "data curation" play in preparing data for fine-tuning a foundation model?
189. 기초 모델 미세 조정을 위한 데이터 준비에서 "데이터 큐레이션"의 역할은 무엇인가?

a) Ensuring that the data is appropriately labeled for supervised learning tasks (지도 학습 작업에 적절히 라벨링된 데이터 보장)

b) Selecting and organizing data to ensure quality and relevance for the model's training objectives (모델의 훈련 목표에 맞는 품질과 관련성을 보장하기 위한 데이터 선택 및 조직)

c) Implementing continuous pre-training to update the model with new data (모델을 최신 데이터로 업데이트하기 위한 지속적 사전 학습 구현)

d) Applying governance policies to manage data privacy and security (데이터 프라이버시 및 보안을 관리하기 위한 거버넌스 정책 적용)

190. Which technique involves adjusting a model to apply its learned knowledge to new but related tasks?
190. 학습된 지식을 새롭지만 관련된 작업에 적용하기 위해 모델을 조정하는 기법은 무엇인가?

a) Instruction tuning (지시 튜닝)

b) Transfer learning (전이 학습)

c) Continuous pre-training (지속적 사전 학습)

d) Reinforcement learning from human feedback (RLHF) (인간 피드백을 통한 강화 학습)

191. In foundation model fine-tuning, what is the significance of "data labeling"?
191. 기초 모델 미세 조정에서 "데이터 라벨링"의 중요성은 무엇인가?

a) It provides data for continuous pre-training (지속적 사전 학습을 위한 데이터 제공)

b) It ensures data quality by removing irrelevant information (관련 없는 정보를 제거하여 데이터 품질 보장)

c) It assigns labels to data to enable supervised learning tasks and guide model training (지도 학습 작업을 가능하게 하고 모델 훈련을 안내하기 위해 데이터에 라벨 할당)

d) It creates synthetic data for augmenting training sets (훈련 세트 증대를 위한 합성 데이터 생성)

192. What is the main difference between "fine-tuning" and "continuous pre-training" in the context of foundation models?
192. 기초 모델에서 "미세 조정"과 "연속 사전 학습"의 주요 차이점은 무엇인가?

a) Fine-tuning adapts the model to specific tasks, while continuous pre-training updates the model with new data over time (미세 조정은 특정 작업에 모델을 적응시키는 반면, 연속 사전 학습은 새로운 데이터로 모델을 지속적으로 업데이트)

b) Fine-tuning updates the model with new data, while continuous pre-training adapts the model to specific tasks (미세 조정은 새로운 데이터로 모델을 업데이트하고, 연속 사전 학습은 모델을 특정 작업에 적응)

c) Fine-tuning and continuous pre-training are identical processes (미세 조정과 연속 사전 학습은 동일한 과정)

d) Fine-tuning involves using reinforcement learning, while continuous pre-training does not (미세 조정은 강화 학습을 포함하며, 연속 사전 학습은 그렇지 않음)

193. Which approach is best for assessing the performance of a foundation model in a way that incorporates human judgment and qualitative feedback?
193. 사람의 판단과 질적 피드백을 포함하는 방식으로 기초 모델의 성능을 평가하는 데 가장 적합한 접근 방식은 무엇인가?

a) Benchmark datasets (벤치마크 데이터셋)

b) Human evaluation (인간 평가)

c) Automated metrics (자동화된 지표)

d) Cross-validation (교차 검증)

194. Which metric is commonly used to evaluate the quality of generated text in natural language processing (NLP) tasks by comparing the generated output with reference texts?
194. 생성된 텍스트의 품질을 참조 텍스트와 비교하여 평가하는 데 일반적으로 사용되는 자연어 처리(NLP) 작업의 지표는 무엇인가?

a) ROUGE (루즈)

b) BLEU (블루)

c) BERTScore (버트스코어)

d) F1 Score (F1 점수)

195. What is the primary use of ROUGE (Recall-Oriented Understudy for Gisting Evaluation) in evaluating foundation models?
195. 기초 모델을 평가할 때 ROUGE(요약 평가를 위한 리콜 지향 지표)의 주요 용도는 무엇인가?

a) Measuring the accuracy of text classification tasks (텍스트 분류 작업의 정확도 측정)

b) Evaluating the quality of generated text by comparing it with reference summaries (참조 요약과 비교하여 생성된 텍스트의 품질 평가)

c) Assessing the model's performance in real-time applications (실시간 응용 프로그램에서 모델 성능 평가)

d) Calculating the model's precision in image classification tasks (이미지 분류 작업에서 모델의 정밀도 계산)

196. Which metric measures the semantic similarity between the generated text and reference text by considering contextual embeddings rather than exact word matches?

196. 정확한 단어 일치를 고려하는 대신, 문맥적 임베딩을 사용하여 생성된 텍스트와 참조 텍스트 간의 의미적 유사성을 측정하는 지표는 무엇인가?

a) ROUGE (루즈)

b) BLEU (블루)

c) BERTScore (버트스코어)

d) Precision (정밀도)

197. When evaluating whether a foundation model effectively meets business objectives, which of the following metrics would be least relevant?

197. 기초 모델이 비즈니스 목표를 효과적으로 충족하는지 평가할 때 가장 관련성이 낮은 지표는 무엇인가?

a) Productivity (생산성)

b) User engagement (사용자 참여)

c) Task engineering (작업 엔지니어링)

d) Model training time (모델 학습 시간)

198. Which method involves using a set of pre-defined tasks and data to benchmark and compare the performance of different foundation models?

198. 미리 정의된 작업과 데이터를 사용하여 다양한 기초 모델의 성능을 벤치마크하고 비교하는 방법은 무엇인가?

a) Human evaluation (인간 평가)

b) Benchmark datasets (벤치마크 데이터셋)

c) Real-time user feedback (실시간 사용자 피드백)

d) Model adaptation (모델 적응)

199. Which of the following is not a direct metric for evaluating the performance of foundation models in NLP tasks?

199. 다음 중 NLP 작업에서 기초 모델의 성능을 평가하는 직접적인 지표가 아닌 것은 무엇인가?

a) ROUGE (루즈)

b) BLEU (블루)

c) BERTScore (버트스코어)

d) Click-through rate (CTR: 클릭률)

200. In the context of evaluating foundation models, which of the following best describes "task engineering"?
200. 기초 모델을 평가하는 맥락에서, "작업 엔지니어링"을 가장 잘 설명하는 것은 무엇인가?

a) Measuring how well the model handles different types of data (모델이 다양한 데이터 유형을 얼마나 잘 처리하는지 측정)

b) Assessing the model's performance in completing specific business tasks (특정 비즈니스 작업을 수행하는 모델의 성능 평가)

c) Evaluating the model's ability to generate human-like text (모델이 인간 같은 텍스트를 생성하는 능력 평가)

d) Analyzing the model's computational efficiency (모델의 계산 효율성 분석)

201. Which evaluation approach is useful for understanding how a model's outputs align with human expectations in real-world scenarios?
201. 실제 시나리오에서 모델의 출력이 인간의 기대와 어떻게 일치하는지 이해하는 데 유용한 평가 접근법은 무엇인가?

a) Automated metrics (자동화된 메트릭)

b) Cross-validation (교차 검증)

c) Human evaluation (인간 평가)

d) Benchmark datasets (벤치마크 데이터셋)

202. Which of the following features of responsible AI is concerned with ensuring that AI models operate consistently across various demographic groups without unfair advantages or disadvantages?
202. 책임 있는 AI의 다음 특징 중 AI 모델이 다양한 인구 그룹에서 일관되게 작동하고 불공정한 유불리가 없도록 보장하는 데 관련 있는 것은 무엇인가?

a) Robustness (강건성)

b) Fairness (공정성)

c) Inclusivity (포용성)

d) Safety (안전성)

203. What is the primary purpose of using Guardrails for Amazon Bedrock in the context of responsible AI?
203. 책임 있는 AI의 맥락에서 Amazon Bedrock의 Guardrails 사용의 주요 목적은 무엇인가?

a) To improve model training speed (모델 학습 속도 향상)

b) To identify and mitigate bias in AI models (AI 모델의 편향 식별 및 완화)

c) To enhance the transparency of AI decision-making processes (AI 의사 결정 과정의 투명성 향상)

d) To ensure model interpretability for end-users (최종 사용자에게 모델 해석 가능성 보장)

204. When selecting an AI model, which responsible practice focuses on minimizing the environmental impact and promoting sustainability?
204. AI 모델을 선택할 때 환경 영향을 최소화하고 지속 가능성을 촉진하는 데 중점을 두는 책임 있는 관행은 무엇인가?

a) Data diversity (데이터 다양성)

b) Model robustness (모델 강건성)

c) Environmental considerations (환경적 고려)

d) Fairness (공정성)

205. Which legal risk associated with generative AI involves the potential for a model to produce outputs that infringe upon existing intellectual property rights?
205. 생성형 AI와 관련된 법적 위험 중 기존 지적 재산권을 침해할 수 있는 출력을 생성할 가능성이 있는 것은 무엇인가?

a) Biased model outputs (편향된 모델 출력)

b) Intellectual property infringement claims (지적 재산권 침해 주장)

c) Loss of customer trust (고객 신뢰 상실)

d) Hallucinations (환각)

206. Which characteristic of datasets ensures that they are representative of all relevant demographic and social groups to avoid biased outcomes?
206. 데이터셋의 어떤 특성이 모든 관련 인구 및 사회 그룹을 대표하여 편향된 결과를 피하도록 보장하는가?

a) Inclusivity (포용성)

b) Curated data sources (선별된 데이터 출처)

c) Balanced datasets (균형 잡힌 데이터셋)

d) Diversity (다양성)

207. How does bias affect AI models, and which issue is related to overfitting due to the model's excessive complexity?
207. 편향이 AI 모델에 어떤 영향을 미치며, 모델의 과도한 복잡성으로 인한 과적합과 관련된 문제는 무엇인가?

a) Bias affects demographic groups; overfitting is related to variance (편향은 인구 그룹에 영향을 미치며, 과적합은 분산과 관련이 있음)

b) Bias affects accuracy; variance affects generalization (편향은 정확도에 영향을 미치고, 분산은 일반화에 영향을 미침)

c) Bias affects trustworthiness; overfitting affects robustness (편향은 신뢰성에 영향을 미치고, 과적합은 강건성에 영향을 미침)

d) Bias affects robustness; variance affects model complexity (편향은 강건성에 영향을 미치고, 분산은 모델 복잡성에 영향을 미침)

208. Which tool or technique helps in analyzing label quality to detect and monitor bias and truthfulness in AI models?
208. AI 모델에서 편향과 진실성을 감지하고 모니터링하기 위해 라벨 품질을 분석하는 도구나 기술은 무엇인가?

a) Amazon SageMaker Clarify (아마존 SageMaker Clarify)

b) Human audits (인간 감사)

c) Subgroup analysis (하위 그룹 분석)

d) Amazon Augmented AI (Amazon A2I) (아마존 증강 AI)

209. Which AWS service is used for human-in-the-loop review to ensure the trustworthiness and ethical use of AI models?
209. AI 모델의 신뢰성과 윤리적 사용을 보장하기 위해 사람의 개입을 통한 검토에 사용되는 AWS 서비스는 무엇인가?

a) Amazon SageMaker Clarify (아마존 세이지메이커 클래리파이)

b) Amazon Augmented AI (아마존 증강 AI)

c) Amazon SageMaker Model Monitor (아마존 세이지메이커 모델 모니터)

d) Amazon Comprehend (아마존 컴프리헨드)

210. Which responsible AI feature is concerned with ensuring that AI models are resilient to adversarial attacks and perform reliably in various scenarios?
210. AI 모델이 적대적 공격에 견고하고 다양한 시나리오에서 신뢰성 있게 작동하도록 보장하는 책임 있는 AI 기능은 무엇인가?

a) Fairness (공정성)

b) Inclusivity (포용성)

c) Robustness (강건성)

d) Veracity (진실성)

211. Which of the following best describes a transparent model in the context of AI?
211. AI의 맥락에서 투명한 모델을 가장 잘 설명하는 것은 무엇인가?

a) A model that provides clear insights into how its internal decision-making processes work (내부 의사 결정 과정이 작동하는 방식을 명확히 보여주는 모델)

b) A model that produces results without the need for user input (사용자 입력 없이 결과를 생성하는 모델)

c) A model that offers high performance but lacks interpretability (높은 성능을 제공하지만 해석 가능성이 낮은 모델)

d) A model that operates in real-time environments without any delay (지연 없이 실시간 환경에서 작동하는 모델)

212. What is a key characteristic of a model that is considered explainable but not necessarily transparent?
212. 설명 가능하지만 반드시 투명하지는 않은 모델의 주요 특징은 무엇인가?

a) It provides detailed information about its internal algorithms and data handling (내부 알고리즘과 데이터 처리에 대한 자세한 정보를 제공)

b) It allows users to understand its decisions through post-hoc explanations (사후 설명을 통해 결정 내용을 사용자에게 이해시킴)

c) It operates without requiring any data preprocessing (데이터 전처리 없이 작동)

d) It can adapt to new tasks without additional training (추가 학습 없이 새로운 작업에 적응 가능)

213. Which tool helps in providing a comprehensive overview of a model's behavior, including its strengths and limitations?
213. 모델의 강점과 한계를 포함한 행동을 포괄적으로 개요하는 데 도움이 되는 도구는 무엇인가?

a) Amazon SageMaker Model Cards (아마존 세이지메이커 모델 카드)

b) Open-source model repositories (오픈 소스 모델 저장소)

c) Data governance frameworks (데이터 거버넌스 프레임워크)

d) Licensing agreements (라이선스 계약)

214. What is the primary benefit of using open-source models when assessing transparency and explainability?
214. 투명성과 설명 가능성을 평가할 때 오픈 소스 모델을 사용하는 주요 이점은 무엇인가?

a) They are always free to use and modify (항상 무료로 사용 및 수정 가능)

b) They offer detailed documentation and community insights on model behavior (모델 행동에 대한 자세한 문서와 커뮤니티 통찰 제공)

c) They guarantee high performance across all tasks (모든 작업에서 높은 성능 보장)

d) They require less computational power for deployment (배포에 적은 계산 능력 필요)

215. Which of the following trade-offs is often encountered between model safety and transparency?
215. 모델 안전성과 투명성 간에 자주 발생하는 트레이드오프는 무엇인가?

a) Increasing transparency usually reduces model performance (투명성을 높이면 모델 성능이 감소)

b) Ensuring safety often requires complex models that are less interpretable (안전을 보장하려면 해석하기 어려운 복잡한 모델이 필요)

c) Models with high transparency always have better safety features (투명성이 높은 모델은 항상 더 나은 안전 기능을 갖춤)

d) Safety and transparency are mutually exclusive and cannot be balanced (안전성과 투명성은 상호 배타적

이며 균형을 맞출 수 없음)

216. When balancing model interpretability and performance, what is a common approach to mitigate the trade-offs?
216. 모델 해석 가능성과 성능 간 균형을 맞출 때 트레이드오프를 완화하기 위한 일반적인 접근 방식은 무엇인가?

a) Use only transparent models regardless of their performance (성능에 상관없이 투명한 모델만 사용)

b) Employ techniques that provide post-hoc explanations while maintaining high performance (고성능을 유지하면서 사후 설명을 제공하는 기법을 사용)

c) Focus solely on enhancing model performance at the expense of interpretability (해석 가능성을 희생하여 모델 성능 향상에만 집중)

d) Limit the scope of the model to ensure it remains highly interpretable (모델의 범위를 제한하여 높은 해석 가능성을 유지)

217. Which principle of human-centered design ensures that AI models are understandable and usable by end-users?
217. 인간 중심 설계 원칙 중 AI 모델이 최종 사용자가 이해하고 사용할 수 있도록 보장하는 것은 무엇인가?

a) User feedback integration (사용자 피드백 통합)

b) Data privacy (데이터 프라이버시)

c) Computational efficiency (계산 효율성)

d) Model complexity reduction (모델 복잡성 감소)

218. What is a key consideration when designing explainable AI systems to ensure they meet human-centered design principles?
218. 설명 가능한 AI 시스템을 설계할 때 인간 중심 설계 원칙을 충족하기 위해 고려해야 할 주요 사항은 무엇인가?

a) Ensuring the AI system has the lowest possible cost (AI 시스템의 비용을 가능한 낮게 유지)

b) Providing clear and actionable explanations for AI decisions (AI 결정에 대한 명확하고 실행 가능한 설명 제공)

c) Limiting the AI system's functionality to reduce complexity (AI 시스템의 기능을 제한하여 복잡성 줄임)

d) Maximizing the computational resources used by the AI system (AI 시스템이 사용하는 계산 자원 최대화)

219. A company has thousands of customer support interactions per day and wants to analyze these interactions to identify frequently asked questions and develop insights. Which AWS service can the company use to meet this requirement?
219. 하루에 수천 건의 고객 지원 상호 작용이 발생하는 회사가 자주 묻는 질문을 파악하고 인사이트를 얻기 위해 이 상호 작용을 분석하고자 할 때 사용할 수 있는 AWS 서비스는 무엇인가?

a) Ensuring the AI system has the lowest possible cost (AI 시스템의 비용을 가능한 낮게 유지)

b) Providing clear and actionable explanations for AI decisions (AI 결정에 대한 명확하고 실행 가능한 설명 제공)

c) Limiting the AI system's functionality to reduce complexity (AI 시스템의 기능을 제한하여 복잡성 줄임)

d) Maximizing the computational resources used by the AI system (AI 시스템이 사용하는 계산 자원 최대화)

220. A company has a database of petabytes of unstructured data from internal sources. The company wants to transform this data into a structured format so that its data scientists can perform machine learning (ML) tasks. Which service will meet these requirements?

220. 회사가 내부 소스에서 수집한 페타바이트 단위의 비정형 데이터를 보유하고 있으며, 이를 구조화된 형식으로 변환하여 데이터 과학자가 머신 러닝(ML) 작업을 수행할 수 있도록 하려 한다. 이러한 요구 사항을 충족할 수 있는 서비스는 무엇인가?

a) Amazon Lex (아마존 렉스)

b) Amazon Comprehend (아마존 컴프리헨드)

c) Amazon Transcribe (아마존 트랜스크라이브)

d) Amazon Translate (아마존 트랜스레이트)

221. Which AWS service or feature can help an AI development team quickly deploy and consume a foundation model (FM) within the team's VPC?

221. AI 개발 팀이 팀의 VPC 내에서 기초 모델(FM)을 빠르게 배포하고 사용할 수 있도록 돕는 AWS 서비스 또는 기능은 무엇인가?

a) Amazon Personalize (아마존 퍼스널라이즈)

b) Amazon SageMaker JumpStart (아마존 세이지메이커 점프스타트)

c) PartyRock, an Amazon Bedrock Playground (파티록, 아마존 베드록 플레이그라운드)

d) Amazon SageMaker endpoints (아마존 세이지메이커 엔드포인트)

222. A company wants to use a large language model (LLM) on Amazon Bedrock for sentiment analysis. The company wants to classify the sentiment of text passages as positive or negative. Which prompt engineering strategy meets these requirements?

222. 한 회사가 아마존 베드록에서 대형 언어 모델(LLM)을 사용하여 감성 분석을 수행하려고 합니다. 회사는 텍스트 문장의 감성을 긍정 또는 부정으로 분류하고자 합니다. 이 요구 사항을 충족하는 프롬프트 엔지니어링 전략은 무엇인가?

a) Provide examples of text passages with corresponding positive or negative labels in the prompt followed by the new text passage to be classified (프롬프트에 긍정 또는 부정 레이블이 포함된 텍스트 예시를 제공하고 분류할 새 텍스트 문장을 추가)

b) Provide a detailed explanation of sentiment analysis and how LLMs work in the prompt (프롬프트에 감성 분석과 LLM의 작동 방식에 대한 자세한 설명을 제공)

c) Provide the new text passage to be classified without any additional context or examples (추가적인 맥락이나 예시 없이 분류할 새 텍스트 문장을 제공)

d) Provide the new text passage with a few examples of unrelated tasks, such as text summarization or question answering (텍스트 요약 또는 질문 답변과 같은 관련 없는 작업의 예시와 함께 새 텍스트 문장을 제공)

223. A company has installed a security camera. The company uses an ML model to evaluate the security camera footage for potential thefts. The company has discovered that the model disproportionately flags people who are members of a specific ethnic group. Which type of bias is affecting the model output?

223. 한 회사가 보안 카메라를 설치했습니다. 회사는 보안 카메라 영상을 평가하기 위해 ML 모델을 사용하고 있으며 잠재적인 절도 행위를 탐지합니다. 회사는 모델이 특정 민족 그룹의 사람들을 불균형적으로 표시하고 있음을 발견했습니다. 모델 출력에 영향을 미치는 편향 유형은 무엇인가?

a) Measurement bias (측정 편향)

b) Sampling bias (표본 편향)

c) Observer bias (관찰자 편향)

d) Confirmation bias (확증 편향)

224. A company wants to make a chatbot to help customers. The chatbot will help solve technical problems without human intervention. The company chose a foundation model (FM) for the chatbot. The chatbot needs to produce responses that adhere to the company's tone. Which solution meets these requirements?

224. 한 회사가 고객을 돕기 위해 챗봇을 만들고자 합니다. 챗봇은 인간의 개입 없이 기술적 문제를 해결하도록 도울 것입니다. 회사는 챗봇을 위한 기초 모델(FM)을 선택했습니다. 챗봇은 회사의 어조에 맞는 응답을 생성해야 합니다. 이러한 요구 사항을 충족하는 솔루션은 무엇인가?

a) Set a low limit on the number of tokens the FM can produce (FM이 생성할 수 있는 토큰 수에 낮은 제한 설정)

b) Use batch inferencing to process detailed responses (배치 추론을 사용하여 자세한 응답을 처리)

c) Experiment and refine the prompt until the FM produces the desired responses (FM이 원하는 응답을 생성할 때까지 프롬프트를 실험하고 조정)

d) Define a higher number for the temperature parameter (온도 매개변수에 더 높은 숫자를 지정)

225. To achieve consistent and contextually accurate translations for marketing materials across different languages using Amazon Translate, which feature should be utilized?

225. Amazon Translate를 사용하여 다양한 언어로 된 마케팅 자료에 대해 일관되고 맥락적으로 정확한 번역을 달성하려면 어떤 기능을 활용해야 하는가?

a) Custom Terminology (맞춤 용어)

b) Real-Time Translation (실시간 번역)

c) Batch Translation (배치 번역)

d) Document Translation (문서 번역)

226. Which AWS service provides fine-grained access control to AI resources and ensures that only authorized users and applications can access them?

226. 어떤 AWS 서비스가 AI 리소스에 대한 세밀한 접근 제어를 제공하며, 승인된 사용자와 애플리케이션만 접근할 수 있도록 보장하는가?

a) AWS Shield (AWS Shield)

b) AWS Identity and Access Management (IAM) (AWS 아이덴티티 및 접근 관리)

c) Amazon CloudWatch (아마존 클라우드와치)

d) AWS Key Management Service (KMS) (AWS 키 관리 서비스)

227. Which AWS feature helps in protecting data in transit and at rest by using encryption and secure connections for AI workloads?

227. 어떤 AWS 기능이 AI 워크로드에 대해 데이터 전송 중 및 저장 중 암호화 및 안전한 연결을 통해 데이터를 보호하는 데 도움이 되는가?

a) AWS WAF (AWS WAF)

b) Amazon Macie (아마존 메이시)

c) AWS PrivateLink (AWS 프라이빗 링크)

d) AWS CloudTrail (AWS 클라우드트레일)

228. Which AWS service helps document and manage the lineage and cataloging of data used in AI models?

228. 어떤 AWS 서비스가 AI 모델에 사용된 데이터의 계보와 카탈로그화를 문서화하고 관리하는 데 도움을 주는가?

a) Amazon Athena (아마존 아테나)

b) AWS Glue Data Catalog (AWS 글루 데이터 카탈로그)

c) Amazon SageMaker Model Cards (아마존 세이지메이커 모델 카드)

d) AWS Data Pipeline (AWS 데이터 파이프라인)

229. What is the purpose of using SageMaker Model Cards in AI projects?

229. AI 프로젝트에서 SageMaker 모델 카드를 사용하는 목적은 무엇인가?

a) To automate model deployment (모델 배포 자동화)

b) To provide documentation about the model's performance and usage (모델 성능 및 사용에 대한 문서 제공)

c) To manage data lineage and cataloging (데이터 계보 및 카탈로그 관리)

d) To implement real-time threat detection (실시간 위협 탐지 구현)

230. Which of the following best practices is essential for ensuring data integrity in a secure data engineering pipeline?

230. 다음 모범 사례 중 안전한 데이터 엔지니어링 파이프라인에서 데이터 무결성을 보장하기 위해 필수적인 것은 무엇인가?

a) Encrypting data only during transfer (전송 중에만 데이터 암호화)

b) Implementing strong data access controls and validation checks (강력한 데이터 접근 제어 및 유효성 검증 체크 실행)

c) Limiting the use of data cataloging tools (데이터 카탈로그 도구 사용 제한)

d) Avoiding data encryption for performance reasons (성능 이유로 데이터 암호화 회피)

231. What is the primary method for implementing privacy-enhancing technologies in a data engineering workflow?
231. 데이터 엔지니어링 워크플로우에서 프라이버시 강화 기술을 구현하는 주요 방법은 무엇인가?

a) Reducing data redundancy (데이터 중복성 감소)

b) Using data anonymization and encryption techniques (데이터 익명화 및 암호화 기술 사용)

c) Increasing data storage capacity (데이터 저장 용량 증가)

d) Limiting data access to specific users (특정 사용자에게 데이터 접근 제한)

232. Which of the following security measures is specifically designed to protect AI models from adversarial attacks and prompt injections?
232. 다음 보안 조치 중 AI 모델을 적대적 공격과 프롬프트 삽입으로부터 보호하기 위해 특별히 설계된 것은 무엇인가?

a) Application security (애플리케이션 보안)

b) Threat detection (위협 탐지)

c) Vulnerability management (취약점 관리)

d) Infrastructure protection (인프라 보호)

233. In the context of AI systems, why is it important to implement encryption at rest and in transit?
233. AI 시스템의 맥락에서, 데이터가 저장 중일 때와 전송 중일 때 암호화를 구현하는 것이 중요한 이유는 무엇인가?

a) To improve model training efficiency (모델 훈련 효율성 향상)

b) To ensure data privacy and integrity throughout the entire lifecycle (전체 수명 주기 동안 데이터 프라이버시와 무결성 보장)

c) To minimize the use of encryption keys (암호화 키 사용 최소화)

d) To reduce the need for regular security audits (정기 보안 감사 필요성 감소)

234. Which AWS service can be used to monitor and protect data access and usage within AI systems by identifying sensitive data and setting up data access policies?
234. AI 시스템 내에서 민감한 데이터를 식별하고 데이터 접근 정책을 설정하여 데이터 접근 및 사용을 모니터링하고 보호하는 데 사용할 수 있는 AWS 서비스는 무엇인가?

a) AWS CloudTrail (AWS 클라우드트레일)

b) Amazon Macie (아마존 메이시)

c) AWS Config (AWS 콘피그)

d) AWS GuardDuty (AWS 가드듀티)

235. How does AWS Key Management Service (KMS) enhance the security of AI models deployed in the cloud?
235. AWS 키 관리 서비스(KMS)가 클라우드에 배포된 AI 모델의 보안을 어떻게 강화하는가?

a) By enabling automatic scaling of AI instances (AI 인스턴스의 자동 스케일링 지원)

b) By providing encryption for data at rest and controlling encryption keys (저장된 데이터 암호화 제공 및 암호화 키 제어)

c) By offering real-time monitoring of AI model performance (AI 모델 성능의 실시간 모니터링 제공)

d) By managing user access permissions to AI resources (AI 리소스에 대한 사용자 접근 권한 관리)

236. Which AWS service provides a comprehensive record of data access and changes, helping in tracking data origins and ensuring data integrity?
236. 어떤 AWS 서비스가 데이터 접근 및 변경 사항에 대한 종합적인 기록을 제공하여 데이터 출처를 추적하고 데이터 무결성을 보장하는 데 도움이 되는가?

a) AWS CloudTrail (AWS 클라우드트레일)

b) AWS Glue Data Catalog (AWS 글루 데이터 카탈로그)

c) Amazon DynamoDB (아마존 다이나모DB)

d) Amazon S3 (아마존 S3)

237. What role does data lineage play in ensuring the quality of AI models, and which AWS tool assists in this?
237. 데이터 계보는 AI 모델의 품질을 보장하는 데 어떤 역할을 하며, 이를 돕는 AWS 도구는 무엇인가?

a) Data lineage helps trace the origin and flow of data through the AI pipeline; AWS Glue Data Catalog assists in managing this information (데이터 계보는 AI 파이프라인을 통해 데이터의 출처와 흐름을 추적하는 데 도움을 주며, AWS Glue Data Catalog가 이 정보를 관리하는 데 도움)

b) Data lineage improves model accuracy; AWS Lambda helps manage this information (데이터 계보는 모델의 정확도를 향상시키며, AWS Lambda가 이 정보를 관리하는 데 도움)

c) Data lineage is not critical for AI models; AWS Data Pipeline provides related features (데이터 계보는 AI 모델에 중요하지 않으며, AWS Data Pipeline이 관련 기능을 제공)

d) Data lineage ensures compliance only; Amazon QuickSight provides related features (데이터 계보는 준수성만을 보장하며, Amazon QuickSight가 관련 기능을 제공.)

238. Which practice is essential for ensuring privacy and security in a data engineering workflow that handles sensitive AI data?
238. 민감한 AI 데이터를 처리하는 데이터 엔지니어링 워크플로우에서 프라이버시와 보안을 보장하기 위해 필수적인 관행은 무엇인가?

a) Limiting the use of data analytics (데이터 분석 사용 제한)

b) Implementing role-based access control (RBAC, and data encryption) (역할 기반 접근 제어(RBAC) 및 데이터 암호화 구현)

c) Avoiding data backups to prevent unauthorized access (무단 접근을 방지하기 위한 데이터 백업 회피)

d) Using public data sources exclusively (공공 데이터 소스만 사용)

239. In secure data engineering, what is the primary purpose of implementing data access controls?
239. 안전한 데이터 엔지니어링에서 데이터 접근 제어를 구현하는 주요 목적은 무엇인가?

a) To speed up data processing (데이터 처리 속도 향상)

b) To minimize storage costs (저장 비용 최소화)

c) To ensure that only authorized users can access and modify data (허가된 사용자만 데이터에 접근하고 수정할 수 있도록 보장)

d) To reduce data redundancy (데이터 중복성 감소)

240. What is a key consideration when addressing security and privacy issues related to prompt injection attacks in AI systems?
240. AI 시스템에서 프롬프트 삽입 공격과 관련된 보안 및 프라이버시 문제를 해결할 때 중요한 고려사항은 무엇인가?

a) Increasing model size (모델 크기 증가)

b) Implementing input validation and sanitization (입력 검증 및 정화 구현)

c) Using larger training datasets (더 큰 학습 데이터 세트 사용)

d) Optimizing model performance (모델 성능 최적화)

241. When assessing the security of AI systems, which factor is critical for ensuring data protection during model training and inference?
241. AI 시스템의 보안을 평가할 때, 모델 학습 및 추론 중 데이터 보호를 보장하는 데 중요한 요소는 무엇인가?

a) Using the latest model architecture (최신 모델 아키텍처 사용)

b) Ensuring encryption of data both at rest and in transit (휴지 상태 및 전송 중 데이터 암호화 보장)

c) Increasing the number of training epochs (훈련 에포크 수 증가)

d) Selecting the most recent version of the AI framework (가장 최신 AI 프레임워크 버전 선택)

242. Which AWS service allows developers to create original music compositions using artificial intelligence and machine learning techniques?
242. AI 및 ML 기법을 사용하여 개발자가 원본 음악을 작곡할 수 있게 하는 AWS 서비스는 무엇인가?

a) AWS DeepComposer (AWS 딥컴포저)

b) Amazon Polly (아마존 폴리)

c) Amazon Music (아마존 뮤직)

d) AWS Lambda (AWS 람다)

243. What is a primary feature of AWS DeepComposer that enhances the musical creativity of its users?
243. AWS DeepComposer가 사용자들의 음악적 창의성을 향상시키는 주요 기능은 무엇인가?

a) Real-time voice synthesis (실시간 음성 합성)

b) Automated genre classification (자동 장르 분류)

c) AI-generated musical accompaniments (AI가 생성한 음악 반주)

d) Speech-to-text conversion (음성-텍스트 변환)

244. Which AWS service is designed to help healthcare organizations manage and analyze medical imaging data using machine learning and artificial intelligence?
244. 의료 조직이 기계 학습 및 인공지능을 사용하여 의료 영상 데이터를 관리하고 분석하도록 돕기 위해 설계된 AWS 서비스는 무엇인가?

a) AWS HealthOmics (AWS 헬스오믹스)

b) Amazon SageMaker (아마존 세이지메이커)

c) AWS HealthImaging (AWS 헬스이미징)

d) AWS Panorama (AWS 파노라마)

245. What is a key benefit of using AWS HealthImaging in healthcare applications?
245. AWS HealthImaging을 의료 애플리케이션에서 사용할 때 주요 이점은 무엇인가?

a) Real-time weather data integration (실시간 날씨 데이터 통합)

b) Securely managing and analyzing large volumes of imaging data (대량의 영상 데이터를 안전하게 관리하고 분석)

c) Automating customer service responses (고객 서비스 응답 자동화)

d) Enhancing e-commerce transactions (전자상거래 거래 개선)

246. Which AWS service provides tools for integrating and analyzing genomic and omics data to support precision medicine and personalized healthcare?

246. 정밀 의학 및 개인 맞춤형 헬스케어를 지원하기 위해 유전체 및 오믹스 데이터를 통합하고 분석할 도구를 제공하는 AWS 서비스는 무엇인가?

a) AWS HealthImaging (AWS 헬스이미징)

b) AWS HealthOmics (AWS 헬스오믹스)

c) Amazon Comprehend Medical (아마존 컴프리헨드 메디컬)

d) Amazon Lex (아마존 렉스)

247. What is a key feature of AWS HealthOmics that aids in genomic data analysis?
247. AWS HealthOmics의 유전체 데이터 분석 지원을 위한 주요 기능은 무엇인가?

a) Real-time music composition (실시간 음악 작곡)

b) Integration with weather forecasting tools (날씨 예보 도구와 통합)

c) Support for large-scale genomic data processing (대규모 유전체 데이터 처리 지원)

d) Automated document classification (문서 자동 분류)

248. Which AWS service is designed to monitor and detect anomalies in industrial equipment using machine learning?
248. 기계 학습을 사용하여 산업 장비의 이상을 모니터링하고 감지하도록 설계된 AWS 서비스는 무엇인가?

a) AWS Panorama (AWS 파노라마)

b) Amazon Monitron (아마존 모니트론)

c) AWS DeepComposer (AWS 딥컴포저)

d) AWS HealthImaging (AWS 헬스이미징)

249. What is the primary use case of Amazon Monitron?
249. Amazon Monitron의 주요 사용 사례는 무엇인가?

a) Creating music compositions (음악 작곡)

b) Analyzing genomic data (유전체 데이터 분석)

c) Detecting and predicting equipment failures (장비 고장 감지 및 예측)

d) Managing medical imaging data (의료 영상 데이터 관리)

250. Which AWS service enables users to build computer vision applications that can run on edge devices to process video streams locally?
250. 사용자가 엣지 장치에서 실행되어 로컬로 비디오 스트림을 처리할 수 있는 컴퓨터 비전 애플리케이션을 구축할 수 있게 하는 AWS 서비스는 무엇인가?

a) AWS HealthOmics (AWS 헬스오믹스)

b) AWS Panorama (AWS 파노라마)

c) Amazon Monitron (아마존 모니트론)

d) AWS DeepComposer (AWS 딥컴포저)

251. What is a significant advantage of using AWS Panorama for video analytics?

251. 비디오 분석에 AWS Panorama를 사용하는 중요한 이점은 무엇인가?

a) High-cost infrastructure requirements (고비용 인프라 요구사항)

b) Limited to cloud-based processing (클라우드 기반 처리로 제한)

c) Ability to perform video analytics locally on edge devices (엣지 장치에서 로컬 비디오 분석 수행 가능)

d) Inability to handle large-scale video data (대규모 비디오 데이터 처리 불가)

252. When utilizing AWS DeepComposer for generating musical compositions, which of the following factors most directly influences the variety of musical styles produced by AI?

252. AWS DeepComposer를 사용하여 음악 작곡을 생성할 때, 다음 중 AI가 생성하는 음악 스타일의 다양성에 가장 직접적인 영향을 미치는 요인은 무엇인가?

a) The length of the input melody (입력 멜로디 길이)

b) The model architecture used for music generation (음악 생성에 사용되는 모델 아키텍처)

c) The genre tags applied to the input melody (입력 멜로디에 적용된 장르 태그)

d) The number of MIDI tracks in the composition (작곡에 사용된 MIDI 트랙 수)

253. Which feature of AWS HealthImaging would be critical for integrating AI-based analysis of medical images with existing electronic health record (EHR) systems?

253. AWS HealthImaging의 어떤 기능이 의료 이미지의 AI 기반 분석을 기존 전자 건강 기록(EHR) 시스템과 통합하는 데 중요한가?

a) Data cataloging and governance (데이터 카탈로그 및 관리)

b) Real-time video streaming capabilities (실시간 비디오 스트리밍 기능)

c) Custom AI model training (사용자 지정 AI 모델 학습)

d) Data lineage tracking (데이터 계보 추적)

254. How does AWS HealthOmics handle the integration of diverse omics data types for comprehensive analysis, and what AWS service facilitates this integration?

254. AWS HealthOmics는 종합 분석을 위해 다양한 오믹스 데이터 유형의 통합을 어떻게 처리하며, 어떤 AWS 서비스가 이 통합을 지원하는가?

a) Using AWS Data Pipeline for data transformation (데이터 변환을 위한 AWS Data Pipeline 사용)

b) Using Amazon Redshift for data warehousing (데이터 웨어하우징을 위한 Amazon Redshift 사용)

c) Using AWS Glue for data integration and ETL (데이터 통합 및 ETL을 위한 AWS Glue 사용)

d) Using Amazon SageMaker for model training and analysis (모델 학습 및 분석을 위한 Amazon SageMaker 사용)

255. In a scenario where AWS HealthOmics is used to analyze patient genomic data, which AWS service would be best suited for managing and visualizing complex multi-dimensional omics data?
255. AWS HealthOmics가 환자 유전체 데이터를 분석하는 시나리오에서 복잡한 다차원 오믹스 데이터를 관리하고 시각화하는 데 가장 적합한 AWS 서비스는 무엇인가?

a) AWS QuickSight (AWS 퀵사이트)

b) Amazon CloudWatch (아마존 클라우드와치)

c) Amazon SageMaker Studio (아마존 세이지메이커 스튜디오)

d) AWS Glue (AWS 글루)

256. Which approach should be adopted when configuring Amazon Monitron to ensure effective anomaly detection in a manufacturing setting with varying equipment conditions?
256. 다양한 장비 조건이 있는 제조 환경에서 효과적인 이상 감지를 보장하기 위해 Amazon Monitron을 설정할 때 채택해야 하는 접근 방식은 무엇인가?

a) Using a static threshold for all equipment types (모든 장비 유형에 대해 고정 임계값 사용)

b) Applying a generic model across all equipment types (모든 장비 유형에 걸쳐 일반 모델 적용)

c) Customizing models and thresholds based on specific equipment and historical data (특정 장비와 과거 데이터를 기반으로 모델과 임계값 맞춤 설정)

d) Relying solely on manual inspections for anomaly detection (이상 감지를 위해 수동 검사에만 의존)

257. When integrating Amazon Monitron with other AWS services for a comprehensive predictive maintenance solution, which service would provide real-time alerts and automated responses based on detected anomalies?
257. Amazon Monitron을 다른 AWS 서비스와 통합하여 종합적인 예측 유지보수 솔루션을 구축할 때, 감지된 이상 현상을 기반으로 실시간 경고와 자동 응답을 제공하는 서비스는 무엇인가?

a) AWS CloudTrail (AWS 클라우드트레일)

b) Amazon SNS (아마존 SNS)

c) AWS Config (AWS 컨피그)

d) AWS Step Functions (AWS 스텝 펑션)

258. In deploying an AWS Panorama solution for real-time video analytics at the edge, which factor is critical for ensuring optimal performance and minimal latency in video processing?
258. 엣지에서 실시간 비디오 분석을 위한 AWS Panorama 솔루션을 배포할 때, 비디오 처리에서 최적의 성능과 최소 지연을 보장하기 위해 중요한 요소는 무엇인가?

a) The size of the data warehouse used for storing video data (비디오 데이터를 저장하기 위해 사용하는 데

이터 웨어하우스의 크기)

b) The processing power and memory of the edge devices (엣지 장치의 처리 능력과 메모리)

c) The number of users accessing the video streams (비디오 스트림에 접근하는 사용자 수)

d) The frequency of data backups (데이터 백업 빈도)

259. Which AWS Panorama feature helps in managing the deployment of computer vision models across multiple edge devices in a large-scale video surveillance deployment?

259. 대규모 비디오 감시 배포에서 여러 엣지 장치에 컴퓨터 비전 모델을 배포 관리하는 데 도움을 주는 AWS Panorama의 기능은 무엇인가?

a) AWS Systems Manager (AWS 시스템 매니저)

b) AWS IoT Core (AWS IoT 코어)

c) AWS Panorama Device SDK (AWS 파노라마 디바이스 SDK)

d) Amazon Kinesis Video Streams (아마존 키네시스 비디오 스트림)

260. Which feature of Amazon Augmented AI (Amazon A2I) allows users to manage and review human tasks for machine learning model outputs, ensuring that appropriate human reviewers handle these tasks?

260. Amazon Augmented AI (Amazon A2I)의 어떤 기능이 사용자로 하여금 기계 학습 모델 출력에 대한 인간 작업을 관리하고 검토할 수 있도록 하여, 적절한 인간 검토자가 이러한 작업을 처리하도록 보장하는가?

a) Human Review Workflow (인간 검토 워크플로우)

b) Task Categorization (작업 분류)

c) Automated Labeling (자동 레이블링)

d) Model Calibration (모델 보정)

261. When configuring an Amazon A2I workflow to handle exceptions in an image moderation use case, which Amazon service is commonly used to handle the initial image processing before human review?

261. 이미지 검토 사용 사례에서 예외 처리를 위해 Amazon A2I 워크플로우를 설정할 때, 인간 검토 전에 초기 이미지 처리를 담당하는 Amazon 서비스는 무엇인가?

a) Amazon Rekognition (아마존 레코그니션)

b) Amazon Polly (아마존 폴리)

c) Amazon Textract (아마존 텍스트랙트)

d) Amazon Lex (아마존 렉스)

262. In the context of Amazon Bedrock, which of the following best describes the service's ability to streamline foundation model development for specific use cases?

262. Amazon Bedrock에서 특정 사용 사례에 대한 기초 모델 개발을 간소화하는 서비스의 능력을 가장 잘 설명하는 것은 무엇인가?

a) Custom Model Training (맞춤형 모델 학습)

b) Pre-trained Model Customization (사전 학습된 모델 맞춤 설정)

c) AutoML Deployment (AutoML 배포)

d) Multi-model Aggregation (다중 모델 집합)

263. Which component of Amazon Bedrock allows users to evaluate the performance of foundation models using customized benchmarks and datasets?

263. Amazon Bedrock의 어느 구성 요소가 사용자가 맞춤형 벤치마크와 데이터셋을 사용하여 기초 모델의 성능을 평가할 수 있게 하는가?

a) Model Evaluation Toolkit (모델 평가 툴킷)

b) Model Optimization Dashboard (모델 최적화 대시보드)

c) Model Evaluation Lab (모델 평가 연구소)

d) Foundation Model Benchmarking (기초 모델 벤치마킹)

264. Which of the following features of Amazon Comprehend is specifically designed to identify and extract entities from text, such as names, dates, and locations?

264. Amazon Comprehend의 다음 기능 중 이름, 날짜, 위치와 같은 엔티티를 텍스트에서 식별하고 추출하도록 설계된 기능은 무엇인가?

a) Sentiment Analysis (감정 분석)

b) Key Phrases Extraction (핵심 구문 추출)

c) Named Entity Recognition (명명된 엔티티 인식)

d) Language Detection (언어 감지)

265. How does Amazon Comprehend improve accuracy in language understanding for multilingual documents?

265. Amazon Comprehend가 다국어 문서의 언어 이해 정확성을 어떻게 개선하는가?

a) By utilizing translation services (번역 서비스 활용)

b) By employing cross-lingual embeddings (교차 언어 임베딩 활용)

c) By integrating with Amazon Translate (아마존 트랜스레이트와 통합)

d) By leveraging language-specific models (언어별 모델 활용)

266. What is a key benefit of using Amazon Fraud Detector's built-in fraud detection models over creating custom fraud detection models from scratch?

266. Amazon Fraud Detector의 내장된 사기 탐지 모델을 사용하는 것이 처음부터 맞춤형 사기 탐지 모델을 만드는 것보다 가지는 주요 이점은 무엇인가?

a) Faster deployment and easier integration (더 빠른 배포 및 더 쉬운 통합)

b) Higher accuracy for all types of fraud (모든 유형의 사기에 대해 더 높은 정확도)

c) Increased data storage capacity (데이터 저장 용량 증가)

d) Reduced need for data preprocessing (데이터 전처리 필요성 감소)

267. Which AWS service can be integrated with Amazon Fraud Detector to provide real-time decision-making based on detected fraud signals?

267. Amazon Fraud Detector와 통합하여 탐지된 사기 신호에 따라 실시간 의사 결정을 제공할 수 있는 AWS 서비스는 무엇인가?

a) AWS Lambda (AWS 람다)

b) Amazon Kinesis (아마존 키네시스)

c) AWS Step Functions (AWS 스텝 펑션)

d) Amazon S3 (아마존 S3)

268. Which feature of Amazon Kendra allows it to provide relevant search results by understanding the context of the query and the content of documents?

268. Amazon Kendra의 어떤 기능이 쿼리의 맥락과 문서 내용을 이해하여 관련 검색 결과를 제공하는 데 도움이 되는가?

a) Document Embeddings (문서 임베딩)

b) Query Understanding (쿼리 이해)

c) Semantic Search (시맨틱 검색)

d) Auto-Tagging (자동 태깅)

269. When using Amazon Kendra to index a large number of documents, which service should be used to handle document ingestion and transformation?

269. Amazon Kendra를 사용하여 다수의 문서를 색인할 때 문서 수집 및 변환을 처리하는 데 사용해야 하는 서비스는 무엇인가?

a) AWS Glue (AWS 글루)

b) Amazon Textract (아마존 텍스트랙트)

c) Amazon QuickSight (아마존 퀵사이트)

d) AWS Data Pipeline (AWS 데이터 파이프라인)

270. Which component of Amazon Lex is responsible for managing the dialogue flow and context of a conversation in a chatbot application?

270. Amazon Lex의 어떤 구성 요소가 챗봇 애플리케이션의 대화 흐름과 맥락을 관리하는 역할을 하는가?

a) Intents (인텐트)

b) Fulfillment (이행)

c) Slots (슬롯)

d) Contextual Prompts (맥락적 프롬프트)

271. In Amazon Lex, which feature would you use to handle a scenario where the chatbot needs to request additional information from the user based on previous responses?

271. Amazon Lex에서 챗봇이 이전 응답을 바탕으로 사용자에게 추가 정보를 요청해야 하는 시나리오를 처리하기 위해 사용할 수 있는 기능은 무엇인가?

a) Session Attributes (세션 속성)

b) Lambda Functions (람다 함수)

c) Slot Types (슬롯 유형)

d) Prompts (프롬프트)

272. Which Amazon Personalize feature allows you to build personalized recommendation models using user behavior data and item attributes?

272. Amazon Personalize의 어떤 기능이 사용자 행동 데이터와 항목 속성을 사용하여 개인 맞춤형 추천 모델을 구축할 수 있도록 하는가?

a) Personalization Recipes (개인화 레시피)

b) User Segmentation (사용자 세분화)

c) Real-Time Personalization (실시간 개인화)

d) Custom Data Schemas (사용자 정의 데이터 스키마)

273. When implementing Amazon Personalize for a recommendation system, which dataset is crucial for creating accurate user preferences?

273. 추천 시스템을 위해 Amazon Personalize를 구현할 때 정확한 사용자 선호도를 생성하는 데 필수적인 데이터 세트는 무엇인가?

a) Interaction Dataset (상호작용 데이터 세트)

b) User Profile Dataset (사용자 프로필 데이터 세트)

c) Item Metadata Dataset (항목 메타데이터 데이터 세트)

d) Evaluation Dataset (평가 데이터 세트)

274. Which feature of Amazon Polly enables the generation of speech that closely mimics human emotions and intonation?

274. Amazon Polly의 어떤 기능이 인간의 감정과 억양을 가깝게 모방하는 음성 생성을 가능하게 하는가?

a) Neural TTS (신경 TTS)

b) Speech Synthesis Markup Language (SSML) (음성 합성 마크업 언어)

c) Custom Voice Models (맞춤형 음성 모델)

d) Real-Time Streaming (실시간 스트리밍)

275. Which Amazon Polly feature allows users to customize the pronunciation of specific words or phrases in generated speech?
275. Amazon Polly의 어떤 기능이 생성된 음성에서 특정 단어나 구문의 발음을 사용자 정의할 수 있도록 하는가?

a) Lexicons (사전)
b) Speech Marks (음성 마크)
c) Voice Variants (음성 변형)
d) Speech Synthesis Markup Language (SSML) (음성 합성 마크업 언어)

276. Which primary use case for Amazon Q involves leveraging generative AI models to enhance customer interactions and provide personalized responses?
276. Amazon Q의 주요 사용 사례 중 어떤 것이 생성형 AI 모델을 활용하여 고객 상호작용을 강화하고 맞춤형 응답을 제공하는가?

a) Conversational AI (대화형 AI)
b) Image Recognition (이미지 인식)
c) Sentiment Analysis (감정 분석)
d) Fraud Detection (사기 탐지)

277. Which AWS service can be used in conjunction with Amazon Q to analyze customer interactions and improve response quality based on conversation history?
277. Amazon Q와 함께 사용할 수 있으며 고객 상호작용을 분석하고 대화 기록을 바탕으로 응답 품질을 개선할 수 있는 AWS 서비스는 무엇인가?

a) Amazon Comprehend (아마존 컴프리헨드)
b) Amazon QuickSight (아마존 퀵사이트)
c) Amazon Kinesis (아마존 키네시스)
d) AWS Glue (아마존 글루)

278. Which Amazon Rekognition feature is best suited for identifying and tracking people across multiple video frames in a surveillance application?
278. 감시 애플리케이션에서 여러 비디오 프레임에 걸쳐 사람을 식별하고 추적하는 데 가장 적합한 Amazon Rekognition 기능은 무엇인가?

a) Face Comparison (얼굴 비교)
b) Object Detection (객체 탐지)
c) Person Tracking (사람 추적)
d) Facial Analysis (얼굴 분석)

279. In Amazon Rekognition, which functionality allows for detecting and analyzing specific facial attributes such as age, emotion, and gender?
279. Amazon Rekognition에서 나이, 감정, 성별과 같은 특정 얼굴 속성을 감지하고 분석할 수 있는 기능은 무엇인가?

a) Face Comparison (얼굴 비교)

b) Facial Analysis (얼굴 분석)

c) Face Detection (얼굴 탐지)

d) Object and Scene Detection (객체 및 장면 탐지)

280. Which component of Amazon SageMaker provides a fully managed environment for building, training, and deploying machine learning models?
280. Amazon SageMaker의 어떤 구성 요소가 머신 러닝 모델을 구축, 훈련, 배포하기 위한 완전 관리형 환경을 제공하는가?

a) SageMaker Studio (세이지메이커 스튜디오)

b) SageMaker Autopilot (세이지메이커 오토파일럿)

c) SageMaker Ground Truth (세이지메이커 그라운드 트루스)

d) SageMaker Model Monitor (세이지메이커 모델 모니터)

281. Which Amazon SageMaker feature helps automate the process of hyperparameter tuning to improve model performance?
281. 모델 성능을 향상시키기 위해 하이퍼파라미터 튜닝을 자동화하는 Amazon SageMaker 기능은 무엇인가?

a) SageMaker Autopilot (세이지메이커 오토파일럿)

b) SageMaker Hyperparameter Tuning Jobs (세이지메이커 하이퍼파라미터 튜닝 잡스)

c) SageMaker Ground Truth (세이지메이커 그라운드 트루스)

d) SageMaker Neo (세이지메이커 네오)

282. Which Amazon Textract feature is particularly useful for extracting structured data from complex documents such as forms and tables?
282. 양식과 테이블과 같은 복잡한 문서에서 구조화된 데이터 추출에 특히 유용한 Amazon Textract 기능은 무엇인가?

a) Text Extraction (텍스트 추출)

b) Form Extraction (폼 추출)

c) Table Extraction (테이블 추출)

d) Document Classification (문서 분류)

283. When processing a scanned document using Amazon Textract, which feature helps in identifying and extracting specific fields like names and addresses from a form?
283. 스캔된 문서를 처리할 때 이름과 주소와 같은 특정 필드를 식별하고 추출하는 데 도움이 되는 Amazon Textract 기능은 무엇인가?

a) Text Detection (텍스트 감지)

b) Form Data Extraction (폼 데이터 추출)

c) Key-Value Pair Extraction (키-값 쌍 추출)

d) Document Analysis (문서 분석)

284. Which Amazon Transcribe feature allows for distinguishing between multiple speakers in an audio recording and providing separate transcriptions for each?

284. 오디오 녹음에서 여러 화자를 구분하고 각 화자에 대한 별도의 전사를 제공하는 Amazon Transcribe 기능은 무엇인가?

a) Speaker Identification (화자 식별)

b) Language Detection (언어 감지)

c) Custom Vocabulary (사용자 정의 어휘)

d) Real-Time Transcription (실시간 전사)

285. How can Amazon Transcribe be integrated with Amazon Comprehend to enhance the analysis of transcribed audio content?

285. Amazon Transcribe를 Amazon Comprehend와 통합하여 전사된 오디오 콘텐츠의 분석 향상법은 무엇인가?

a) By using Transcribe to pre-process audio for sentiment analysis (Transcribe를 사용하여 오디오를 감정 분석용으로 전처리)

b) By combining Transcribe's output with Comprehend's entity recognition (Transcribe의 출력을 Comprehend의 엔터티 인식과 결합)

c) By storing transcriptions in Comprehend's data lake (전사 내용을 Comprehend의 데이터 레이크에 저장)

d) By using Comprehend to translate the transcribed text into multiple languages (Comprehend를 사용하여 전사된 텍스트를 여러 언어로 번역)

286. Which Amazon Translate feature enables real-time translation of user-generated content in a web application to support multilingual user interactions?

286. 웹 애플리케이션에서 사용자가 생성한 콘텐츠를 실시간으로 번역하여 다국어 사용자 상호작용을 지원하는 Amazon Translate 기능은 무엇인가?

a) Batch Translation (배치 번역)

b) Real-Time Translation (실시간 번역)

c) Custom Translation (사용자 정의 번역)

d) Document Translation (문서 번역)

287. To improve translation quality for domain-specific terms and jargon using Amazon Translate, which feature allows customization of translation models?

287. Amazon Translate를 사용하여 특정 분야의 용어와 전문 용어의 번역 품질을 향상시키기 위해, 번역 모델을 맞춤화할 수 있는 기능은 무엇인가?

a) Translation Memory (번역 메모리)

b) Custom Terminology (사용자 정의 용어)

c) Machine Translation Enhancement (기계 번역 향상)

d) Custom Translation Models (사용자 정의 번역 모델)

288. A research team is developing a generative AI model to automatically generate marketing copy for various products. They are considering different approaches for representing textual data and generating content. Which of the following methods would be most effective for encoding and generating text, and why?

288. 연구팀이 다양한 제품에 대한 마케팅 카피를 자동으로 생성하는 생성 AI 모델을 개발하고 있다. 이들은 텍스트 데이터를 표현하고 콘텐츠를 생성하는 다양한 방법을 고려하고 있다. 텍스트 인코딩 및 생성에 가장 효과적인 방법은 무엇이며, 그 이유는 무엇인가?

a) Using Tokens and Embeddings: Implement a tokenizer to convert text into tokens, then use embeddings to represent these tokens in a continuous vector space, and finally leverage a transformer-based model for generation (토큰 및 임베딩 사용: 텍스트를 토큰으로 변환하기 위해 토크나이저를 구현하고, 이러한 토큰을 연속 벡터 공간으로 표현하기 위해 임베딩을 사용한 후, 생성에는 변환 기반 모델을 활용)

b) Using Chunking and Vectors: Chunk the text into predefined segments, represent each segment with vectors, and use a sequence-to-sequence model for content generation (청킹 및 벡터 사용: 텍스트를 미리 정의된 세그먼트로 청킹하고 각 세그먼트를 벡터로 표현한 후, 콘텐츠 생성을 위해 시퀀스-투-시퀀스 모델을 사용)

c) Using Diffusion Models: Apply diffusion models to generate textual data by progressively refining a noisy input until it resembles a coherent marketing copy (확산 모델 사용: 노이즈 입력을 점진적으로 정제하여 일관된 마케팅 카피와 유사하게 텍스트 데이터를 생성하는 확산 모델을 적용)

d) Using Multi-modal Models: Combine text with image data to generate marketing copy by jointly training on text and visual features (멀티모달 모델 사용: 텍스트와 이미지 데이터를 결합하여 텍스트 및 시각적 특징을 공동 학습하여 마케팅 카피를 생성)

289. A financial institution wants to implement a chatbot capable of answering customer queries about their accounts and transaction history. What are the most appropriate generative AI models to consider for this use case, and what capabilities should these models have?

289. 금융 기관이 고객의 계좌 및 거래 기록에 대한 질문에 답변할 수 있는 챗봇을 구현하려고 한다. 이 사용 사례에 적합한 생성 AI 모델은 무엇이며, 이 모델이 갖추어야 할 기능은 무엇인가?

a) Text Summarization Models: Use summarization models to condense long customer service documents into concise responses (텍스트 요약 모델: 긴 고객 서비스 문서를 요약하여 간결한 응답으로 변환)

b) Code Generation Models: Implement code generation models to produce backend logic for the chatbot's integration with customer data (코드 생성 모델: 챗봇이 고객 데이터와 통합될 수 있도록 백엔드 로직을 생성하는 코드 생성 모델 구현)

c) Conversational AI Models: Use transformer-based language models fine-tuned for dialogue to generate contextually accurate responses to customer queries (대화형 AI 모델: 고객 질문에 대한 맥락적으로 정확한 응답을 생성하기 위해 대화에 맞춰 미세 조정된 변환 기반 언어 모델 사용)

d) Image Generation Models: Employ image generation models to create visual representations of account information (이미지 생성 모델: 계좌 정보를 시각적으로 표현하는 이미지를 생성하는 모델 사용)

290. A company wants to create a new foundation model for generating legal documents. They have gathered a large dataset of existing legal texts. What should be the order of steps in the model lifecycle to ensure the successful development and deployment of this foundation model?

290. 회사가 법률 문서를 생성하는 새로운 기초 모델을 만들고자 한다. 이들은 기존 법률 텍스트의 대규모 데이터셋을 수집했다. 이 기초 모델의 성공적인 개발 및 배포를 보장하기 위한 모델 라이프사이클의 단계 순서는 무엇인가?

a) Data Selection → Pre-training → Fine-tuning → Evaluation → Deployment → Feedback (데이터 선택 → 사전 학습 → 미세 조정 → 평가 → 배포 → 피드백)

b) Model Selection → Data Curation → Fine-tuning → Evaluation → Pre-training → Deployment (모델 선택 → 데이터 큐레이션 → 미세 조정 → 평가 → 사전 학습 → 배포)

c) Data Selection → Model Selection → Pre-training → Fine-tuning → Evaluation → Feedback → Deployment (데이터 선택 → 모델 선택 → 사전 학습 → 미세 조정 → 평가 → 피드백 → 배포)

d) Data Curation → Pre-training → Model Selection → Fine-tuning → Deployment → Evaluation → Feedback (데이터 큐레이션 → 사전 학습 → 모델 선택 → 미세 조정 → 배포 → 평가 → 피드백)

291. A media company wants to build an AI system that can generate short video clips based on text descriptions provided by users. Which generative AI approach should they use, and what are the key components of the model?

291. 미디어 회사가 사용자가 제공한 텍스트 설명을 기반으로 짧은 동영상 클립을 생성할 수 있는 AI 시스템을 구축하려고 한다. 이들이 사용할 생성 AI 접근 방식은 무엇이며, 모델의 주요 구성 요소는 무엇인가?

a) Use Transformer-Based Models: Apply transformers to generate video scripts from text, then use separate models for video synthesis (변환 기반 모델 사용: 텍스트에서 비디오 스크립트를 생성하고, 별도의 모델을 사용해 비디오 합성 수행)

b) Use Multi-Modal Models: Employ a multi-modal generative model that can simultaneously process text and video data to generate video clips directly from text descriptions (멀티모달 모델 사용: 텍스트 설명에서 직접 비디오 클립을 생성할 수 있도록 텍스트와 비디오 데이터를 동시에 처리하는 멀티모달 생성 모델 사용)

c) Use Embeddings and Vectors: Generate video clips by mapping text descriptions into embeddings and using a vector-based approach for video generation (임베딩 및 벡터 사용: 텍스트 설명을 임베딩으로 매핑하고 벡터 기반 접근 방식으로 비디오 생성)

d) Use Diffusion Models: Implement diffusion models to iteratively refine initial video frames generated from text descriptions (확산 모델 사용: 텍스트 설명에서 생성된 초기 비디오 프레임을 반복적으로 정제하는 확산 모델 사용)

292. After deploying a foundation model for summarizing news articles, you receive feedback that the model is generating summaries that are too lengthy. What steps should be taken to improve the model's performance?

292. 뉴스 기사 요약을 위한 기초 모델을 배포한 후, 모델이 생성하는 요약이 너무 길다는 피드백을 받았다. 모델 성능을 향상시키기 위한 조치는 무엇인가?

a) Increase the size of the training dataset to improve generalization (훈련 데이터셋 크기 증가: 일반화 개선을 위해 데이터셋 크기 증가)

b) Fine-tune the model with a focus on summarization tasks, using shorter summaries as training examples (미

세 조정: 요약 작업에 집중하여 짧은 요약을 훈련 예제로 사용)

c) Switch to a different pre-trained model with more advanced summarization capabilities (모델 교체: 더 발전된 요약 기능을 갖춘 사전 학습 모델로 교체)

d) Adjust the model's hyperparameters to increase the length of generated summaries (하이퍼파라미터 조정: 생성된 요약 길이를 늘리기 위해 하이퍼파라미터 조정)

293. You are building an image moderation system using Amazon A2I and Amazon Rekognition. You need to ensure that flagged images are reviewed by human moderators only if the confidence level of the detection is below a certain threshold. How would you configure the workflow in Amazon A2I to achieve this?

293. Amazon A2I와 Amazon Rekognition을 사용하여 이미지 검열 시스템을 구축하고 있다. 감지 신뢰도가 특정 임계값 이하일 경우에만 사람이 검토하도록 설정하려면 어떻게 구성해야 하나?

a) Configure a manual review task to be triggered for all images regardless of confidence level (수동 검토 작업 설정: 신뢰도와 상관없이 모든 이미지에 수동 검토 작업 트리거)

b) Set up an Amazon Rekognition Custom Labels model to filter out low-confidence images before sending them to Amazon A2I (커스텀 라벨 모델 설정: Amazon Rekognition 커스텀 라벨 모델을 통해 신뢰도가 낮은 이미지를 Amazon A2I로 보내기 전 필터링)

c) Create an A2I workflow with a conditional step that sends images to human reviewers only if the confidence level from Amazon Rekognition is below the defined threshold (조건부 단계 설정: Amazon Rekognition의 신뢰도가 정의된 임계값 이하일 때만 사람 검토로 이미지를 보내는 조건부 단계 생성)

d) Use Amazon A2I to automatically process all images and then filter out low-confidence results manually (자동 처리 후 필터링: Amazon A2I로 모든 이미지를 자동 처리한 후, 수동으로 신뢰도가 낮은 결과를 필터링)

294. Your company wants to implement an automated content moderation system using Amazon A2I to handle sensitive content in user-uploaded images. How can you ensure the system meets compliance requirements and maintains high-quality reviews?

294. Amazon A2I를 사용하여 사용자 업로드 이미지에서 민감한 콘텐츠를 처리하는 자동 콘텐츠 검열 시스템을 구현하려 한다. 시스템이 규정 준수를 충족하고 고품질 리뷰를 유지하도록 보장하려면 어떻게 해야 하나?

a) Use a pre-built model in Amazon A2I and configure it to handle all types of content without human review (사전 구축 모델 사용: Amazon A2I의 사전 구축 모델을 사용하여 모든 콘텐츠를 사람 검토 없이 처리하도록 설정)

b) Regularly update the moderation models and perform periodic audits of human reviews to ensure compliance and quality (정기 업데이트 및 감사: 규정 준수 및 품질을 보장하기 위해 검열 모델을 정기적으로 업데이트하고, 사람 검토의 주기적인 감사를 수행)

c) Set up automated email alerts for every image processed and manually review each alert for compliance (자동 이메일 알림 설정: 처리된 각 이미지에 대해 자동 이메일 알림을 설정하고, 각 알림을 수동으로 검토하여 규정 준수 확인)

d) Rely solely on machine learning models for content moderation and skip human reviews to save costs (비용 절감: 콘텐츠 검열을 위해 머신러닝 모델에만 의존하고, 사람 검토는 생략)

295. You are tasked with customizing a pre-trained foundation model for a customer service application using Amazon Bedrock. The customer has specific needs for handling complex queries and providing accurate responses. How would you approach this customization?

295. Amazon Bedrock을 사용하여 고객 서비스 애플리케이션을 위한 사전 학습된 기초 모델을 맞춤화하는 작업을 맡았다. 고객의 복잡한 질문 처리 및 정확한 응답 제공 요구 사항을 충족하기 위해 어떻게 접근할 것인가?

a) Use Amazon Bedrock's pre-trained models without further customization, as they are already optimized for general use (사전 학습 모델 사용: 일반 사용을 위해 최적화된 Amazon Bedrock의 사전 학습 모델을 추가 맞춤화 없이 사용)

b) Fine-tune the pre-trained model with domain-specific data and customer queries to improve accuracy for complex queries (도메인 데이터로 미세 조정: 복잡한 질문에 대한 정확도를 향상시키기 위해 도메인 데이터와 고객 질문을 사용해 사전 학습 모델을 미세 조정)

c) Develop a new model from scratch using Amazon Bedrock's tools to fully customize the model's responses (새 모델 개발: Amazon Bedrock의 도구를 사용하여 완전히 맞춤화된 응답을 제공하는 새로운 모델을 개발)

d) Use only general-purpose embeddings from the pre-trained model without further adjustments (일반 임베딩 사용: 추가 조정 없이 사전 학습 모델의 일반 목적 임베딩만 사용)

296. You need to evaluate different foundation models for a new product recommendation system using Amazon Bedrock. Which approach would you take to ensure you select the best model for your needs?

296. Amazon Bedrock을 사용하여 새 제품 추천 시스템을 위한 여러 기초 모델을 평가해야 한다. 필요에 가장 적합한 모델을 선택하기 위해 어떤 접근 방식을 택해야 하나?

a) Compare models based on their general performance metrics provided by Amazon Bedrock (일반 성능 지표 비교: Amazon Bedrock이 제공하는 일반 성능 지표를 기반으로 모델 비교)

b) Test each model with your product data and use custom benchmarks to evaluate their performance in real-world scenarios (맞춤 벤치마크 테스트: 제품 데이터를 사용하여 각 모델을 테스트하고, 실제 시나리오에서 성능을 평가하기 위해 맞춤 벤치마크 사용)

c) Rely on the most recent model release, assuming it has the latest improvements (최신 모델 신뢰: 최신 개선 사항이 반영되었을 것으로 가정하여 가장 최근에 출시된 모델을 신뢰)

d) Choose the model with the highest number of pre-trained parameters, assuming it will have better performance (매개변수 수 기반 선택: 더 나은 성능을 기대하며 사전 학습된 매개변수 수가 가장 많은 모델 선택)

297. Your team is building a sentiment analysis tool for customer feedback using Amazon Comprehend. You want to ensure the tool accurately detects sentiment across multiple languages. How should you configure Amazon Comprehend to handle this requirement?

297. Amazon Comprehend를 사용하여 고객 피드백에 대한 감정 분석 도구를 구축 중이다. 여러 언어에서 감정을 정확하게 감지하도록 하려면 어떻게 Amazon Comprehend를 구성해야 하나?

a) Use Amazon Comprehend's built-in language detection to process feedback in different languages separately (내장 언어 감지 사용: Amazon Comprehend의 내장 언어 감지 기능을 사용하여 각기 다른 언어의 피드백을 별도로 처리)

b) Combine Amazon Comprehend with Amazon Translate to first translate all feedback to a single language before analysis (번역 후 분석: Amazon Translate와 Amazon Comprehend를 결합하여 모든 피드백을 단일 언어로 번역한 후 분석)

c) Use Amazon Comprehend's multi-language support feature to analyze sentiment directly in the original languages (다중 언어 지원 기능 사용: Amazon Comprehend의 다중 언어 지원 기능을 사용하여 원본 언어로 직접 감정 분석 수행)

d) Manually translate feedback into English before using Amazon Comprehend for sentiment analysis (수동 번역 후 분석: 감정 분석을 위해 Amazon Comprehend를 사용하기 전에 피드백을 영어로 수동 번역)

298. You are developing a customer support application using Amazon Comprehend to categorize incoming support tickets into predefined categories. The system needs to handle diverse ticket formats and ensure accurate categorization. What approach should you take?

298. Amazon Comprehend를 사용하여 들어오는 고객 지원 티켓을 미리 정의된 카테고리로 분류하는 애플리케이션을 개발 중이다. 다양한 티켓 형식을 처리하고 정확한 분류를 보장하기 위해 어떤 접근 방식을 택해야 하나?

a) Use Amazon Comprehend's entity recognition to extract relevant information and manually categorize tickets based on extracted data (엔터티 인식 사용: 관련 정보를 추출하고 추출된 데이터를 기반으로 티켓을 수동 분류)

b) Train a custom classification model in Amazon Comprehend using labeled examples of each ticket category to improve categorization accuracy (맞춤형 분류 모델 훈련: Amazon Comprehend에서 각 티켓 카테고리에 대한 레이블 예시를 사용해 맞춤형 분류 모델을 훈련하여 분류 정확도 향상)

c) Rely on Amazon Comprehend's built-in classification without customization for handling diverse ticket formats (기본 분류 기능 사용: 다양한 티켓 형식을 처리하기 위해 Amazon Comprehend의 기본 분류 기능에 의존)

d) Pre-process all tickets into a uniform format before feeding them into Amazon Comprehend for categorization (사전 처리 후 입력: 분류를 위해 모든 티켓을 일관된 형식으로 사전 처리한 후 Amazon Comprehend에 입력)

299. Your e-commerce platform is using Amazon Fraud Detector to identify fraudulent transactions. You want to improve detection accuracy by incorporating historical transaction data and patterns. What should you do?

299. 전자상거래 플랫폼에서 Amazon Fraud Detector를 사용하여 사기 거래를 식별하고 있다. 탐지 정확도를 높이기 위해 과거 거래 데이터와 패턴을 통합하려면 어떻게 해야 하나?

a) Use Amazon Fraud Detector's built-in models without customization to leverage historical data (기본 모델 사용: 맞춤화 없이 Amazon Fraud Detector의 기본 모델을 사용해 과거 데이터 활용)

b) Create a custom fraud detection model in Amazon Fraud Detector by training it with historical transaction data to capture patterns (맞춤형 모델 생성: 과거 거래 데이터를 사용하여 패턴을 포착하는 맞춤형 사기 탐지 모델을 Amazon Fraud Detector에서 훈련)

c) Rely solely on real-time data for fraud detection and ignore historical patterns (실시간 데이터만 의존: 사기 탐지에 실시간 데이터만 의존하고 과거 패턴은 무시)

d) Manually review all transactions flagged as suspicious by the built-in models to improve accuracy (수동 검토: 기본 모델에 의해 의심 거래로 표시된 모든 거래를 수동으로 검토하여 정확도 향상)

300. To enhance the fraud detection capabilities of your system using Amazon Fraud Detector, you need to integrate with additional AWS services. Which integration would be most effective for real-time fraud detection and response?

300. Amazon Fraud Detector를 사용하여 시스템의 사기 탐지 기능을 강화하려면 추가 AWS 서비스와 통합이 필요하다. 실시간 사기 탐지 및 대응에 가장 효과적인 통합은 무엇인가?

a) Amazon S3 for storing transaction logs (아마존 S3: 거래 로그 저장용)

b) Amazon DynamoDB for storing user profiles (아마존 다이나모DB: 사용자 프로필 저장용)

c) AWS Lambda for executing custom fraud response logic (AWS 람다: 맞춤형 사기 대응 로직 실행용)

d) Amazon CloudWatch for monitoring fraud detection metrics (아마존 클라우드워치: 사기 탐지 지표 모니터링용)

적중문제 정답 해설집 받기

본 적중문제에 대한 해설집(PDF)은 [책바세.com] - [도서목록] - [AWS 국제공인 AI 전문가 자격시험] - [학습자료] 폴더 안에 포함되어 있다.

▶ 독자들을 위한 [연봉 5억 AI 무자본 창업 아이템 50선]이 담긴 선물

본 도서를 구입한 독자분들에게는 480페이지 분량의 "연봉 5억 N잡러가 되기 위한 AI 무자본 창업 50선" 도서(PDF)를 무료로 제공한다. 이 도서는 생성형 AI 활용 대중화를 통해 누구나 도전해 볼 수 있는 AI 무자본 창업에 대한 영감과 아이디어를 샘솟게 해주는 아주 실험적인 내용이 담긴 전자책(PDF) 형태의 도서로, 현재 교보, 알라딘 등에서 실물(종이책)로 판매되고 있는 것으로, 본 도서의 독자들을 위해 특별한 선물로 제공하고 있다.

부록 전자책 비밀번호 요청하기

본 도서에 포함된 전자책(PDF)은 [책바세.com] - [도서목록] - [(해당 도서) 학습자료] 폴더 안에 포함되어 있으며, 부록 전자책을 보기 위한 비밀번호는 다음과 같이 스마트폰 카메라를 이용해 QR 코드를 스캔한 후 "책바세 톡톡" 카카오톡 채널로 접속해서 요청하면 된다.

◀ 이름과 직업을 지워지지 않는 펜으로 쓴 후 촬영하여 QR 코드 스캔을 통해 접속한 카카오 톡에, 촬영한 이미지와 함께 요청한다. (후기글 작성해 주기)

적중문제 해답

1번 정답: c
2번 정답: b
3번 정답: b
4번 정답: c
5번 정답: c
6번 정답: b
7번 정답: c
8번 정답: a
9번 정답: a
10번 정답: b
11번 정답: b
12번 정답: b
13번 정답: c
14번 정답: a
15번 정답: b
16번 정답: b
17번 정답: c
18번 정답: b
19번 정답: b
20번 정답: b
21번 정답: a
22번 정답: b
23번 정답: b
24번 정답: b
25번 정답: b
26번 정답: b
27번 정답: a
28번 정답: b
29번 정답: b
30번 정답: a
31번 정답: a
32번 정답: a
33번 정답: a
34번 정답: c
35번 정답: c
36번 정답: c
37번 정답: c
38번 정답: a
39번 정답: b
40번 정답: c
41번 정답: b
42번 정답: b
43번 정답: d
44번 정답: b
45번 정답: c
46번 정답: a
47번 정답: a
48번 정답: c
49번 정답: a
50번 정답: a
51번 정답: d
52번 정답: b
53번 정답: b
54번 정답: b
55번 정답: c
56번 정답: c
57번 정답: c
58번 정답: a
59번 정답: b
60번 정답: a
61번 정답: c
62번 정답: b
63번 정답: a
64번 정답: b
65번 정답: c
66번 정답: c
67번 정답: d
68번 정답: c
69번 정답: a
70번 정답: b
71번 정답: c
72번 정답: b
73번 정답: b
74번 정답: c
75번 정답: c
76번 정답: b
77번 정답: b
78번 정답: b
79번 정답: b
80번 정답: d
81번 정답: b
82번 정답: b
83번 정답: b
84번 정답: c
85번 정답: b
86번 정답: c
87번 정답: a
88번 정답: b
89번 정답: b
90번 정답: b
91번 정답: d
92번 정답: c
93번 정답: c
94번 정답: c
95번 정답: c
96번 정답: a
97번 정답: c
98번 정답: d
99번 정답: b
100번 정답: a
101번 정답: a
102번 정답: c
103번 정답: b
104번 정답: c
105번 정답: d
106번 정답: c
107번 정답: b
108번 정답: d

109번 정답: b
110번 정답: a
111번 정답: c
112번 정답: b
113번 정답: b
114번 정답: d
115번 정답: a
116번 정답: c
117번 정답: a
118번 정답: b
119번 정답: a
120번 정답: a
121번 정답: a
122번 정답: c
123번 정답: b
124번 정답: b
125번 정답: c
126번 정답: b
127번 정답: b
128번 정답: b
129번 정답: a
130번 정답: b
131번 정답: b
132번 정답: b
133번 정답: c
134번 정답: a
135번 정답: c
136번 정답: c
137번 정답: b
138번 정답: b
139번 정답: c
140번 정답: b
141번 정답: a
142번 정답: b
143번 정답: a
144번 정답: b

145번 정답: b
146번 정답: b
147번 정답: a
148번 정답: c
149번 정답: b
150번 정답: b
151번 정답: a
152번 정답: c
153번 정답: a
154번 정답: a
155번 정답: c
156번 정답: a
157번 정답: b
158번 정답: b
159번 정답: c
160번 정답: b
161번 정답: a
162번 정답: a
163번 정답: c
164번 정답: b
165번 정답: c
166번 정답: b
167번 정답: c
168번 정답: b
169번 정답: b
170번 정답: b
171번 정답: b
172번 정답: b
173번 정답: c
174번 정답: b
175번 정답: c
176번 정답: b
177번 정답: b
178번 정답: a
179번 정답: b
180번 정답: b

181번 정답: c
182번 정답: b
183번 정답: b
184번 정답: b
185번 정답: b
186번 정답: a
187번 정답: d
188번 정답: b
189번 정답: b
190번 정답: b
191번 정답: c
192번 정답: a
193번 정답: b
194번 정답: b
195번 정답: b
196번 정답: c
197번 정답: d
198번 정답: b
199번 정답: d
200번 정답: b
201번 정답: c
202번 정답: b
203번 정답: b
204번 정답: c
205번 정답: b
206번 정답: a
207번 정답: a
208번 정답: a
209번 정답: b
210번 정답: c
211번 정답: a
212번 정답: b
213번 정답: a
214번 정답: b
215번 정답: b
217번 정답: a

218번 정답: b
219번 정답: b
220번 정답: d
221번 정답: d
222번 정답: a
223번 정답: b
224번 정답: c
225번 정답: a
226번 정답: b
227번 정답: c
228번 정답: b
229번 정답: b
230번 정답: b
231번 정답: b
232번 정답: a
233번 정답: b
234번 정답: b
235번 정답: b
236번 정답: a
237번 정답: a
238번 정답: b
239번 정답: c
240번 정답: b
241번 정답: b
242번 정답: a
243번 정답: c
244번 정답: c
245번 정답: b
246번 정답: b
247번 정답: c
248번 정답: b
249번 정답: c
250번 정답: b
251번 정답: c
252번 정답: b
253번 정답: a
254번 정답: c
255번 정답: a
256번 정답: c
257번 정답: b
258번 정답: b
259번 정답: c
260번 정답: c
261번 정답: a
262번 정답: b
263번 정답: d
264번 정답: c
265번 정답: b
266번 정답: a
267번 정답: a
268번 정답: c
269번 정답: a
270번 정답: d
271번 정답: d
272번 정답: a
273번 정답: c
274번 정답: a
275번 정답: a
276번 정답: a
277번 정답: a
278번 정답: c
279번 정답: b
280번 정답: a
281번 정답: b
282번 정답: c
283번 정답: c
284번 정답: a
285번 정답: b
286번 정답: b
287번 정답: d
288번 정답: a
289번 정답: c
290번 정답: a
291번 정답: b
292번 정답: b
293번 정답: c
294번 정답: b
295번 정답: b
296번 정답: b
297번 정답: c
298번 정답: b
299번 정답: b
300번 정답: c